ॐ

ह्रां ह्रीं ह्रौं सः
सूर्याय नमः

ASTROLOGY

Mystery Unravelled

365 Questions and Answers with Logics

DR ARUN KUMAR TREHAN
M.B.B.S., JYOTISH ACHARAYA

NAVIN MALHOTRA
JYOTISH DEEWAKAR

F-2/16, Ansari Road, Daryaganj, New Delhi-110002
E-mail: info@unicornbooks.in • Website: www.unicornbooks.in
☎ 011-23275434, 23262683, 23250704

Branch : Mumbai
23-25, Zaoba Wadi, Thakurdwar, Mumbai-400002
☎ 022-22010941, 022-22053387
E-mail: rapidex@bom5.vsnl.net.in

ISBN: 978-81-7806-401-7

Edition: 2018

Printed at : *Param Offsetters, Okhla, New Delhi-110020*

INDEX

PREFACE

This book has been written to answer the day-to-day queries of everyone regarding *jyotish*. My interest in astrology was aroused by my first *guru*, respected late Shri Hakim Shyam Lal Mehta. I am thankful to Dr. Rajesh Mehta for all the guidance, inspiration and motivation in astrology. Whatever I am trying to sum up here is due to zest for astrology, which I have learned from ICAS and *BHARTIYA VIDYA BHAWAN* while I did *Jyotish* Praveen, *Jyotish Alankar* and *Jyotish Acharya* under the guidance of great scholars like Shri Z. Ansari, Shri K.N. Rao, Shri Shukla ji, Shri Mishra ji, Shri M.S. Mehta, Shri Deepak Kapoor and many others. This was followed by teaching, sharing, practical application and research at *Vastu VIDYA MANDIR* which was established under the guidance of Dr. Rajesh Mehta, Shri J.L. Sharma, Shri Y.K. Bansal, Dr. Sanjeev Dhaumya, Shri Lalit and myself. My special thanks to all the students who have helped me in providing innumerable questions as well as data from time to time on different subjects.

The main aim of the book is to make people aware about the preventive measures to be taken to ward off or dilute certain problems.

The subject matter in the book is based on personal observations of mine and in no way binding on the readers. I have no responsibility whatsoever regarding the effects of the contents. After 20 years in medical profession, I realised the limitations of medical science. Doctors of any field like Allopathic, *Ayurvedic*, Homeopathic, *Unani* etc., get struck at some point of treatment. Some serious patients recover fast, while others keep on suffering due to minor illness for a very long time. These patients at some stage of life accept the disease as part of their lives. The only way they console themselves is: *shaayad meri kismat hee kharab hai* (it is my bad fortune), *yay sub mere karmo kaa phal hai* (All this is because of my bad past *karmas*). This made me think about, the past *karmas* as well as destiny. That day I as a doctor decided, that 'Astrology Begins Where Medicine Ends". Now, after almost 25 years in astrology and 40 years in medical practice, I realise that astrology begins much before you are born or even the concept materializes.

My first experience with astrology was way back around 1970. I accompanied my mother to an old man's place for astrological advice regarding my career.

The old man: "How many questions you want to ask?"

I said, "Two".

Old man: "Think about the questions you want to ask."

He wrote something on two papers, rolled them, then he gave me two papers and asked me to write the questions on papers. He asked me to wrap up the papers and leave in front of him. He never picked up the papers or read them. Then he asked me to pick the two papers which he had rolled earlier and asked me to read the answer. I was so shocked and surprised to see the answers written on the papers for the questions which he never read or knew.

The questions I had written were :–

1. "Will my sister get married to the boy we were in touch with?"
2. "Will I get a seat in M.B.B.S. in Delhi?"

The answers were yes to both the queries and both happened positively. My sister got married to the boy we were in touch with and I got a seat in M.B.B.S. in Delhi. He gave me two mantras to recite.

1. *Om gan, ganpatay namah.*
2. *Om hraam, hareem, hraum sah suryay namah.* I recited these mantras very sincerely, but now after I entered into astrology, I realize the importance of these mantras.

Everyone is born at a particular place, particular time, to a particular mother. The position of planets at that particular moment is the secret of unfolding of *karmas* throughout life. So, everyone is born in a particular *mahurat* which is predestined.

I am greatly indebted to my associate Navin Malhotra for this book.

Vastu Vidya Mandir
Dr. Arun Kumar Trehan
M.B.B.S. *Jyotish Acharaya*
Arun108786@yahoo.co.in

INTRODUCTION TO JYOTISH

What is *jyotish*? If we break the word, it is *jyoti* (light) + *ish* (God). This means torch or search light of Lord *Shiva*. *Jyotish* (astrologer) is the person who tries to see the future with the torch of Lord *Shiva*. *Jyotish* can mishandle the torch or may not focus the light at a proper place but the torch of Lord *Shiva* never fluctuates in its illumination or intensity. So, the first thing one has to remember is that "An Astrologer Can Fail, But Astrology Never Fails."

Parashri is the study of effects of nine planets and twelve signs as per country, person and culture over a period of 120 years of *dasha*.

Lal Kitab is the study of horoscope along with *Varshphals* to see if any remedy is required to safeguard against any ill effects during a particular year.

Astrology is a divine science and to utilise it, one should have faith, devotion, and commitment.

Nobody in this universe can change your destiny. A noble charitable personality can however, definitely minimise the impact or avoid the following in your life:

- Diseases
- Distresses
- Disasters
- Diversions
- Dangers
- Divorces
- Death like situations etc.

But, what is really required is the acceptance of the shortcomings of one's present and past *karmas*. Before learning astrology or practising it, the learner should have the following qualities to be a good astrologer:

Be honest.

Be optimistic.

Never be proud.

Have full faith in God.

Never be greedy.

Should be egoless.

Be impartial or unbiased.

Learn from your failures.

Try to boost the morale of everyone.

Have faith in the remedies with full devotion before you apply.

Destiny cannot be denied, but can definitely be diluted.

May God bless you with all the happiness and prosperity.

Try to follow *satvik* lifestyle.

Pray for the person who is suffering.

Always try to uplift the society by using astrology.

Never disclose the problem of your client to anyone.

Suggest remedies which are practical and feasible.

Avoid doing astrological analysis on *amavasya*, *poornima* and *grahan* (eclipse) days.

Suggest remedies which can be done easily.

Suggest remedies which can be useful for the society specially the suffering, needy and helpless people:

Feeding lepers (*Rahu* remedy),

Feeding blinds (Saturn remedy),

Feeding dogs (*Ketu* remedy),

Feeding crows (*Rahu* and Saturn) remedies,

Distributing books and study material to poor children (Mercury and Jupiter)

Donating blood, medicines for needy (Mars remedy)

As per *desh kaal paatr*, try to show other side of astrology (*karmas* and spiritualism etc.).

When you apply the principles of astrology everything goes right but when the astrologer starts giving his personnel verdict everything goes wrong.

(*Jab Tak Jyotish Bolta Hai, Tab Tak Sab Theek, Jab Jyotshi Bolta Hai toh Sab Gallat*)

KARMAS AND ASTROLOGY

Astrology is totally based on your past *karmas. Karma* is the net Balance of one's physical, mental, emotional and spiritual deeds done in different births. Astrology is based on the past *karmas* which get unfolded in the form of a fixed *dasha* pattern depending upon the degrees of your birth—Moon. Some of our *karmas* get unfolded immediately in this birth while some may take many more births. The past *karmas* form the basic horoscope and can't be changed. It is the present *karmas* which can help in promoting a positive event or may even aggravate a negative event depending upon your attitude, deeds, charity, religious activities etc. It has been said in *Gita*, "*karam kar, phal kee ichha mat kar*". The fruits of your actions, whether sweet or bitter, will get unfolded in this birth or in further births to come. If you don't believe in past *karmas*, then I don't think astrology will be of much use to you. *Rishis* have clearly described the rebirth as like changing of clothes, but a person can easily be identified though he changes his clothes daily. In the same way, your past *karmas* track you and identify you. After identifying, they give you favourable or unfavourable results as per the *Bal*ance of your *karmas*. This is done by planets who rule in a fixed pattern of *dasha* system depending upon the degrees of birth—Moon.

The results are further dependent on the:

Strength of *dasha* Lord

Placement of *dasha* Lord

Aspects on *dasha* Lord

Conjunction of *dasha* Lord

This is managed in astrology by nine planets. The nine planets are Sun, Moon, Mars, Mercury, Jupiter, Venus, Saturn, *Rahu* and *Ketu*. Out of these nine planets, Jupiter, Venus, Moon, Mercury are comparatively more beneficial than Saturn, Mars, *Rahu*, *Ketu* and Sun.

Whatever one has sowed in the past births as *karmas* comes as good or bad in the present birth. All planets are associated with certain relations, activities, items etc. By taking note of the strength of the planet one can have an idea about the past *karmas* of a person. If you are ready to accept the good results of the past *karmas* then you have to accept and repay the loans of past *Karma* also in this birth. These are recognized in astrology in the form of "*rins*" like (*pitr rin*, *matri rin*, self *rin*, *jaalimana rin* etc.)

Grahans (eclipse):--we have two sources of light in the universe that is the Sun and the Moon. They are like positive and negative of electricity which have to be *Bal*anced and grounded by the e*Arth* wire (*Lagan* Lord).

In the horoscope *Lagan*, 4th house, 5th house are like 3 pin plug. If one of this pin is not working, the light will not glow and can give you shock. If these sources of light—the Sun and the Moon are having any PAC (position, aspect, conjunction) with Saturn, *Rahu*, *Ketu* (sources of darkness), it is like dim light or darkness. In order to get proper light, we have to either increase the voltage further (promoting Sun and Moon) or reduce the darkness of Saturn, *Rahu*, and *Ketu*. To enjoy or suffer as per past *karmas* one has to take birth (*Lagan* Lord) as human being. One of these power points (Sun, Moon and *Lagan*) has to be in afflicted situation to get human birth. I believe, it is hard to see any horoscope which doesn't have PAC of malefic with Sun/Moon/*Lagan*/*Lagan* Lord.

Before the *dasha* starts, the planets start giving their results e.g., Saturn starts giving the results almost six months before its *mahadasha* starts. Other planets like Jupiter, *Rahu*, *Ketu* (outer planets) etc. also start giving their results much before their *dasha* starts. This is the crucial time to take preventive measures in the form of different remedies.

The difference to be observed by us is the role of—

Natural benefics

Natural malefic

Functional benefics

Functional malefic

The benefics always bring:

Beneficial results

Blessings

Bag full of money

Brotherhood

The malefic will bring:

Miseries

Melancholy

Meanness

Money problems

Mrityu-tulaye kasht

Sometimes, the natural benefics also change their role when they become functional malefic depending upon the rising *Lagan*. This leads to malefic results even in the *dasha* of natural benefic.

In the same way, the natural malefics also change their role when they become functional benefic depending upon the rising *Lagan*. This leads to benefic results even in the *dasha* of natural malefics.

The end results are dependent on the *mahadasha*, *antardasha*, *pratyanter dasha* at the time of event.

Right *Dasha* at the Right Age Makes Everything Right.

This has to be co-related with the *gochar* and present *karmas*.

The results should further be analyzed as per *Desh*, *Kaal*, and *Paatr*.

This means the *dasha* will give results as per country or place, surrounding atmosphere and the personality of the person.

PREVENTIONS IN ASTROLOGY

"Prevention is the best medicine" this saying proves hundred percent true in health sciences and it is perfectly true as far as astrology is concerned. Normally, when a person comes to an astrologer, he already has a problem and there is no miracle if an astrologer tells him that he has this or that sort of problems.

In the case of health and medicine, normally people have family doctors who know the minute details of the person and his family. A Doctor can correlate the problem with any hereditary feature, such as *asthma*. So is true in astrology, but this is not used in the day-to-day practices. The job and the duty of the doctor as well as the astrologer is to forewarn the person in a tactful manner and advise him to take preventive measures at the right time before the problem aggravates. How this is done, is what I would like to discuss here. As we often read that the planet starts giving their results much before their *dasha*. Saturn gives its results almost six months before the beginning of its *mahadasha*. This principle can help us in taking either preventive or promotional measures before the *dasha* begins.

Natural benefics such as Jupiter, full Moon, Venus and unafflicted Mercury should ideally be giving benefic results. However, when they start giving unfavourable results that really hurts us, because we hope for the best of the benefic results during the *dasha* of natural benefics.

In the same way one may get pleasantly surprised by benefic results during *dasha* of natural malefic when they become functional benefic. e.g. Mars is yog *karaka* planet for Cancer and Leo *Lagan*. Saturn is yog *karaka* planet for Taurus and Libra *Lagan*. Though both are natural malefic but are functional benefic for the abovesaid *Lagan*s. As in medicine, the vaccinations are given to children to protect them from diseases. Similarly, in astrology, measures are taken to prevent the ill effects of *dasha* of natural malefic or functional malefic before it starts.

The first thing to be done before giving astrological advice is to see the manner in which the planet is going to behave. This is very important that we should be crystal clear before deciding the remedy as this will decide the results. You must have heard the saying:

'*Jo Dam Duaon May Hai Woh Dawaon May Nahin*'

(Blessings are More Powerful than Medicines.)

By taking the blessings of live *karaka*s of planets, the unfavourable results of planets can be diluted to a certain extent.

Live *Karaka*s of different planets are as follows : —

	Planet	**Live *Karakas***
1.	Sun	Father, father-in-law, government officials, boss
2.	Moon	Mother, mother-in-law, elderly ladies
3.	Mars	Younger brother
4.	Mercury	Younger sister, mother's sister
5.	Jupiter	Elder brother, priest, teacher
6.	Venus	Wife, younger females, subordinate females in office
7.	Saturn	Servants, workers at office, peon
8.	*Rahu*	Paternal grandfather, lepers, maternal grandmother
9.	*Ketu*	Paternal grandmother, son, dog, maternal grandfather

As we know the benefic results are always welcomed at whatever time they come to you. What a person does not want in life is the role of malefic and their bad to worst results. God always gives you warning and time before any major event in life. What a common man cannot foresee should be seen well in advance by an astrologer. Nature gives you warning and time, depending upon your *kaal* (time) and *karmas* (deeds), which are reflected in astrology by the placement of planets in different signs and *dasha* pattern in one's life. The *dasha* pattern depends upon the position of Moon at birth.

Everyone in this world wants to know the future for himself and his family members. Astrology is based on the following things for prediction:

— date of birth

— time of birth

— place of birth

— *dasha* pattern

— *gocher* or transit and

— *desh kaal paatr*

The horoscope has twelve houses, twelve signs and nine planets. The houses are controlled by seven planets:-

Sun is Lord of Leo,

Moon is Lord of Cancer,

Mars is Lord of Aries and Scorpio,

Mercury is Lord of Gemini and Virgo,

Jupiter is Lord of Sagittarius and Pisces,

Venus is Lord of Taurus and Libra,

Saturn is Lord of Capricorn and Aquarius and

Rahu and *Ketu* don't own any sign.

Sun and Moon are the Lords of one sign each and all the other planets are the Lords of two signs.

Total number of planets are nine from the astrological point of view but only seven are the true planets:--Sun, Moon, Mars, Jupiter, Mercury, Venus, and Saturn. Here, the first four planets belong to "A" group and the rest three in "B" group. Whereas, *Rahu* and *Ketu* are shadowy planets and are in "C" group. *Rahu* and *Ketu* are not true planets but are highly sensitive points in zodiac. Planets of 'C' group behave more or less like the planets of 'B' group. The planets of 'A' group are inimical to 'B' group and *vice-versa*.

The other classification of the planets is natural benefic and natural malefic.

Natural benefics : Jupiter, Venus, unafflicted Mercury, and *Paksh Bali* Moon.

Natural malefic: Mars, Saturn, *Rahu*, *Ketu*.

Sun is a cruel planet.

By the above statement it means that the natural benefic planets give favourable results, while the natural malefic give bad results. So, the astrological predictions should be very simple.

'Easier Said Than Done'. This will be explained under functional benefics and malefic.

In today's competitive life, one is forced to fight for a very small fraction of marks in the exam, so the astrological predictions should also be very superfine.

For making a beautiful photograph or scenery etc., one needs (paper, pencil, brush, colour, drawing board, drawing pins, good light, favourable atmosphere, positive thinking, patience, learning from mistakes, prior knowledge, fresh imagination etc.).

All these factors are needed in astrology as well (accurate data, accurate horoscope, divisional charts, *dasha* pattern, *desh*, *kaal*, *paatr*, strength of houses, strength of Lords, strength of planets, good intuition, patience and so on.)

Before moving to predictive astrology, certain datas have to be memorized.

"WELL BEGUN IS HALF DONE"

This principle can be of great use in choosing a good *mahurat* for any auspicious activity. The *mahurat* part of astrology helps in getting the events fullfilled with least of troubles and lots of gains and prosperity.

Any suggestions, improvements, corrections by the readers will be highly appreciated.

The book is in question answer form. This being a book on basic astrology, a very simple and common man's language/words have been used in describing different principles. Details are available in my other books on remedial astrology, *Vastu* and feng shui, *Lal Kitab* etc.

OM GANESHAYAY NAMAH

As Lord *Ganesha* is *Adidev* and Lord *Shiva* is the *Kal purush* (represented by *kaal purush kundli*), they should always be worshipped before venturing into any event of astrology. In *kalyug* each and every problem can be diluted or can be rectified by worshipping. Without getting into any religious controversies, my personal opinion is to worship the following mantras etc.

Twelve names of Lord Ganesh are as Follows:

1. *Om Sumukhayay Namah*
2. *Om Ekdantayay Namah*
3. *Om Kapilayay Namah*
4. *Om Gaj Karan Kayay Namah*
5. *Om Lambodrayay Namah*
6. *Om Vikatayay Namah*
7. *Om Vighan Nashnayay Namah*
8. *Om Vinakayay Namah*
9. *Om Dhumra Ketuvay Namah*
10. *Om Gana Dhakshayay Namah*
11. *Om Bhal Chandrayay Namah*
12. *Om Gajananyay Namah*

Saraswati Mantra

Om Saraswati Maha Bhagay, Vidya Kamal Lochanay

Vidya Rupay Vishal Laakshi, Vidyam Dahi Namo Suttay

Hare Krishan Hare Krishan, Krishan Krishan Hare Hare

Hare Rama Hare Rama, Rama Rama Hare Hare

Individual *Nav Graha Mantras*

Sun : *Om hraam hreem hraum sah sooryaay namah*

Moon : *Om shraam shreem shraum sah chandrayay namah*

Mars : *Om kraam kreem kraum sah bhaumayay namah*

Mercury : *Om braam breem braum sah budhayay namah*

Jupiter : *Om graam greem graum sah gurve namah*

Venus : *Om draam dreem draum sah shukrayay namah*

Saturn : *Om praam preem praum sah shanichrayay namah*

Rahu : *Om bhraam bhreem bhraum sah raahvay namah*

Ketu : *Om sraam sreem sraum sah ketvay namah*

Nav Graha Mantra

Brahmaa Muraari –Sah -Tripuraantakaarii
Bhaanuh Shashii Bhuumisuto Budhash-Cha
Gurush-Cha Shukrah Shani-Raahu-Ketavah
Kuruvantu Sarve Mam Suprabhaatam.

After reciting these *mantras*,

Panchang for the day and time should be noted everyday.

In astrology following parameters are required:

Namc and sex

Date of birth

Time of birth

Place of birth

These help in making the horoscope.

The horoscope is clubbed with the *panchang*

Day (Vaar)

Tithi

Nakshatra

Yog

Karan

Special yogas

The *Lagan* sign

The Moon sign

The Sun sign

Dasha and *dasha* pattern

Gochar/transit

Desh kaal paatr

Divisional charts

Ashtakvargas

Shadbal etc.

The parameters mentioned above may look like too many, but when you gradually learn the flow of these parameters, the predictions become easy. My experience in astrology so far has taught me not to bypass the basic parameters. These basic threads only help us in getting a strong bond of principles. The astrology has advanced and progressed a lot after the introduction of softwares and computers, laptops. Whether you practice *Parashri*, *Lal Kitab*, Krishanmurthy *paddhati* or *nadi* astrology, the basics will never change. With the help of computers and softwares, we are able to calculate macro and micro parameters of astrology in a few seconds. Here I would like to warn you about the mistakes which we can commit when we go to micro labels without accurate data.

Parashri system will always remain the base, whether you study Krishanmurthy *paddhati* or *nadi* system or *Lal Kitab*. The importance of *Parashri* and its advancement will be clear to you in my books on *Lal Kitab*, Remedial Astrology and Krishanmurthy *Paddhati*.

In the end, let me tell you that my aim is to share the knowledge with everyone and not get any financial gains. I have learned a lot from my teachers, students, books, and internet and by personal interaction with lots of respected traditional pandits.

The book is dedicated to my respected parents.

This book has been a reality because of overwhelming support, motivation, blessings of my parents Late Shri Jagdish Mitter Trehan and Late Smt. Lalita Rani Trehan. This book is also due to unconditional support of my wife Vandana, all my students and friends. My special thanks to Navin Malhotra for extraordinary efforts in making this publication a reality. For smooth completion of any work, one needs a peaceful, healthy and refreshing atmosphere and you cannot get a better place than Barog station in Himachal on Kalka-Shimla toy train route.

Final proof reading, editing and setting of the book was done under the blessings of Lord Krishan at holy city of VRINDAVAN by Ms. Anu Sindhwani and Shri Vinod *Kumar*. Our special thanks to Shri A. P. Sharma for proof reading and valuable suggestions. The question bank was prepared by Shri Navin Malhotra, Mrs Raj Arora, Shri Vinod *Kumar*, Mrs Anshu Tyagi and many others.

The book is in question answer form. Very simple and common man's language has been used in describing different principles.

In my twenty years of teaching experience, what I have observed is that all students know all the aspects of astrology, but what they lack is the application of the parameters.

My request to all my readers is that they may learn few principles but must know how to apply those principles for different purposes.

For example, what are moveable signs? Every student will know that 1, 4, 7, 10 (Aries, Cancer, Libra, Capricorn) are moveable signs. Does the role of moveable signs finish here?

Will I recover from disease? Moveable *Lagan*, yes you will recover.

Will I get transferred? Moveable *Lagan*, yes you will get transferred.

Should I give my money to someone? Moveable *Lagan*, your money gone.

Will I be able to buy property? Moveable *Lagan*, no you will not.

Why can't my child sit quietly? Moveable *Lagan*, *Lagan* Lord in moveable sign.

If majority of the planets in moveable signs, person keeps on moving with frequent transfers.

So, the utility of moveable should be realized. In the same way, the above methods should be applied to fixed and dual signs.

In this book, I will try to answer all the important principles and their application in day to day analysis. Principles of *Parashri* along with *Lal Kitab* will be covered. I presume that you are well aware of the basics of astrology

Before you start predicting, you must understand that no planet is absolutely benefic or malefic.

Every planet gives mixed results depending upon:—

— its basic nature

— its Lordship of different houses

— its PAC (position, aspect and conjunction)

— it's *dasha* at particular age

— *Desh, kaal, paatr*.

As astrology is a non-ending subject, I will try to give important principles of astrology with their practical utility.

Questions by Navin Malhotra

Answers by Dr. Arun *Kumar* Trehan

M.B.B.S. Jyotish Acharya

Answer to the Following questions is based on their utility in practical analysis.

QUESTIONS AT A GLANCE

1. What is Astrology?
2. What is Horoscope?
3. What is the basic data required to make a Horoscope?
4. What is the importance of date of birth?
5. What is the importance of time of birth?
6. What is the importance of place of birth?
7. What is *Lagan*/ascendant?
8. What is *Kal purush kundli*?
9. What are the three most important parameters of Astrology?
10. What is a house in Astrology?
11. What are *rashis*/signs?
12. What is celestial kingdom?
13. What are planets?
14. How many planets are there?
15. What are real planets?
16. What are shadowy planets?
17. Name the friends of different planets?
18. Name the neutral of different planets?
19. Name the enemies of different planets?
20. How many houses are there and what do they represent?
21. What are the significances of 1st house?
22. What are the significances of 2nd house?
23. What are the significances of 3rd house?
24. What are the significances of 4th house?
25. What are the significances of 5th house?
26. What are the significances of 6th house?

27. What are the significances of 7th house?
28. What are the significances of 8th house?
29. What are the significances of 9th house?
30. What are the significances of 10th house?
31. What are the significances of 11th house?
32. What are the significances of 12th house?
33. What are the different groups of houses?
34. What are Trine houses and their use?
35. What are *Kendra* houses and their use?
36. What does different houses indicate? How to use them?
37. What are *Laxmi Sthans*?
38. What are *Vishnu Sthans*?
39. What are the *Upchaya* houses and their use?
40. What are the *Dushtsthan* houses and their use?
41. What are the longevity houses and their use?
42. What are the *Marak* houses and their use?
43. What are *Badhak* houses and their use?
44. What are *panphar* houses and their use?
45. What are the apoklime houses and their use?
46. What are the *trishadaya* houses and their use?
47. What are the Trik houses and their use?
48. What are *Dharam*, *Arth*, *Kaam*, *Moksh* houses?
49. What are *Dharam*, *Arth*, *Kaam*, *Moksh* signs?
50. What are *Dharma* houses and their use?
51. What are *Arth* houses and their use?
52. What are *Kaam* houses and their use?
53. What are *Moksh* houses and their use?
54. What are *Satwik* houses and their use?

55. What are *Rajsik* houses and their use?
56. What are *Tamsik* houses and their use?
57. What are natural benefic planets?
58. What are natural malefic planets?
59. What are the significances of Sun?
60. What are the significances of Moon?
61. What are the significances of Mars?
62. What are the significances of Mercury?
63. What are the significances of Jupiter?
64. What are the significances of Venus?
65. What are the significances of Saturn?
66. What are the significances of *Rahu*?
67. What are the significances of *Ketu*?
68. What are *Satwik* planets and their uses?
69. What are *Rajsik* planets and their uses?
70. What are *Tamsik* planets and their uses?
71. What are the male planets and their uses?
72. What are the female planets and their uses?
73. What are eunuch planets and their uses?
74. What is the conjunction of the planets?
75. How does conjunction of two or more planets affect each other?
76. What are the different ways of conjunctions and its effects?
77. What, if exalted and debilitated planet conjunct with each other?
78. Give examples of conjunct exalted and debilitated planets.
79. What are inner planets?
80. What are outer planets?
81. Why do outer planets have more aspects?

82. What are aspects of planets and what is their importance?
83. What are *tatwas* of planets and signs?
84. What are significaters/*karakas*?
85. Name different *Karkas* of 12 houses and their importance?
86. Name the different *Karka* of houses as per *Parashri* and *Lal Kitab*?
87. How do you see *Karakas* in astrology?
88. Does the placement of planets in certain signs of *kaal purush kundli* of any use in studying your personal relationship with certain personalities?
89. Does the strength of a *Karka* planet in transit of any use?
90. How many *nakshatras* are there?
91. Name all the *nakshatras*?
92. What are *Nakshatras* and how do they help in prediction?
93. How do you see day and night birth in horoscope?
94. How do you see *Pooranmashi* birth in a horoscope?
95. How do you see *Amavasya* birth in horoscope?
96. How do you make out *Shukal paksh* birth in horoscope?
97. How do you make out *Krishan paksh* birth in horoscope?
98. Which houses represent which relative in horoscope?
99. How do you see debilitation in horoscope?
100. What are Yog *karaka* planets?
101. Which planets can become Yog *karaka* for different *Lagan*?
102. Which are comparatively bad houses in horoscope?
103. How do planets behave differently for odd or even *Lagans*?
104. Are 6th, 8th, and 12th bad for everyone?
105. What are *Digbali* planets?
106. What is exaltation of planets?

107. What does exaltation mean?
108. What is extreme exaltation?
109. Does degrees of exalted planet matter in prediction?
110. What does debilitation mean?
111. What is extreme debilitation?
112. Does degrees of debilitated planet matter in prediction?
113. Name the *mool trikone* signs of planets?
114. What do you understand by grading of planetary strength?
115. How does planet become strong?
116. How do you analyze a planet?
117. What are functional malefic planets?
118. What are functional benefic planets?
119. What is the difference between a natural benefic and functional benefic?
120. What is *Badhakpati*? Show *Badhakpatis* for different *Lagan*?
121. What is *Kendrapati* dosh?
122. What is dispositer?
123. What is *Vipreet raj* yog?
124. What are *Raj* yogas?
125. How do you see body parts in horoscope?
126. What is the effect of placement of *Lagan* Lord in *Dushtsthans* (6/8/12)?
127. What are the effects of 5th Lord in 6th?
128. Which house indicates about your service or business?
129. What are the combinations for successful business man?
130. Which house indicates about your problems in profession?
131. Which house indicates professional satisfaction/dissatisfaction?
132. Which are money houses in Astrology?

133. Which house indicates about your gains in life (money)?
134. Which house indicates about your wife/partner's profession?
135. Which house indicates whether you have a working partner?
136. How do you see short journeys/transfer?
137. How do you see long journeys and foreign trips?
138. How do you make out whether the person will come back from abroad?
139. How does a house become strong?
140. What are the qualities of benefic houses?
141. What are malefic houses?
142. How do you analyze a house?
143. Name the Lords of different signs?
144. What is the use of signs?
145. What are the qualities of Aries sign and its uses?
146. What are the qualities of Taurus sign and its uses?
147. What are the qualities of Gemini sign and its uses?
148. What are the qualities of Cancer sign and its uses?
149. What are the qualities of Leo sign and its uses?
150. What are the qualities of Virgo sign and its uses?
151. What are the qualities of Libra sign and its uses?
152. What are the qualities of Scorpio sign and its uses?
153. What are the qualities of Sagittarius sign and its uses?
154. What are the qualities of Capricorn sign and its uses?
155. What are the qualities of Aquarius sign and its uses?
156. What are the qualities of Pisces sign and its uses?
157. How does the nature of planet changes as per nature of sign?
158. How many types of signs are there?
159. What is a sign Lord?

160. What is the difference between sign Lord and house Lord?
161. What are moveable signs and their uses?
162. What are fixed signs and their uses?
163. What are dual signs and their uses?
164. How to see short, medium and long assertion in Horoscope?
165. How do you analyze different significances?
166. What is the difference between sign and house?
167. What is the importance of degree of planets?
168. Does degree of *Lagan* and degree of planets have any combined use?
169. Who are the live *Karaka*s of different planets and their importance?
170. What are the *Avasthas* of planets and how does it affect the results?
171. What are separative planets?
172. What is the role of separative planets?
173. Name the exaltation, debilitation and *mool trikone* signs of planets?
174. How to use planets/houses and signs together?
175. What are *Shirshodaya*, *Pirshodaya* and *Upbhodaya* signs?
176. What are the uses of *Shirshodaya*, *Pirshodaya* and *Upbhodaya* signs?
177. How to give strength to the house in the horoscope?
178. What are the important factors in predicting an event?
179. What are odd *Lagan*s and how do they affect the nature of a person?
180. What are even *Lagan*s and how do they affect the nature of a person?
181. What are the effects of own sign Sun in 4th house?
182. What are the effects of exalted sign Sun in 4th house?

183. What are the effects of debilitated sign Sun in 4th house?
184. What are the effects of *mool trikone* sign Sun in 4th house?
185. What are the effects of friendly sign Sun in 4th house?
186. What are the effects of inimical sign Sun in 4th house?
187. What are the effects of neutral sign Sun in 4th house?
188. What is sade-sati?
189. What are the effects of *Sadesati*?
190. What is the role of Moon sign in *Sadesati*?
191. Does *Nakshatra* play any role in analysis of *Sadesati*?
192. Do *Tatwa* play any role in *Sadesati*?
193. Does degree of Moon play any role in *Sadesati*?
194. What is the importance of *Lagan* degree in the horoscope?
195. What is *Dinmaan/Ratrimaan* and their importance?
196. What is *Rahu kalam* and its effects?
197. What is *Mahurat* and its importance?
198. What is *Gaudhuli Mahurat* and its importance?
199. What is *Abhijeet Mahurat*?
200. What is *Panchang* and its importance?
201. Which is the most popular *dasha* used by astrologers?
202. Give the *dasha* pattern of *vimshotri dasha*?
203. What are the uses of *dasha*?
204. What are the sub divisions of *dasha*?
205. How do you calculate *Vimshotari dasha* in detail?
206. How do you calculate *antardasha*?
207. How do planets give their results during *dasha* and *antardasha* etc.?
208. How do you find out the timing of events through *vimshotari dasha*?

209. How do you find out the timing of events through transit of planets?
210. What are the important factors in predicting an event?
211. Name the favourable *dashas* in Astrology?
212. What are the important principles to study results and time period for an event by *dasha* of different planets?
213. Does *dasha* of blood relatives play any role in the life of a person?
214. What are the effects of *dasha* when it is Lord of Trines and *Dushtsthan*?
215. What are the important aspects of *dasha*?
216. Is there any method to improve the *dasha* results?
217. Does *dasha* pattern play any role in life?
218. Out of the two signs of a planet, which house results will be felt first?
219. What are the main ways by which a planet can give results?
220. Name the basics of *dasha* analysis?
221. What is *gochar* or transit?
222. What is double transit and its importance in predictions?
223. What is the role of Mars in transit timings?
224. What is the role of Sun in transit timings?
225. What is the role of Moon in transit timings?
226. Can transit supersede birth chart (d-1)?
227. How the strength of the transit planet useful in astrology?
228. Does the strength of a transit planet affect the *mahadasha/antardasha*?
229. Does weakness of transit planet affect the *mahadasha/antardasha*?
230. Does the strength of a *karaka* planet in transit is of any use?
231. Do planets give immediate results when they enter a sign during transit?

232. Which is the single most important principle to analyze health?
233. Which is the single most important principle to analyze wealth?
234. How can you know about your past *karmas* by your Horoscope?
235. Does natural malefic sheds its maleficence by becoming a functional benefic?
236. Does natural benefic sheds its beneficence by becoming a functional malefic?
237. Name the *mool trikone* signs of all the planets and their importance?
238. How are *panch maha purush* yogas formed?
239. What are the results of *panch maha purush* yogas?
240. Can one mix more than one system while analyzing a horoscope?
241. What are the parameters for analyzing a horoscope as per *Parashri*?
242. What are the parameters for analyzing a Horoscope as per *Lal Kitab*?
243. Can one club *Parashri* and *Lal Kitab* systems together?
244. What are the guidelines before giving any prediction, remedial measure?
245. What are the rules to be kept in mind?
246. What is the single most important principle of astrology?
247. What do you understand by the physical and functional results of a planet?
248. What are divisional charts?
249. How many divisional charts are there and what is the relative numerical value of different charts?
250. What are the different significances of sixteen divisional charts?
251. How do you use divisional charts for the prediction?
252. What is the importance of divisional charts?
253. What are the results when natural benefics are placed in Trines?

254. What are the results when natural benefics are placed in *Kendras*?

255. What are the results when natural benefics are placed in 6/8/12 house?

256. What are the results when natural benefics are placed in 3, 6, 10, and 11th house?

257. What are the results when natural malefic are placed in 2/11 house?

258. What are the results when natural malefic are placed in Trines?

259. What are the results when natural malefic are placed in *Kendras*?

260. What are the results when natural malefic are placed in 6th/8th/12th house?

261. What are the results when functional benefics are placed in 3, 6, 10, and 11 house?

262. What are the results when functional benefics are placed in 2nd/11th house?

263. What are the results when functional benefics are placed in Trines?

264. What are the results when functional benefics are placed in *Kendras*?

265. What are the results when functional malefic are placed in 6/8/12?

266. What are the results when functional malefic are placed in 3, 6, 10, 11?

267. What are the results when functional malefic are placed in 2/11?

268. Should functional benefics be strong?

269. Should functional malefic be strong?

270. What is the importance of Moon *Lagan*?

271. What are the uses of moon?

272. What are the uses of *janam rashi* (birth moon sign)?

273. What are the uses of prachalit name (popular or legal name)?
274. What is the importance of Sun *Lagan*?
275. What is the importance of *Sudershan Chakra*?
276. What are the factors which should be considered before giving results?
277. What are the important factors in predicting an event?
278. What does *Rahu* represent?
279. What does *Ketu* represent?
280. What is eclipse?
281. When do the eclipses take place?
282. How to calculate your events from the horoscopes of your blood relations?
283. How do you see relation between person and father?
284. How do you see relation between person and mother?
285. How do you see relation between person and elder sister/ brother?
286. How do you see relation between person and younger sister/ brother?
287. How do you see relation between person and wife?
288. How do you see relation between person and mother-in-law?
289. Are there any factors to be considered by the astrologer before giving astrological predictions?
290. How to go ahead in astrology?
291. What will decide the results of planets and horoscope as a whole?
292. How to differentiate whether live personality or significances will suffer?
293. How to do all these practically?
294. How will you decide the results?
295. What are static factors of astrology?

296. What are dynamic factors of Astrology?
297. How to decide the results of a planet as per particular *Lagan*?
298. What are the best positions of the benefics in the horoscope?
299. What are the best positions of the malefic in the horoscope?
300. What are the results of exchange of planets?
301. What are the result of house Lords?
302. Which are the houses and planets to be studied for gains of money?
303. What are the results of exalted planet getting debilitated in *Navmansha*?
304. What are the results of debilitated planet getting exalted in *Navmansha*?
305. Does *Rahu* and *Ketu* influence the results of planet?
306. How malefic and benefic planets in house influence the results of the house?
307. How exaltation/debilitation of a planet in transit does affect significances of planets?
308. How do you catch a disease of different parts of body?
309. How can you be sure about the disease and its severity?
310. How does a planet get afflicted as far as disease is concerned?
311. What is the significance of Sun and parts of body being affected, if afflicted by separative planets?
312. What are the significance of Moon and parts of body being affected, if afflicted by separative planets?
313. What are the significance of Mars and parts of body bang affected, if afflicted by separative planets?
314. What are the significance of Mercury and parts of body being affected, if afflicted by separative planets?
315. What are the significances of Jupiter and parts of body being affected, if afflicted by separative planets?

316. What are the significances of Venus and parts of body being affected, if afflicted by separative planets?

317. What are the significance of Saturn and parts of body being affected, ifafflicted by separative planets?

318. What are the significance of *Rahu* and parts of body being affected, if afflicted by separative planets?

319. What are the significances of *Ketu* and parts of body being affected, if afflicted by separative planets?

320. What are the significances of 1st house and parts of body getting affected, if afflicted by separative planets?

321. What are the significance of 2nd house and parts of body being affected, if it is afflicted by separative planet?

322. What are the significance of 3rd house and parts of body being affected, if it is afflicted by separative planets?

323. What are the significance of 4th house and parts of body being affected, if it is afflicted by separative planets?

324. What are the significance of 5th house and parts of body being affected, if it is afflicted by separative planets?

325. What are the significance of 6th house and parts of body being affected, if it is afflicted by separative planets?

326. What are the significance of 7th house and parts of body being affected, if it is afflicted by separative planets?

327. What are the significance of 8th house and parts of body being affected, if it is afflicted by separative planets?

328. What are the significance of 9th house and parts of body being affected, if it is afflicted by separative planets?

329. What are the significance of 10th house and parts of body being affected, if it is afflicted by separative planets?

330. What are the significance of 11th house and parts of body being affected, if it is afflicted by separative planets?

331. What are the significance of the 12th house and parts of body being affected, if it is afflicted by separative planets?

332. Does slow moving planets play a role in diseases?

333. What are the factors regarding progeny which should be avoided while doing *Kundli milan*?

334. What are the factors which help us in arriving at a decision in astrology? Explain with example.

335. Which horoscope to study, *Lagan* or Moon?

336. What are the different important methods of catching an event?

337. Can one give some interpretation without accurate horoscope?

338. How to catch an event in horoscope as per *Prashna kundli*?

339. How to catch an event in horoscope as per *Lagan kundli*?

340. How to catch an event in Horoscope as per Moon *kundli*?

341. How to catch an event as per transit from Moon?

342. How to catch an event as per transit from *Lagan*?

343. How to catch the event as per running *dasha*?

344. How to do all this practically?

345. How to catch a query after getting the above factors?

346. How do you analyze *Prashna kundli*?

347. How do you decide the time frame after analysis?

348. What are the guidelines while analyzing an event or query?

349. Give some simple hints on analysis?

350. When the planet will be favourable?

351. Does the age and position of planets in horoscope helps in analysis?

352. How to judge a horoscope?

353. What are fertile signs?

354. Are there any specific periods during a year when women are most fertile?

355. How can one use this principle?

356. Is *Prashna kundli* useful in analyzing child birth?

357. How to analyze an event as per different *Varshphals* and *dasha* pattern?

358. How to make a proforma to analyze the position of different factors?

359. What are the effects of Moon in *Rahu/Ketu* axis?

360. What are the main ways by which a planet can give results? Make flow chart?

361. How can you modify the results of a planet by remedies?

362. What do you mean by charity begins at home and what can be achieved by doing charity for different relations?

363. What is the importance of universal remedies in Astrology?

364. What is the use of regular purification and how to do purification?

365. What are the logics behind different steps of purification?

BASIC INFORMATION ABOUT ASTROLOGY

1. What is Astrology?

Astrology is a divine science dealing with the study of interaction between planets, signs, houses, *dasha* along with *gochar*. These five factors are the pillars of astrology. One must know the basics about these five factors before giving any prediction. All this is done on a chart called horoscope, which displays houses, signs, degrees etc. *Desh*, *kaal*, *paatr* (age, living standard and place of living) should always be kept in mind before predicting. Accuracy in prediction is possible only when we study these above factors in totality.

2. What is Horoscope?

Horoscope is a representation of picture of different planets in different signs at a particular day, time and place. This is the main base which shows interaction between different planets, signs and houses etc. North Indian and South Indian are the two most popular types of horoscopes.

North Indian

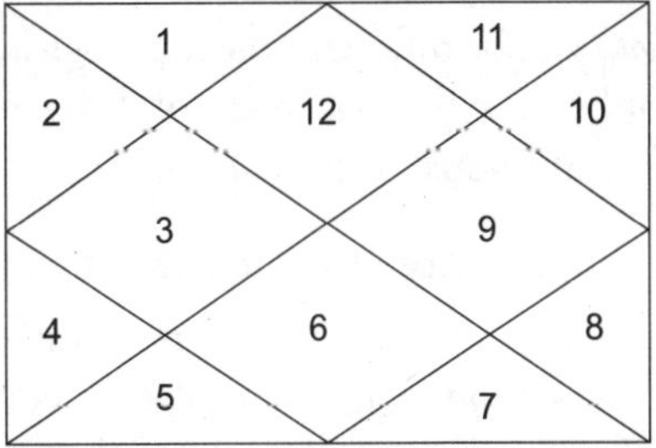

12 Asc. Pisces	1 Aries	2 Taurus	3 Gemini
11 Aquar			4 Cancer
10 Capro			5 Leo
9 Saggit	8 Scorpio	7 Libra	6 Virgo

South Indian Horoscope (Houses are fixed as Shown)

In south Indian horoscopes, the signs are fixed while the houses change as per birth time and place.

In north Indian horoscopes, the houses are fixed and the signs in *Lagan* and twelve houses change as per time and place of birth.

3. What is the basic data required to make a horoscope?

For making a horoscope, one needs

- Date of birth
- Time of birth
- Place of birth

4. What is the importance of date of birth?

The astronomical position of planets is different everyday. The earth is elliptical in shape. The time of Sunrise is different every day at different places and there is variation in *Lagan* also at different places. As the *Lagan* will be different, the astrological predictions would also be different because the placement of different planets will change to different houses as per *Lagan*.

5. What is the importance of time of birth?

The astronomical position of planets is different every minute. Sometimes, the *rashis* of planets will be same but degrees/signs/*nakshatras* can be different. The time of Sunrise is different every day at different places and there is variation in *Lagan* also at different places. As the *Lagan* will be different, the astrological predictions also would be different because the placement of different planets change degrees, *Nakshatra*, and house as per *Lagan*.

6. What is the importance of place of birth?

The e*Arth* is elliptical in shape. The Sunrise is different at different places and there is variation in *Lagan* also at different places. As the *Lagan* will be different, the astrological predictions would also be different because the placement of different planets change house as per *Lagan*.

7. What is lagan/ascendant?

The rising sign in the Eastern horizon determines the ascendant/*Lagan* of the horoscope. The degrees at that particular time indicates the exact degree and strength of *Lagan*/ascendant. This is the most important house of horoscope. "Well Begun Is Half Done ". In this context, if *Lagan*/*Lagan* Lord are strong, the horoscope is strong and person gets a promise of achieving a lot in life. The *Lagan* in the beginning 0°-3° or 27°-30° degrees is supposed to be weak.

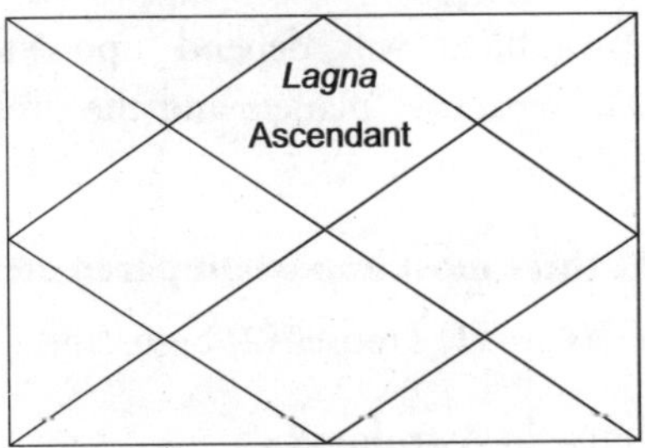

8. What is *Kal Purush Kundli*?

Kaal Purush Kundli is supposed to be the horoscope of Lord *Shiva*. The first house is always treated as Aries, 2nd as Taurus,3rd as Gemini, 4th as Cancer, 5th as Leo, 6th as Virgo, 7th as Libra,8th as Scorpio, 9th as Sagittarius,10th as Capricorn, 11th as Aquarius and 12th as Pisces. This is the rule followed in *Lal Kitab* irrespective of the sign rising in *Lagan*. In *Lal Kitab*, *Lagan* is always treated as Aries/Mesh.

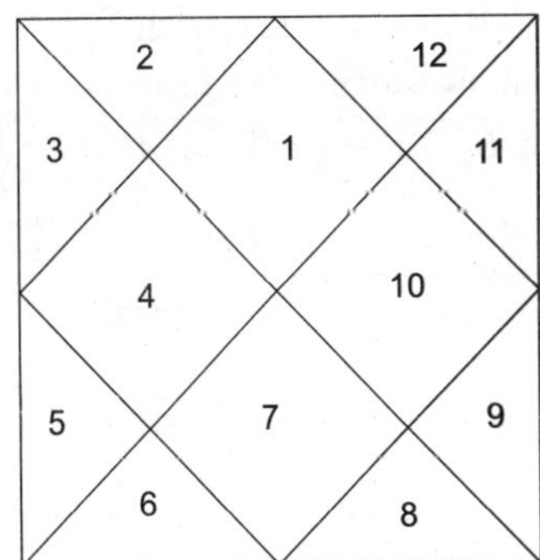

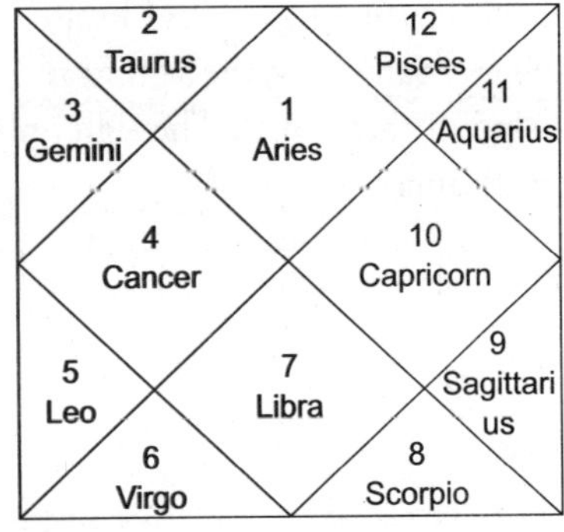

Kaal Purush Kundli should always be kept in mind. If Cancer sign and Moon are afflicted in your horoscope, you are likely to suffer from chest problems. The reason behind this is the representation of fourth house by Cancer sign and its Lord Moon in *Kaal Purush Kundli*.

In addition to this, if your fourth house and fourth Lord of *Lagan kundli* are also afflicted by separative planets, your proneness to chest problems increases further. In addition to this, if your fourth house and fourth Lord of Moon *kundli* are also afflicted by separative planets, your proneness to chest problems becomes almost a certainty.

The intensity of problem will depend upon the strength of destructive forces of separative planets and the protective forces of natural benefics.

9. What are the three most important parameters of astrology?

The three parameters are (1) Houses (2) Signs and (3) Planets.

10. What is a house in Astrology?

Like 12 *rashis* or signs, the horoscope is divided into 12 houses. The houses are fixed and *Lagan* is always the first house followed by second, third, fourth and so on. The houses represent certain things which are universal in nature and same for everyone irrespective of age, sex etc. They are like twelve boxes containing specified items. One must know what is to be seen from which house. These are called as the significances of a house. Whether your *Lagan* is Aries or Virgo or Capricorn or any of the twelve *Lagans*, the *Lagan*/or 1st house will always indicate self/health/brain etc. 2nd house will indicate about wealth/family/cash etc. Same way, the significance of all houses are fixed irrespective of sign in that house. The sign only changes the quality or effects of significances.

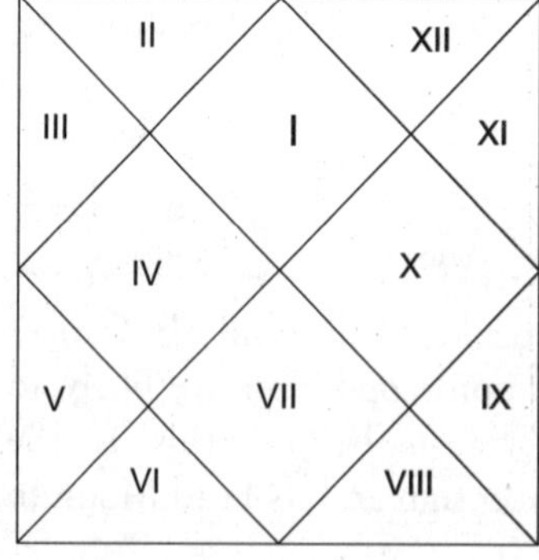

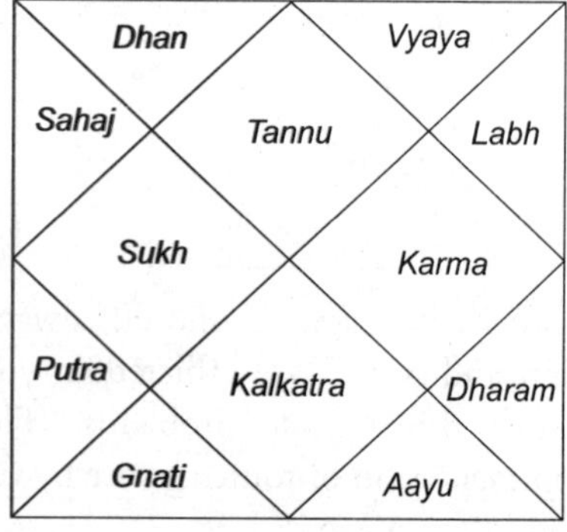

11. What are *Rashis*/signs?

Rashis or signs are the 12 divisions which control the quality and quantity of different houses and planets. There are twelve *rashis* in a horoscope. Each planet is Lord of two *rashis* except Sun and Moon, who have Lordship over one *rashi* only. *Rahu* and *Ketu* do not own any *rashi*. Each *rashi* is of 30 degrees.

Whole circle of the universe is divided into twelve houses/signs of 30 degree each. By taking note of the degree of planet, as per astronomical studies and observations, it is placed in that particular sign.

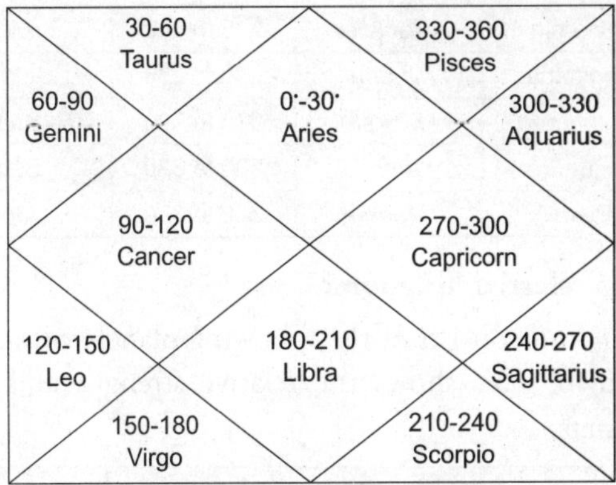

Lord of Aries and Scorpio is Mars so the strength of Mars determines the results of houses wherever Aries or Scorpio happen to fall as per ascendant/*Lagan*, eg. if Aries is the *Lagan*-Mars strength will determine your body (1st house) and longevity (8th house). If Leo is the *Lagan*, Mars strength will decide your residence/*sukh* (4th Lord) and fortune (9th Lord) Lordship. Analyze other planets in the same way.

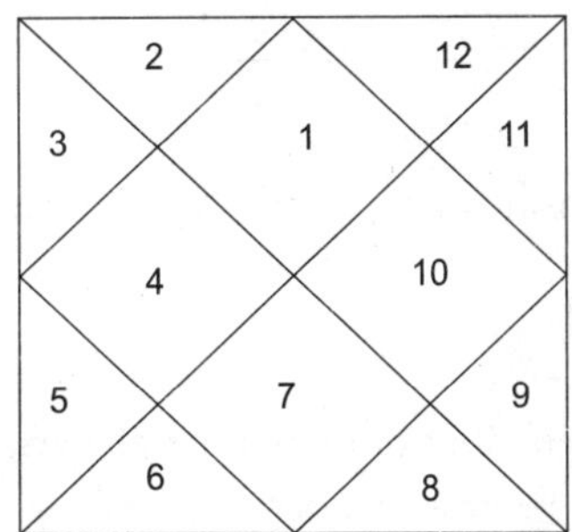

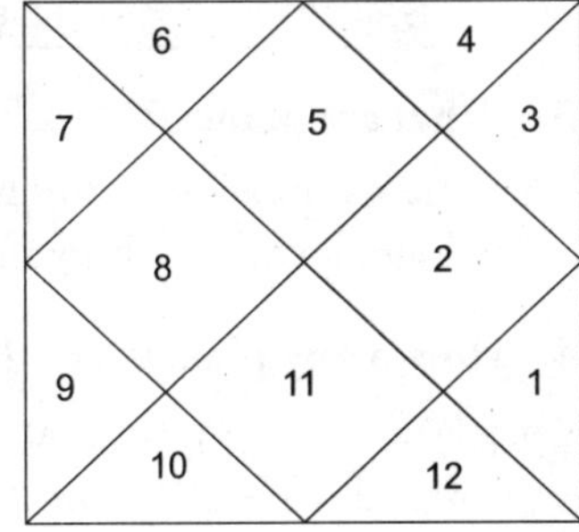

The twelve signs, their Lords and their range is as Follows:

No.	Sign	*Rashi*	Extent	Lord of sign
1	Aries	*Mesha*	00° to 30°	Mars
2	Taurus	*Vrisha*	30 to 60	Venus
3	Gemini	*Mithuna*	60 to 90	Mercury
4	Cancer	*Karka*	90 to 120	Moon
5	Leo	*Simha*	120 to150	Sun
6	Virgo	*Kanya*	150 to 180	Mercury
7	Libra	*Tula*	180 to 210	Venus
8	Scorpio	*Vrischika*	210 to 240	Mars
9	Sagittarius	*Dhanu*	240 to 270	Jupiter
10	Capricorn	*Makar*	270 to 300	Saturn
11	Aquarius	*Kumbha*	300 to 330	Saturn
12	Pisces	*Meena*	330 to 360	Jupiter

12. What is celestial kingdom?

Celestial kingdom consists of the following planets with the relative status as shown. This shows the relative strength and powers of different planets.

Planet	Position/status in kingdom
Sun	King
Moon	Queen
Mars	Commander
Mercury	Prince
Jupiter	Minister
Venus	Minister
Saturn	Servant

13. What are planets?

Planets are the moving bodies in the cosmos with continuous effects on e*Arth* along with the human beings.

14. How many planets are there?

As per *Vedic* astrology, there are 9 planets. Out of these nine planets, seven are real while *Rahu* and *Ketu* are shadowy planets.

Sun	Moon	Mars	Mercury	Jupiter
Venus	Saturn	*Rahu*	*Ketu*	

15. What are real planets?

There are seven real planets which can be seen in the sky with the help of naked eye or telescope.

Sun	Moon	Mars	Mercury
Jupiter	Venus	Saturn	

16. What are shadowy planets?

Rahu and *Ketu* are shadowy planets and cannot be seen with naked eye or telescopes. These are the strong intersection points of path of Sun and Moon as they move in celestial sphere.

17. Name the friends of different planets.

The table given below indicates friends of the various planets.

Planet	Friends
Sun	Moon, Mars, Jupiter
Moon	Sun, Mercury
Mars	Sun, Moon, Jupiter
Mercury	Sun, Venus
Jupiter	Sun, Moon, Mars
Venus	Mercury, Saturn
Saturn	Mercury, Venus, *Rahu*
Rahu	Jupiter,Venus, Saturn
Ketu	Mars, Venus, Saturn

The utility of this table helps in deciding the potential of results for any horoscope. "A Friend In Need Is A Friend Indeed". The principle holds true in astrology also as explained below :

If a planet is

— posited in a friendly sign

— conjunct with a friendly planet

— aspected by a friendly planet.

Then, this planet gets a free hand to deliver it's significances as it is comfortable to act and is fully supported by the friendly planet or planets as per P.A.C. (Position, Aspect and Conjunction). This potentiates the beneficial results of the unafflicted benefic planet. In case the benefic planet is afflicted by melefics or separative planets, the friendly planets help in diluting the bad results by their P.A.C.

18. Name the neutral of different planets.

Note the neutrals in the table given below:

Planet	Neutrals
Sun	Mercury
Moon	Jupiter, Venus, Mars, Saturn
Mars	Venus, Saturn, *Rahu* silent
Mercury	Mars, Jupiter, Saturn, *Ketu*
Jupiter	Saturn, *Rahu*, *Ketu*
Venus	Mars, Jupiter
Saturn	*Ketu*, Jupiter
Rahu	Mercury
Ketu	Mercury, Jupiter

The utility of this table helps in deciding the potential of results for any horoscope.

If a planet is

— posited in a neutral sign

— conjunct with a neutral planet

— aspected by a neutral planet

Then this planet gets a free hand to deliver it's significances as it is comfortable to act but is not supported.

19. Name the enemies of different planets.

In the table given below, note the enemies:-

Planet	Enemies
Sun	Venus,Saturn, *Rahu*, *Ketu*
Moon	*Rahu*, *Ketu*
Mars	Mercury, *Ketu*
Mercury	Moon
Jupiter	Mercury, Venus
Venus	Sun, Moon, *Rahu*
Saturn	Sun, Moon, Mars
Rahu	Sun,Venus, Mars
Ketu	Moon, Mars

The utility of this table helps in deciding the potential of results for any horoscope.

If a planet is

— posited in inimical sign

— conjunct with inimical planet

— aspected by inimical planet

The above factors make the planet weak.

In an inimical sign, a planet gets restricted to deliver it's significances as it is opposed by the inimical planets to act in a free way.

20. How many houses are there and what do they represent?

There are twelve houses in every horoscope which control different items as given below :—

No.	House	Name of House	Significances of the house
1	First	*Tannu*	Physical body, self
2	Second	*Dhan*	Money,wealth
3	Third	*Sahaj*	Self-efforts, youngers
4	Fourth	*Matri*	Mother, residence, *sukh*, vehicles

5	Fifth	*Putra*	Child, education, romance, Speculation, past *karmas*, intelligence
6	Sixth	*Gnati*	Acute diseases, debts, maternal relations, competition
7	Seventh	*Kalatar*	Life partner, business partner
8	Eighth	*Aayu*	Longevity, in-laws, obstructions, chronic diseases
9	Ninth	*Dharam*	Religion, father, fortune, higher education, foreign
10	Tenth	*Karam*	Profession , mother-in-law
11	Eleventh	*Labh*	Gains, elder brother/sister
12	Twelfth	*Vyaya*	Foreign, hospital, jail, expenditures

Family members are also – represented by different houses as shown below.

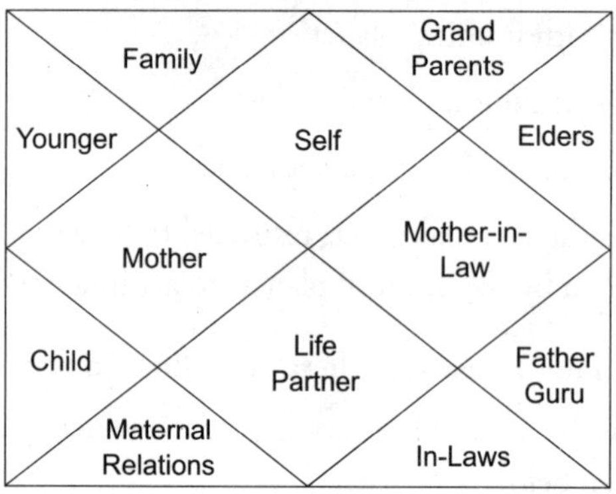

In case where we do not have the horoscope of a blood relation, limited predictions can still be given by making that house as *Lagan*. Make the horoscope by treating that house number as *Lagan*. Analysis is done in the same way as we analyze horoscope.

For example, if one does not have his horoscope, then one can try to analyze from the horoscope of son or daughter's horoscope. The 9th house of son/daughter's horoscope should be treated as *Lagan* and analyzed with the running *dasha*. This is especially useful nowadays because of availability of birth certificates of young generation.

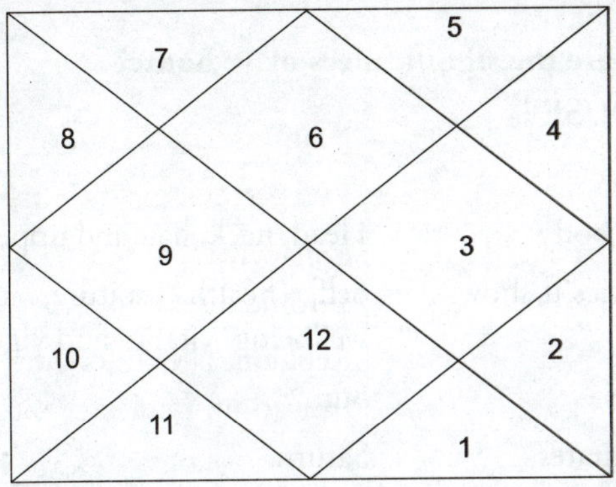

Horoscope of person

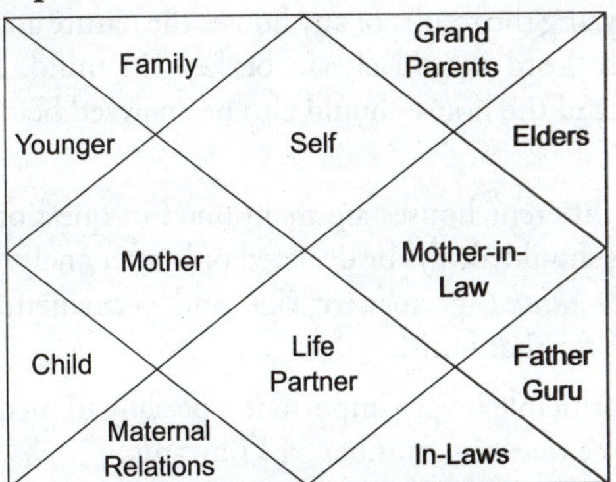

Analysis of father by treating 9th house sign Taurus as *Lagan*

Same *dasha* and *gocher* is applied in both the horoscopes.

SIGNIFICANCES OF HOUSES

21. What are the significances of 1st house?

FIRST HOUSE :

Karaka : Sun

Parts of the body	:	Head, neck, hair and upper part of face.
Characteristics it shows	:	Self, health, stature, temperament, wellbeing, vitality and vigour.
Planet exalts	:	Sun.
Planet debilitates	:	Saturn.
Relatives and relations	:	Self

Before analyzing the results of any house, the nature and significances of the house Lord should always be kept in mind. Besides house Lord, *karaka* of the house should also be analyzed before giving final prediction.

*Karaka*s of different houses are mentioned in question number 87. Final results should always be declared only after analyzing the house, house Lord, *karaka*, permanent sign and permanent sign Lord of *Kaal Purush* for that house.

The above principle is very important especially in medical astrology. For details see question number 313 onwards.

22. What are the significances of 2nd house?

SECOND HOUSE:

Karaka : Jupiter

Parts of the body	:	Face, eyes, cheek, teeth, chin and throat.
Characteristics it shows	:	Family, wealth, speech, second marriage, teachers, bankers, stocks and right eye.
Planet exalts	:	Moon.
Planet debilitates	:	Nil.
Relatives and relations	:	family.

23. What are the significances of 3rd house?

THIRD HOUSE:

Karaka : Mars

Parts of the body	:	Throat, ears, shoulders, nervous system.
Characteristics it shows	:	Younger brother, courage, stamina, telephone, writer, publishing, paper.
Planet exalts	:	nil.
Planet debilitates	:	nil.
Relatives and relations	:	Neighbours, younger siblings.

24. What are the significances of 4th house?

FOURTH HOUSE:

Karaka : Moon.

Parts of the body	:	Chest, heart, lungs, arteries and diaphragm.
Characteristics it shows	:	Mother, peace of mind, intelligence, savings, farms and orchids.
Planet exalts	:	Jupiter.
Planet debilitates	:	Mars.
Relatives and relations	:	Mother.

25. What are the significances of 5th house?

FIFTH HOUSE:

Karaka : Jupiter

Parts of the body	:	Abdomen, liver, gall bladder, heart, intestines.
Characteristics it shows	:	Intelligence, wealth, good morals, dance, love affairs and courtship.
Planet exalts	:	nil.
Planet debilitates	:	nil.
Relatives and relations	:	Paternal grandfather, eldest child.

26. What are the significances of 6th house?

SIXTH HOUSE:

Karaka : Mars

Parts of the body	:	Kidneys, large intestine
Characteristics it shows	:	Miseries, obstacles, accidents, competitive spirit, scandals and sorrow.
Planet exalts	:	Mercury.
Planet debilitates	:	Venus.
Relatives and relations	:	Maternal uncles/aunts, servants and pet animals.

27. What are the significances of 7th house?

SEVENTH HOUSE:

Karaka : Venus

Parts of the body	:	Uterus, bladder, urinary organs, prostate.
Characteristics it shows	:	Partner, marriage, general happiness, sexual diseases, foreign travels.
Planet exalts	:	Saturn.
Planet debilitates	:	Sun.
Relatives and relations	:	Wife, husband, second child.

28. What are the significances of 8th house?

EIGHTH HOUSE:

Karaka : Saturn.

Parts of the body	:	Seminal vesicles, external genitalia.
Characteristics it shows	:	Death, sorrow, hidden wealth, occult sciences and mysteries.
Planet exalts	:	nil.
Planet debilitates	:	Moon.
Relatives and relations	:	In-laws, adopted child.

29. What are the significances of 9th house?

NINTH HOUSE:

Karaka : Jupiter

Parts of the body	:	Thighs and femoral arteries.
Characteristics it	:	Religion, father, son, luck, fortune, pilgrimage, charity, faith.
Planet exalts	:	nil.
Planet debilitates	:	nil.
Relatives and relations	:	Guru, father, third child.

30. What are the significances of 10th house?

TENTH HOUSE:

Karaka	:	Mercury, Jupiter, Sun and Saturn.
Parts of the body	:	Shins.
Characteristics it shows	:	Dignity, honours, power, command, reputation, election, rank, government job.
Planet exalts	:	Mars.
Planet debilitates	:	Jupiter.
Relatives and relations	:	mother-in-law.

31. What are the significances of 11th house?

ELEVENTH HOUSE :

Karaka : Jupiter.

Parts of the body	:	Legs, right foot, left hand, left ear.
Characteristics it shows	:	Longevity of mother, gains, wishes, ambitions, fulfilment of desire.
Planet exalts	:	nil.
Planet debilitates	:	nil.
Relatives and relations	:	Elder siblings.

32. What are the significances of 12th house?

TWELFTH HOUSE:

Karaka : Jupiter

Parts of the body	:	Feet.
Characteristics it shows	:	Sexual enjoyment, foreign travels, hospitalization, jail, *Moksh*a, expenses.
Planet exalts	:	Venus.
Planet debilitates	:	Mercury.
Relatives and relations	:	Paternal grandmother, maternal grandfather.

33. What are the different groups of houses?

Houses have been further divided into different groups like:

Trines/ *Trikones* 1, 5, 9 houses

*Kendra*s 1, 4, 7, 10 houses

Upchaya 3, 6, 10, 11 houses

Dushtsthan 6, 8, 12 houses

Maarak 2, 7 houses

Panphar 2, 5, 8, 11 houses

Apokolime 3, 6, 9, 12 houses

*Trishaday*ay 3, 6,11 houses

Trik 6, 8, 12 houses

Longevity 3, 8 houses

Badhak (11th Lord for moveable *Lagan*, 9th Lord for fixed *Lagan* and 7th Lord for dual *Lagan*s)

2nd and 12th houses are considered as neutral houses. They behave as per the Lordship of their other sign as *Kendra* /trine or dushtstan.

Out of these, comparatively the Trines or *Kendra*'s are favourable houses and *dushtstanas* are unfavourable houses.

34. What are the Trines houses and their use?

Trines houses are first, fifth and ninth.

First house is the most important house as it represents the person as a whole personality. It represents the whole physical body. First house is extra powerful being a *trikone* as well as *Kendra* so represents stability of *Kendra* and fortune of trines.

Fifth house is the house of our past *karmas* and represents the most important aspect of human race i.e., children.

Ninth house represents our present *karmas* and represents father.

So, the Trine houses represents our three generations. These are also called as *Lakshmi* houses and represent money besides second and eleventh houses (Money houses).

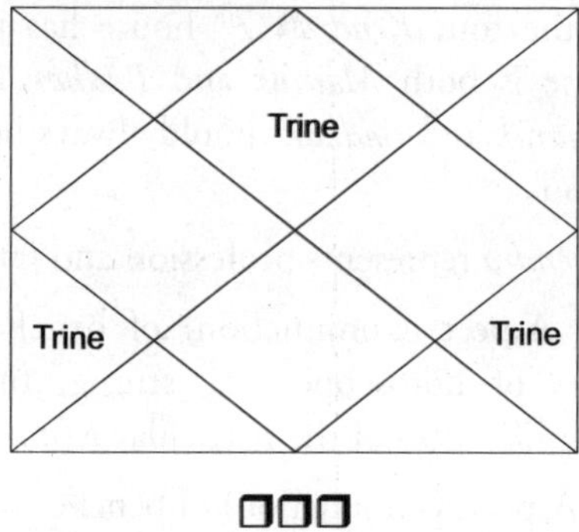

❑❑❑

DIFFERENT HOUSES AND THEIR USES

35. What are *Kendras* and their uses?

Kendras are the stability houses of Horoscope. These are called as pillars of horoscope.

1st, 4th, 7th and 10th houses represent *Kendras*.

First house as *Kendra* represents self, whole personality.

Fourth house as *Kendra* represents mother, vehicles, happiness and home.

Seventh house as *Kendra* represents wife or husband besides business partner. Out of the four *Kendras*, 7th house has the negativity of *Maarak*. 7th house is both *Maarak* and *Badhak* for dual *Lagans*. The effects of *maarak* and *Badhak* should always be co-related with longevity of person.

Tenth house as *Kendra* represents profession and father.

P.A.C. (Position, Aspect, Conjunction) of benefics with *Kendra's* makes the pillars of horoscope very strong, thereby providing strength to the significances of the particular *Kendra*/house.

P.A.C. (Position, Aspect, Conjunction) of benefics with *Kendra* Lords makes the pillars of horoscope very strong, thereby providing strength to the significances of the particular *Kendra*/house.

Melefics as *Kendra* Lords shed their malefic nature.

Benefics as *Kendra* Lords shed their benefic nature.

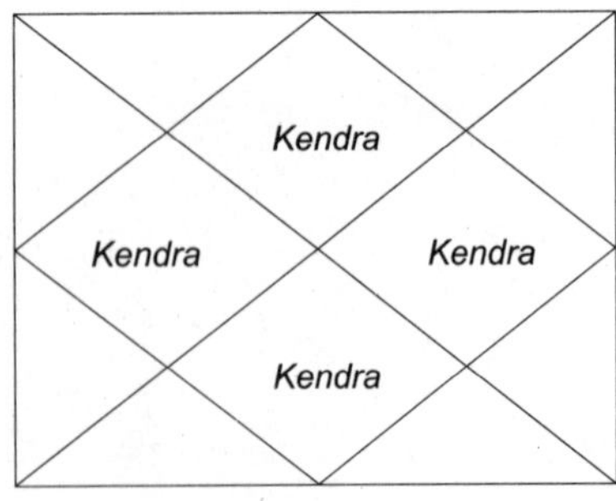

36. What does different houses indicate and how to use them?

1st – house is mainly concerned with the physical body

2nd – *dhan*/money

3rd – *sahaj*/self-efforts

4th – *sukh*/happiness

5th – *putra*/children

6th – *gnati*/diseases

7th – *kalkatra*/life partner

8th – *aayu*/longevity

9th – *dharam*/religion

10th – *karma*/profession

11th – *labh*/gains

12th – *vyaya*/expenses

So, when you want to analyze something, consider the following for gains:-

— 11th house P.A.C.

— 11th Lord P.A.C.

— *Karaka* Jupiter's P.A.C. etc.

In astrology, everything is analyzed by

1 position or placement of planet ..... P

2 aspects on the planet/house ..... A

3 conjunction of other planets C

1, 2, 3 GO (apply the above 1, 2, 3 to house, house Lord and *Karaka* followed by *Gocher* (GO).

Apply P.A.C. to house, house Lord and *karaka* along with *dasha* and transit to assess any event.

The basic utility lies in the fact that one must know about the significances of a house before prediction. For example, one wants to know about one's profession, then the main focus should be on

10th house and 10th Lord. In the same way different events are to be analyzed by picking up the specific house and its Lord.

37. What are *Laxmi sthanas*?

Laxmi Sthans are also known as Trines/*trikone* houses. P.A.C. (Position, Aspect, and Conjunction) of benefics with Trine houses gives money, wealth, fortune, prosperity, health, religious knowledge etc. Combinations of Trines and *Kendras* house Lords give both status, stability besides wealth and prosperity. More the combinations, better the life.

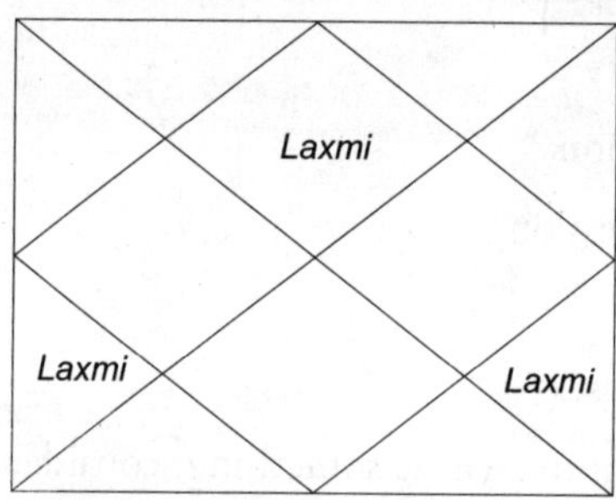

38. What are *Vishnu sthanas*?

Vishnu Sthans are also known as *Kendras*. *Vishnugi* is symbol of status, stability, prosperity, power etc. P.A.C. of *Vishnu Sthans* (*Kendras*) with benefics makes the pillars of horoscope very strong, thereby providing strength to the significances of the particular *Kendra*/ house.

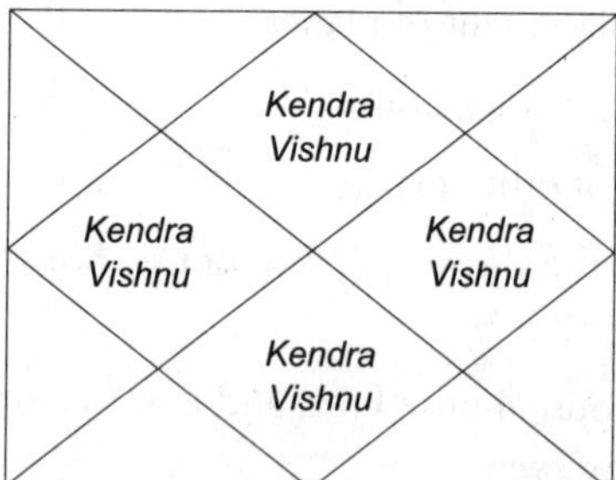

39. What are the *Upchaya* houses and their use?

Upchaya houses are 3rd, 6th, 10th and 11th houses. *Upchaya* houses lift up the person after lot of self-efforts and struggles.

P.A.C. (Position, Aspect and Conjunction) of benefics with these houses gives positive results after sincere efforts.

P.A.C. of benefics with 3rd house gives achievements with good self-effort.

P.A.C. of benefics with 6th house gives competitive spirit.

P.A.C. of benefics with 10th house gives good professional status.

P.A.C. of benefics with 11th house gives gains of life.

More the self-efforts with the healthy competitive spirit, more will be the status along with gains in life.

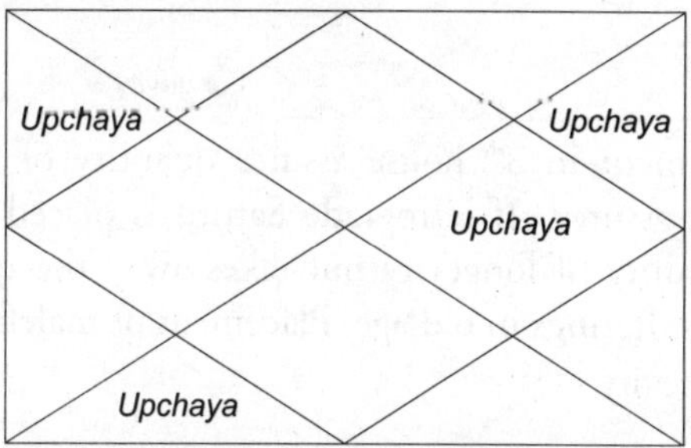

40. What are the *Dushtsthan* houses and their use?

Duststhanas are 6th, 8th and 12th houses. These are comparatively negative houses representing short diseases, long diseases and hospital respectively. The positive side is that 6th house represents competition, 8th house represents research, longevity and 12th house represents *Moksh*, foreign, sleep etc. Placement of natural benefics, functional benefics in *dushtathanas* is a wastage of benefic thereby restricting the positive results of benefics.

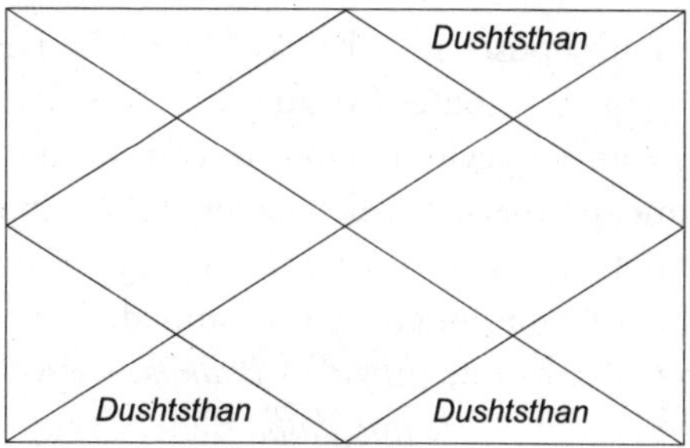

41. What are the longevity houses?

Longevity is indicated by 8th house and 3rd house (8th from 8th). The quality of physical health is indicated by *Lagan*, *Lagan* Lord and *Karaka* Sun. P.A.C. of benefics with the above factors assures good quality of physical health and longevity.

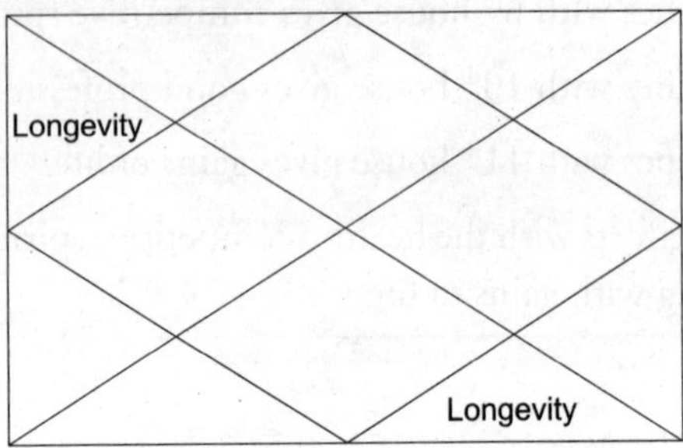

Saturn's placement in 8th house assures quantity of longevity but quality is not assured. If retrograde Saturn is placed in 8th house, it assures quantity of longevity but takes away the quality of life. Rather, gives sufferings in old age. Placement of malefic in 3rd house also gives longevity.

42. What are the *Maarak* houses and their use?

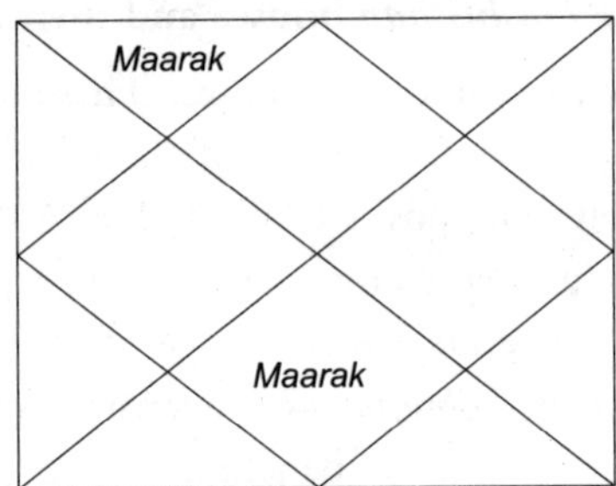

Second and seventh houses are called as *Maarak* houses because they are twelfth to longevity houses (3rd and 8th). They indicate the time of death when your longevity is about to end. In practical life, they give money, fame, partnership when having P.A.C. (position, aspect, conjunction) of benefics. One should not get scared of *Maarak dasha* during life till your longevity is promised. Their role comes in life around your death time provided *Badhak* is also involved. One should never be scared of *Maarak dasha* till longevity is still there.

43. What are *Badhak* houses and their use?

Badhakpati (trouble creator) is a planet, who creates trouble for the *jatak* during its *dasha*. *Badhak* means obstructive, hurdles, hindrances etc.

Badhak houses (11th Lord for moveable *Lagan*, 9th Lord for fixed *Lagan* and 7th Lord for dual *Lagans*) or Lords of *Badhak* houses are more harmful and trouble shooters as compared to *Maaraks*. It is the *Badhak* along with *Maarak* which gives death. Involvement of *Badhak* is more important than *Maarak* while calculating time of death

For moveable *Lagan* (1, 4, 7, and 10) 11th Lord is *Badhakpati.*

For fixed *Lagan* (2, 5, 8, 11) 9th Lord is *Badhakpati.*

For dual *Lagan* (3, 6, 9, 12) 7th Lord is *Badhakpati.*

44. What are *Panphar* houses and their use?

2nd, 5th, 8th, 11th houses are called *Panphar* houses. They give 50 percent results as compared to *Kendras*. P.A.C. of benefics with above houses promote positive results like:—

2nd house : — Wealth

5th house : — Intelligence and higher education

8th house : — Longevity

11th house : — Gains

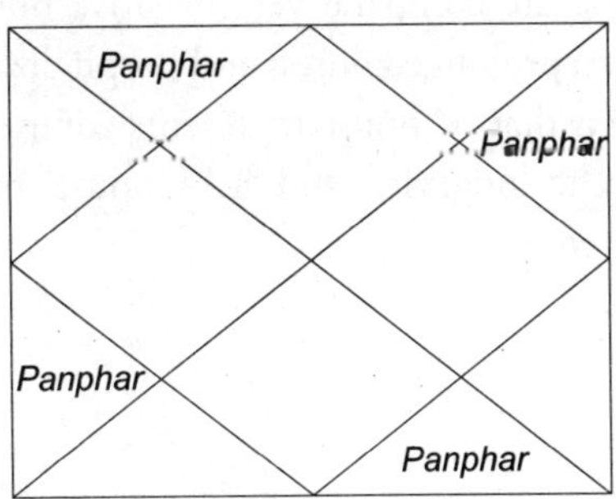

45. What are the Apoklime houses and their use?

3rd, 6th, 9th, and 12th houses are known as Apoklime houses and give 25 percent results as compared to *Kendra*'s. P.A.C. of benefics with the above houses will promote positive results:—

Self-efforts— 3rd house

Competitive spirit— 6th house

Fortune— 9th house

Private life or foreign journey—12th house

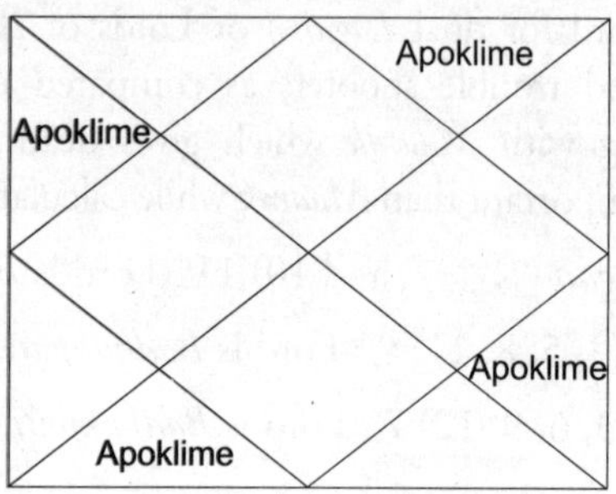

46. What are the *Trishadaya* houses and their use?

Third, sixth and eleventh houses are called as *Trishadaya* houses. They give results after struggles. They are functional malefic for the *Lagan*. *Trishadaya* houses give positive results after struggles if the above houses have benefic P.A.C.

47. What are the *Trik* houses and their use?

Trik houses are 6th, 8th and 12th houses, these are also known as *Duststhanas.* These are comparatively negative houses representing short lived diseases, prolonged illness and hospitalization respectively. The positive side is that 6th house represents competition, 8th house represents research, longevity and 12th house represents *Moksh*, foreign and sleep etc.

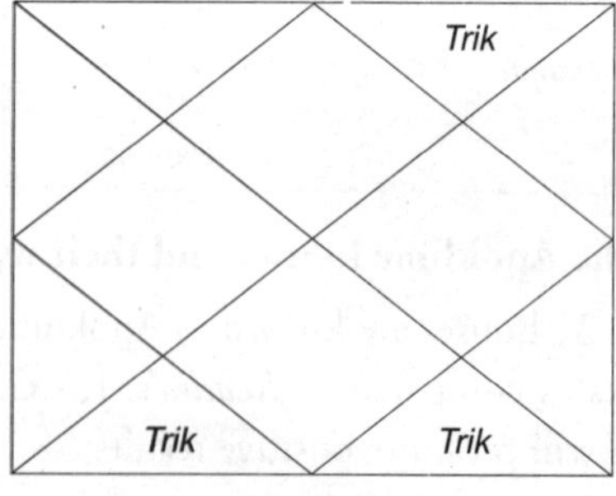

48. What are *Dharam, Arth, Kaam, Moksh* houses?

1st, 5th, 9th houses are permanent *dhram* houses

2nd, 6th, 10th houses are permanent *Arth* houses.

3rd, 7th, 11th houses are permanent *Kaam* houses.

4th, 8th, 12th, are permanent *Moksh* houses.

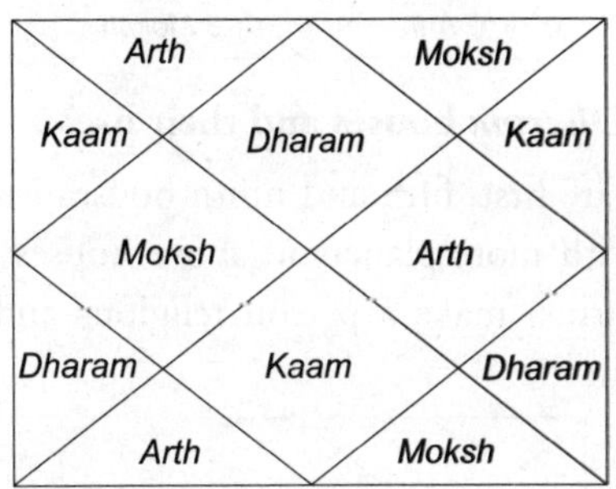

49. What are *Dharam, Arth, Kaam, Moksh* signs?

1st, 5th, 9th (Aries, Leo, Sagittarius) signs are *Dharam* signs.

2nd, 6th, 10th (Taurus, Virgo, Capricorn) signs are *Arth* signs.

3rd, 7th, 11th (Gemini, Libra, Aquarius) are *Kaam* signs.

4th, 8th, 12th (Cancer, Scorpio, and Pisces) are *Moksh* signs.

Placement of planets in different houses indicate the native's inclination towards *Dharam* (religion), *Arth* (wealth), *Kaam* (desires) and *Moksh* (liberation).

More the number of planets in a particular group of houses, more the person will be inclined towards those activities e.g., more planets in 2nd, 6th and 10th houses make one money-minded, wealthy etc.

The final decision should be taken after considering the placement of planets in houses along with signs and strength of planets.

If one has more planets in 1st, 5th, 9th houses along with placement in 1st, 5th, 9th signs, it indicates more of a religious, pious, charitable personality.

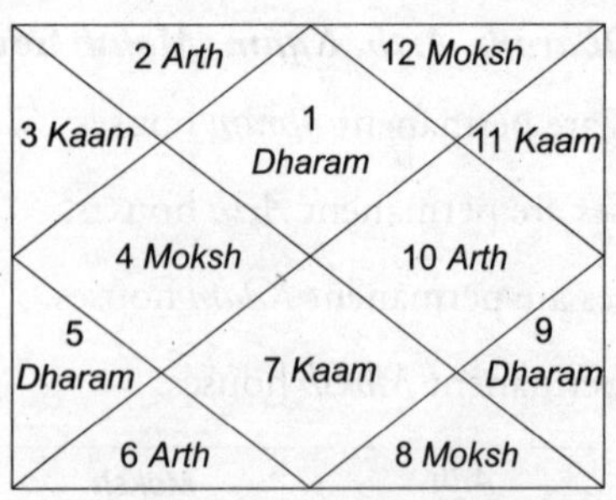

50. What are *Dharma* houses and their use?

Dharma houses are first, fifth and ninth houses irrespective of your *Lagan*. People with more planets in above houses and signs (Aries, Leo, and Sagittarius) make a person religious and truthful with a pious approach in life.

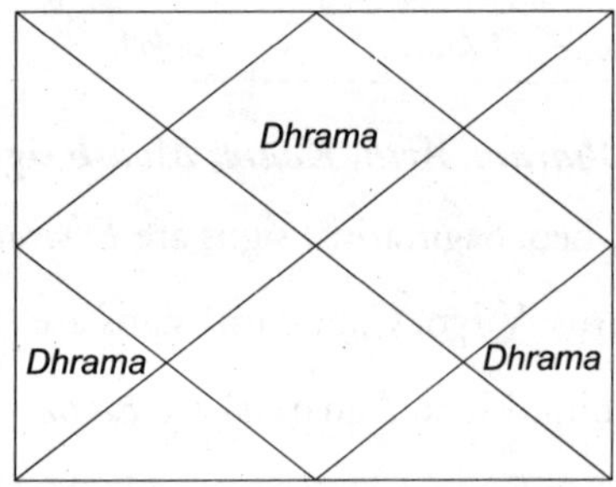

51. What are *Arth* houses and their use?

Arth houses are second, sixth and tenth houses irrespective of your *Lagan*. People with more planets in above houses and signs (Taurus, Virgo, and Capricorn) make a person money-minded with an approach of materialistic gains in life.

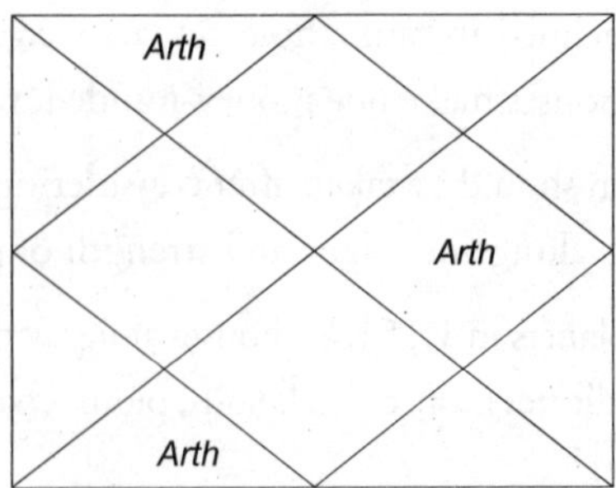

52. What are *Kaam* houses and their use?

Kaam houses are third, seventh and eleventh houses irrespective of your *Lagan*. People with more planets in above houses and signs (Gemini, Libra, Aquarius) make a person more expecting, wishful, sometimes greedy.

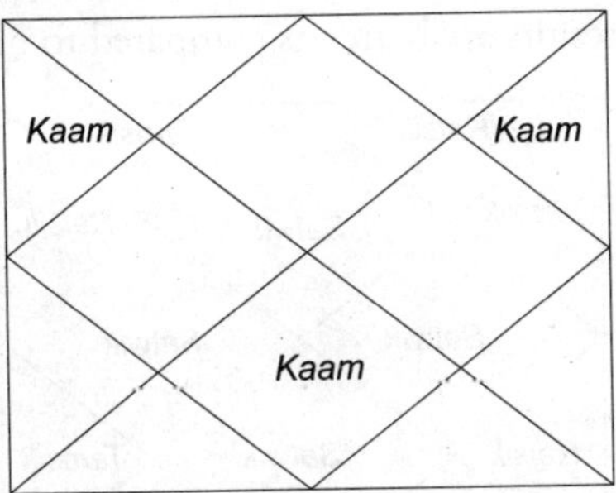

53. What are *Moksha* houses and their use?

Moksha houses are fourth, eighth and twelfth irrespective of your *Lagan*. People with more planets in above houses and signs (Cancer, Scorpio and Pisces) makes a person religious and truthful with an accommodating approach in life.

Note : —

The final outcome should be decided after clubbing the signs and houses both.

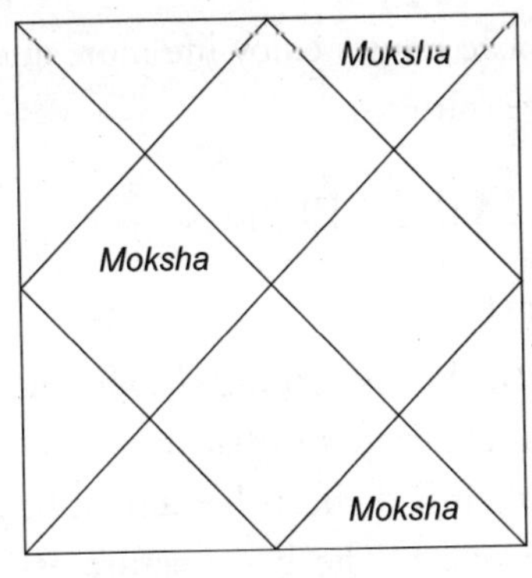

MOKSHA HOUSES

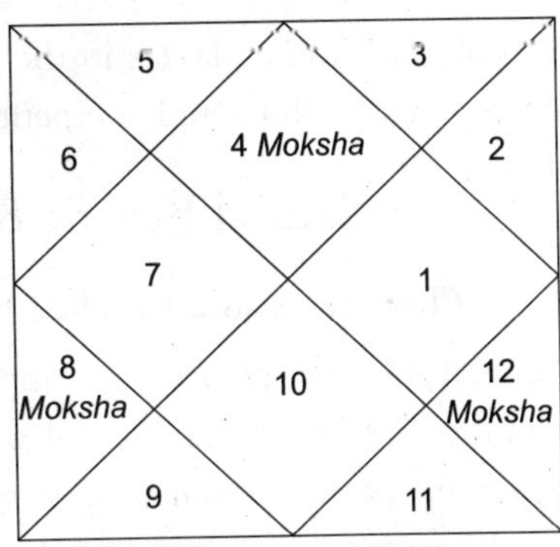

MOKSHA SIGNS

54. What are *Satwik* houses and their use?

Satwik houses are first, fourth, seventh and tenth houses. Persons with more planets in the above houses are blessed, stable in life as all the houses represent the *Kendra*s or the pillars of the horoscope. The *Satwik* houses should preferably be occupied by planets. If occupied by benefics, the results are better as compared to malefics.

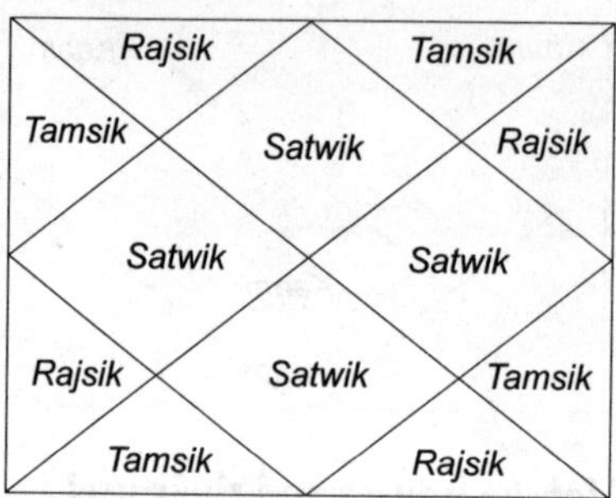

55. What are *Rajsik* houses and their use?

Rajsik houses are second, fifth, eighth and eleventh houses.

Persons with more planets in the above houses are more money-minded and think of materialistic gains and comforts of life.

56. What are *Tamsik* houses and their uses?

Tamsik houses are third, sixth, ninth and twelfth houses.

Persons with more planets in the above houses enjoy life more and believe in self-efforts and competitive spirit.

Natural Benefic & Malefic Planets

57. What are natural benefic planets?

Natural benefic planets are Jupiter, Venus, strong Moon and unafflicted Mercury. The use of natural benefics is that they always give some positive result in spite of their bad effects because of bad Lordship or bad placement in horoscope. The basic nature as a natural benefic is never lost in spite of becoming a functional malefic.

58. What are natural malefic planets?

Natural malefic planets are Saturn, Mars, *Rahu*, and *Ketu*. Sun is a cruel planet. The natural malefic will always give some negative result in spite of their good effects because of good Lordship or good placement in horoscope. The basic nature as a malefic is never lost despite of it becoming a functional benefic.

SIGNIFICANCES OF PLANETS

59. What are the significances of Sun?

SUN:

Sign	:	Leo
Friends of the planet	:	Moon, Mars, Jupiter.
Enemies of the planet	:	Venus, Satun, *Rahu*, *Ketu*.
Neutral to the planets	:	Mercury.
Exaltation of the planet	:	Aries.
Debilitation of the planet	:	Libra.
Mool trikone sign of the planet	:	Leo
Direction of the planet	:	East
Sex of the planet	:	Male
Karaka of the planet	:	Father, power, doctor, physician, blood circulation, heart, brain, bones, forests and deserts etc.
Profession regarding planet	:	Government job, creator, promoter, owner, jeweller, designer, magistrate and ruler.
Items of the planet	:	Wheat, copper, ruby and sandalwood.
Lord of *nakshatras*	:	*Kritika, Uttarphalguni, Uttar shadha.*

Sun being the Lord of planetary kingdom behaves like a boss, leader, commander. He is aggressive and energetic.

The final results of Sun should be declared after studying the P.A.C. of Sun, its sign Leo, 5th house which is permanent house of Sun as per *kaal purush kundli*. Sun is the *Karaka* of 1st and 10th house as per *Parashri* astrology.

Affliction of Sun will affect the results of 1st, and 10th house as *Karaka*.

Affliction of Sun will affect results of 5th house, which is its permanent house as per *kaal purush kundli*.

Affliction of Sun can affect the results of the house as per Lordship of Leo sign depending on *Lagan*. Now the question arises whether all of above will be affected or only some are affected. If in the horoscope 1st house, 1st Lord, 5th house and 5th Lord are not afflicted, then the results of afflicted Sun will be felt over profession as Sun is *Karaka* for tenth house (profession).

60. What are the significances of Moon?

MOON:

Sign	:	Cancer
Friends of the planet	:	Sun, Mercury.
Enemies of the planet	:	*Rahu*, *Ketu*.
Neutral to the planet	:	Mars, Jupiter, Venus and Saturn.
Exaltation of the planet	:	Taurus.
Debilitation of the planet	:	Scorpio.
Mool trikone sign of the planet	:	Taurus.
Direction of the planet	:	North West.
Sex of the planet	:	Female.
Karaka of the planet	:	Mother, heart, mind, liquids, milk and pearl.
Profession regarding planet	:	Water works, liquor, cattle, fish, nursery, mirror and nursing homes.
Items of the planet	:	Milk, rice, silver, pearl and curd.
Lord of *nakshatras*	:	*Hasta, Shravan* and *Rohini*.

The final results of Moon should be declared after studying the P.A.C. of Moon, its sign Cancer, 4th house which is permanent house of Moon as per *kaal purush kundli*. Moon is the *Karaka* of 4th house as per *Parashri* astrology.

Affliction of Moon will affect the results of 4th house as *Karaka*.

Affliction of Moon will affect results of 4th house, which is its permanent house as per *kaal purush kundli*.

Affliction of Moon can affect results of the house as per Lordship of Cancer sign depending on *Lagan*. Now, the question arises whether all of above will be affected or only some are affected. If in the horoscope 4th house, 4th Lord are not afflicted, then the results of afflicted Moon will be felt over house, where Cancer sign falls as per *Lagan*.

61. What are the significances of Mars?

MARS:

Sign	:	Aries and Scorpio.
Friends of the planet	:	Sun, Moon, Jupiter.
Enemies of the planet	:	Mercury, *Ketu*.
Neutral to the planet	:	Saturn and Venus.
Exaltation of the planet	:	Capricorn.
Debilitation of the planet	:	Cancer.
Mool trikone sign of the planet	:	Aries.
Direction of the planet	:	South.
Sex of the planet	:	Male.
Karaka of the planet	:	Younger brother, blood, defence, surgery, violence and fire.
Profession regarding planet	:	Armed forces, chemist, jail, dentist and bakers.
Items of the planet	:	*Gur*, copper and red cloth.
Lord of *nakshatras*	:	*Mrigshira, Chitra* and *Dhanishta*.

The final results of Mars should be declared after studying the P.A.C. of Mars, its signs Aries and Scorpio, 1st house and 8th house which are permanent houses of Mars as per *kaal purush kundli*. Mars is the *Karaka* of 3rd house, 6th house as per *Parashri* astrology.

Affliction of Mars will affect the results of 3rd house, 6th house as *Karaka*.

Affliction of Mars will affect results of 1st house, 8th house, which are its permanent houses as per *kaal purush kundli*.

Affliction of Mars can affect the results of the house as per Lordship of Aries and Scorpio signs depending on *Lagan*. Now, the question arises whether all of above will be affected or only some are affected. If in the horoscope 3rd house, 3rd Lord, 6th house, 6th Lord are not afflicted, then the results of afflicted Mars will be felt over houses, where Aries sign and Scorpio falls as per-*Lagan*.

62. What are the significances of Mercury?

MERCURY:

Sign	:	Gemini and Virgo.
Friends of the planet	:	Sun and Venus.
Enemies of the planet	:	Moon.
Neutral to the planet	:	Saturn, Mars and Jupiter.
Exaltation of the planet	:	Virgo.
Debilitation of the planet	:	Pisces.
Mool trikone sign of the planet	:	Virgo.
Direction of the planet	:	North.
Sex of the planet	:	Male eunuch.
Karaka of the planet	:	Intelligence, publisher, friends, teachers, accountancy, smell and laughter.
Profession regarding planet	:	Business, law, transport, author, astrologer, writer and physician.

Items of the planet: Green cloth, green moong, camphor and ivory.

Lord of *nakshatras*: *Ashlesha, Jyeshtha* and *Rewati*.

The final results of Mercury should be declared after studying the P.A.C. of Mercury, its sign Gemini, Virgo, 3rd house, 6th house, which are permanent houses of Mercury as per *kaal purush kundli*. Mercury is the *karaka* of 10th house as per *Parashri* astrology.

Affliction of Mercury will affect the results of 10th house as *Karaka*.

Affliction of Mercury will affect results of 3rd and 6th houses, which are its permanent houses as per *kaal purush kundli*.

Affliction of Mercury can affect the results of the houses as per Lordship of Gemini and Virgo signs depending on *Lagan*. Now, the question arises whether all of above will be affected or only some are affected. If in the horoscope 3rd house, 3rd Lord, 6th house and 6th Lord are not afflicted, then the results of afflicted Mercury will be felt over profession as Mercury is *Karaka* for tenth house (profession).

63. What are the significances of Jupiter?

JUPITER:

Sign	:	Sagittarius and Pisces.
Friends of the planet	:	Sun, Moon, Mars.
Enemies of the planet	:	Mercury and Venus.
Neutral to the planet	:	Saturn.
Exaltation of the planet	:	Cancer.
Debilitation of the planet	:	Capricorn.
Mool trikone sign of the planet	:	Sagittarius.
Direction of the planet	:	North-East.
Sex of the planet	:	Male.
Karaka of the planet	:	Husband, wealth, guru, knowledge, religion, faith and good acts.
Profession regarding planet	:	Income tax, law, judge, auditors, teachers, priests and councillors.

Items of the planet	:	Gold, Turmeric, *Kesar*, *Chana dal.*
Lord of *nakshatras*	:	*Punarvasu, Vishakha, Poorvbhadra.*

The final results of Jupiter should be declared after studying the P.A.C. of Jupiter, its sign Sagittarius, Pisces 9th house, 12th houses, which are permanent houses of Jupiter as per *kaal purush kundli*. Jupiter is the *Karaka* of 2nd house, 5th house, 9th house,10th house,11th house as per *Parashri* astrology.

Affliction of Jupiter will affect the results of 2nd house, 5th house,9th house,10th house,11th house as *Karaka.*

Affliction of Jupiter will affect results of 9th house,12th house which are its permanent houses as per *kaal purush kundli*.

Affliction of Jupiter can affect the results of the house as per Lordship of Sagittarius, Pisces signs depending on *Lagan*. Now, the question arises whether all of above will be affected or only some are affected. If in the horoscope 9th house,12th house, 9th Lord,12th Lords are not afflicted, then the results of afflicted Jupiter will be felt over profession, money, education, gains etc. as Jupiter is *Karaka* for tenth house(profession), 2nd house (money), 5th house (higher education), 11th house (house of gains).

64. What are the significances of Venus?

VENUS:

Sign	:	Taurus and Libra.
Friends of the planet	:	Saturn and Mercury.
Enemies of the planet	:	Sun, Moon, *Rahu.*
Neutral to the planet	:	Mars and Jupiter.
Exaltation of the planet	:	Pisces.
Debilitation of the planet	:	Virgo.
Mool trikone sign of the planet	:	Libra.

Direction of the planet	:	South-East.
Sex of the planet	:	Female.
Karaka of the planet	:	Wife, luxury items, semen, dance, music, beauty and perfumes.
Profession regarding planet	:	Artists, perfumers, cinema, musicians, poets and jewellers.
Items of the planet	:	*Ghee*, curd, cow and white flowers.
Lord of *nakshatras*	:	*Bharani, Poorvphalugni, Poorvshadha.*

The final results of Venus should be declared after studying the P.A.C. of Venus, its sign Taurus, Libra, 2nd house, 7th house which are permanent houses of Venus as per *kaal purush kundli*. Venus is the *Karaka* of 4th and 7th house as per *Parashri* astrology.

Affliction of Venus will affect the results of 4th house and 7th house as *Karaka*.

Affliction of Venus will affect results of 2nd house, 7th house which are its permanent houses as per *kaal purush kundli*.

Affliction of Venus can affect the results of the house as per Lordship of Taurus, Libra signs depending on *Lagan*. Now, the question arises whether all of above will be affected or only some are affected. If in the horoscope 2nd house, 2nd Lord, 4th house and 4th Lord are not afflicted, then the results of afflicted Venus will be felt over marriage as Venus is *Karaka* for seventh house (marriage).

65. What are the significances of Saturn?

SATURN:

Sign	:	Capricorn and Aquarius.
Friends of the planet	:	Mercury and Venus.
Enemies of the planet	:	Sun, Moon and Mars.

Neutral to the planet	:	Jupiter.
Exaltation of the planet	:	Libra.
Debilitation of the planet	:	Aries.
Mool trikone sign of the planet	:	Aquarius.
Direction of the planet	:	West.
Sex of the planet	:	Female eunuch.
Karaka of the planet	:	Longevity, labourers, poverty, servants, timber, poison and ashes.
Profession regarding planet	:	Hard working jobs, iron and steel, black magic, oil and foot wear.
Items of the planet	:	Iron, musk, black *dal.*
Lord of *nakshatras*	:	*Pushya, Anuradha, Uttarbhadrapad.*

The final results of Saturn should be declared after studying the P.A.C. of Saturn, its sign Capricorn, Aquarius, 10th house, 11th house, which are permanent houses of Saturn as per *kaal purush kundli.* Saturn is the *Karaka* of 6th house, 8th house, 10th house and 12th houses as per *Parashri* astrology.

Affliction of Saturn will affect the results of 6th house, 8th house, 10th house and 12th houses as *Karaka.*

Affliction of Satun will affect results of 10th house, 11th house, which are its permanent houses as per *kaal purush kundli.*

Affliction of Satun can affect the results of the house as per Lordship of Capricorn, Aquarius signs depending on *Lagan.* Now, the question arises whether all of above will be affected or only some are affected. If in the horoscope 6th house,6th Lord,8th house, 8th Lord, 10th house and 10th Lord are not afflicted, then the results of afflicted Saturn will be felt over personal bedroom life as Saturn is *Karaka* for twelfth house (personal bedroom).

66. What are the significances of *Rahu*?

RAHU:

Friends of the planet	:	Venus, Mercury and Saturn.
Enemies of the planet	:	Sun, Venus, Mars.
Neutral to the planets	:	Jupiter, *Ketu.*
Exaltation of the planet	:	Taurus.
Debilitation of the planet	:	Scorpio.
Mool trikone sign of the planet	:	Gemini and Cancer.
Direction of the planet	:	South-West.
Sex of the planet	:	Male.
Karaka of the planet	:	Research, arguments, darkness, gambling, reptiles, and poison.
Profession regarding planet	:	Speculation, slaughter house, dirty places, snake catchers, lawyers.
Items of the planet	:	Black and white blanket, satnaja, lead.
Lord of *nakshatras*	:	*Aradra, Swati, Satbhisha.*

67. What are the significances of *Ketu*?

KETU:

Friends of the planet	:	Mercury, Jupiter.
Enemies of the planet	:	Moon, Mars.
Neutral to the planets	:	Mars, *Rahu*, Venus.
Exaltation of the planet	:	Sagittarius and Capricorn.
Debilitation of the planet	:	Taurus.
Mool trikone sign of the planet	:	Sagittarius and Capricorn.
Direction of the planet	:	North-West.

Sex of the planet	:	Hermaphrodite (a person having both male and female sex organs).
Karaka of the planet	:	*Moksha*, imprisonment, chain smoker, leprosy, suicide and spots on body.
Profession regarding planet	:	Skeletons, bones, slaughter house, sewages, dirty and foul smelling places.
Items of the planet	:	Black and white blanket, satnaja, black and white dog.
Lord of *nakshatras*	:	*Ashwini, Magha, Moola.*

68. What are *Satwik* planets and their uses?

Jupiter and Sun are *satwik* planets and will always take one to the path of truth, honesty, disciplined life etc. *Dasha* of these planets are best for doing *satwik karmas*, charitable activities, donations, disciplined activities etc.

69. Which are *Rajsik* planets and their use?

Moon and Venus are *Rajsik* planets and will always take one to the path of materialism, glamour, enjoyments etc. *Dasha* of these planets are best for enjoying the facilities of the materialistic world.

70. Which are *Tamsik* planets and their uses?

Mercury, Saturn, Mars, *Rahu* and *Ketu* are *Tamsik* planets and takes one towards *Tamsik* activities like enjoyment, cleverness, cunningness etc. *Dasha* of these planets are disease giving, negative thinking, lethargic etc.

71. Which are the male planets and their uses?

Male planets are Sun, Mars and Jupiter and are more dominating in nature as compared to female planets. They are more assertive, commanding, controlling type of persons. When these planets are strong and well placed, the results are more clear and fruitful. These are used while deciding the nature of person, sex of child etc. P.A.C. (Position, Aspect,Conjunction) of male planets with fifth house, fifth Lord, give a tendency to have a male child.

72. Which are the female planets and their uses?

Female planets are Moon and Venus. Female planets are less dominating in nature as compared to male planets. They are less assertive, less commanding. These are used while deciding the nature of person, the sex of child etc. (Position, Aspect, and Conjunction) of female planets with fifth house, fifth Lord, give a tendency to have a female child.

73. Which are eunuch planets and their uses?

The eunuch planets are Mercury and Saturn. Mercury can change its role as per PAC of benefics or melefics.

CONJUNCTION OF PLANETS

74. What is the conjunction of the planets?

When planets are placed in the same sign, it is called as conjunction of planets.

75. How does conjunction of two or more planets affect each other?

Conjunction of planets is a very important aspect of astrology. Conjunction can be "between 01 degree to almost 30 degrees" apart. The closer the conjunction, more influence the planets have on each other.

Normally, conjunction within 3 degrees is effective practically. For real fine tuning of conjunction of two planets, their conjunction should be seen in divisional charts also.

76. What are the different types of conjunctions and their effects?

The conjunction can be

— between two friends

— between two enemies

— between two neutrals

— between a friend and neutral

— between an enemy and neutral etc.

— between a natural benefic and natural malefic

— between a natural benefic and functional malefic

— between a natural benefic and another natural benefic

— between a natural benefic and functional benefic

— between an exalted and debilitated planet etc.

The results will depend according to friendship or enmity between the two planets, as friends will support each other, while enemies will spoil each other.

77. **What if exalted and debilitated planet conjunct with each other?**

As we have heard, a good company can uplift you and a bad company can spoil you, in the same way, a powerful benefic planet tries to improve the results of a bad planet conjunct with it.

But in rectifying a bad planet, the good powerful planet loses some of its positive effects. The results of both the planets should be analyzed accordingly and prediction made during their *dasha* etc.

Somebody's gain is others loss should be fully remembered in analyzing conjunction of planets.

It is the debilitated planet which gains while exalted planet looses its positive or benefic effects.

78. **Give examples of exalted and debilitated planets when conjunct together.**

Debilitated Jupiter and exalted Mars in Capricorn (10)

Debilitated Mars and exalted Jupiter in Cancer (4)

Debilitated Mercury and exalted Venus in Pisces (12)

Debilitated Venus and exalted Mercury in Virgo (6)

It is the exalted planet which looses and debilitated planet which gains during the conjunction. Incidentally, both are friends in all cases.

The results of debilitated will not be as bad as expected while the results of exalted will not be that good as expected.

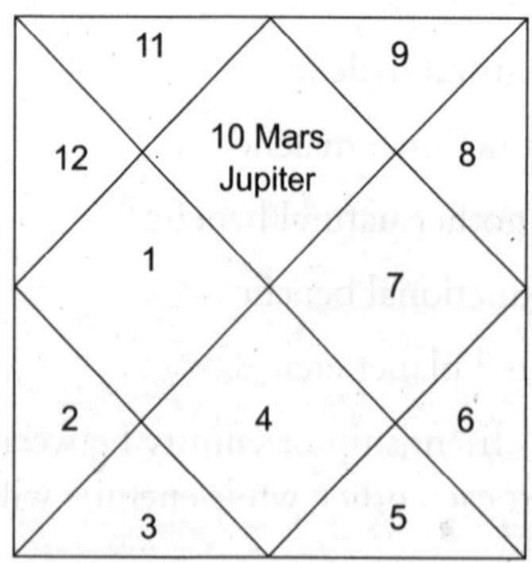

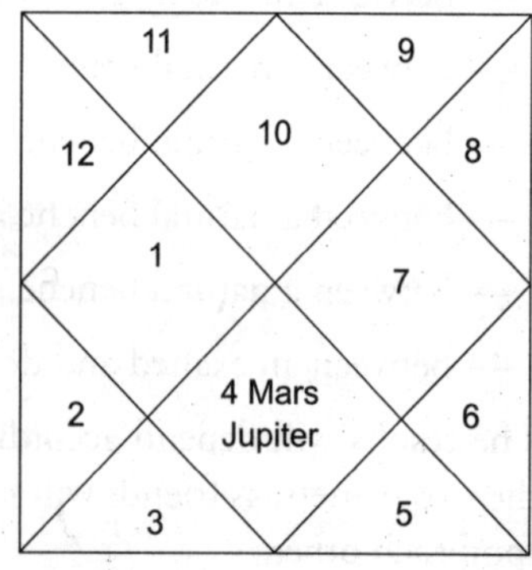

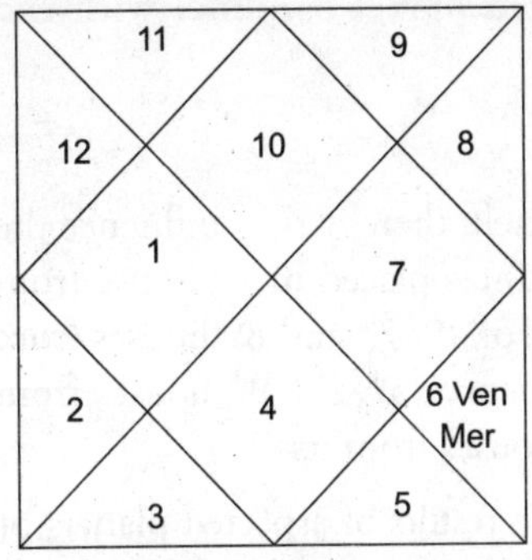

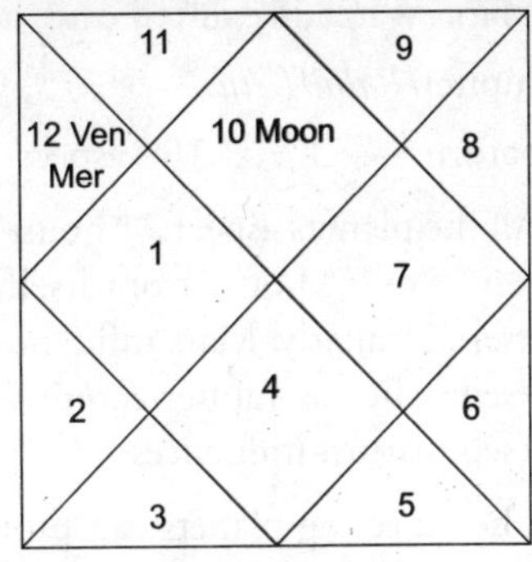

79. What are inner planets?

Inner planets are Sun, Moon, Mercury and Venus. These are fast moving planets.

Their aspects are less powerful as compared to outer planets. These are very useful in fine tuning of timing of an event. These are the ultimate planets, when we apply transit to pin point an event for the exact week, day, hour etc.

80. What are outer planets?

Outer planets are Mars, Jupiter, and Saturn. These are slow moving planets. Their aspects and effects are much more powerful than inner planets. These are useful in calculating the events of life on a broader scale by applying transit.

81. Why do outer planets have more aspects?

Because their distance from earth is much more as compared to inner planets.

The transit of outer planets like Saturn, Jupiter, *Rahu*, *Ketu* and Mars is more important in precipitating the results of planets and houses.

The inner planets help in fine tuning the date of event.

82. What are aspects of planets and what is their importance?

Every planet has its own aspects :—

All planets have seventh aspect.

Sun/Moon/Venus/Mercury—7th

Mars : — 7th, 4th, 8th

Jupiter/*Rahu*/*Ketu*:— 5th, 7th, 9th

Saturn : — 3rd, 7th,10th aspect.

All the planets aspect 7th house from itself, thereby they influence the results of 7th house from itself, the planets placed in 7th house from itself. Similarly, Mars influences result of 4th, 7th and 8th houses from itself, whereas Jupiter/*Rahu*/*Ketu* influences 5th, 7th, 9th houses from itself. Saturn influences 3rd, 7th, 10th houses from itself.

The aspecting planets can promote the results of aspected planets or houses depending upon the friendship and strength of interacting planets.

The aspecting planets can spoil the results of aspected planets or houses depending upon the enmity and strength of interacting planets.

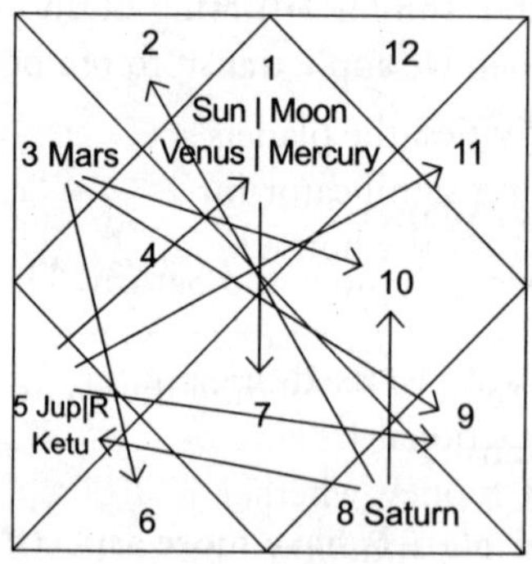

83. What are *Tatwas* of planets and signs?

Tatwas (fire, e*Arth*, air, water) are controlling the basic nature of planets and signs. The *tatwas* are :-

Mars = Lord of Aries and Scorpio : 1 (fiery) + 8 (watery)

Venus = Lord of Taurus and Libra : 2 (e*arthy*) + 7 (airy),

Mercury = Lord of Gemini and Virgo : 3 (airy) + 6 (e*arthy*),

Jupiter = Lord of Sagittarius and Pisces : 9 (fiery) + 12 (watery),

Moon = Lord of Cancer 4 (watery) and

Sun = Lord of Leo 5 (fiery).

Saturn = Lord of Capricorn and Aquarius = 10 (e*Arthy*) +11(airy).

It is to be noted that same planet is the controller of contrasting elements e.g. Mars in Aries give the fiery and aggressive results while in Scorpio (watery) will have an agreeable or comparatively cooler temperament. Jupiter in Sagittarius is fiery in nature, while it is watery and cool in Pisces. The same planet is Lord of a female sign and a male sign. Jupiter in Sagittarius, a male sign will be more dominating while in female sign Pisces will be very accommodating and flexible. Mars in Aries, a male sign will be dominating and aggressive while in Scorpio, a female sign will be more soft and flexible.

84. What are significaters/*Karakas*?

As different houses signify or control certain activities, in the same way planets also represent certain activities and are called the significator of that activity. Like Jupiter signifies money, son, life, healing, worshipping, teacher, adviser, consultant, elder brother, husband etc.

Besides the above activities, the planets act as significators for certain houses. Jupiter acts as a significator for 2nd, 5th, 7th, 9th, 11th houses. They act as caretakers for the house besides the control of sign Lord or house Lord.

The role of significater is fixed irrespective of being a natural benefic/malefic or functional benefic or functional malefic. Jupiter will always represent money whether it is a functional benefic or functional malefic. If it is functional benefic with strength, it gives lots of money. If it is a functional malefic with strength, it gives loss of money or gives illegal or black money.

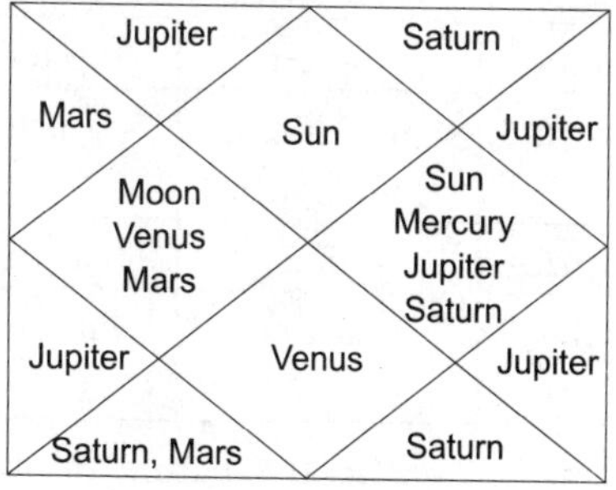

*Karaka*s of Twelve Houses

85. Name different *Karakas* of 12 houses and what is the importance of *Karakas*/significators?

Karakas act like care takers and they are very important in astrology. Before predicting the results of any house, besides PAC of house and house—Lord, strength of *Karaka* should always be considered. Strength of *Karaka* helps in giving favourable results of the concerned house and significations and its weakness affects the positive results.

86. Name the different *Karaka* of all the houses as per *Parashri* and *Lal Kitab*.

The different *Karakas* as per *Parashri* and *Lal Kitab* are displayed as under:

Karaka* Chart as per *Parashri* and *Lal Kitab

House	Lord as per *Parashri*	*Karaka* as per *Parashri*	Lord as per *Lal Kitab*	*Karaka* as per *Lal Kitab*
First	Mars	Sun	Mars	Sun
Second	Venus	Jupiter	Venus	Jupiter
Third	Mercury	Mars	Mercury	Mars, *Ketu*
Fourth	Moon	Mars, Moon, Venus	Moon	Moon
Fifth	Sun	Jupiter	Sun	Jupiter
Sixth	Mercury	Saturn, Mars	Mercury	*Ketu*
Seventh	Venus	Venus, Jupiter	Venus	Mercury
Eighth	Mars	Saturn	Mars	Saturn
Ninth	Jupiter	Jupiter	Jupiter	Jupiter
Tenth	Saturn	Sun, Mer., Jup. Saturn	Saturn	Saturn
Eleventh	Saturn	Jupiter	Saturn	Jupiter
Twelfth	Jupiter, Saturn	Saturn	Jupiter	*Rahu*

Whenever analyzing a *Karaka*, the nature of *Karaka* planet, its strength, placement and P.A.C. should be kept in mind and then only final prediction be given. Besides the above *Karakas*, there is another classification which represents live personalities as per *Karaka* planet as shown in the table.

	Planet	Live *Karakas*
1	Sun	Father, father-in-law, government officials, boss
2	Moon	Mother, mother-in-law, elderly ladies
3	Mars	Younger brother
4	Mercury	Younger sister, mother's sister
5	Jupiter	Elder brother, priest, teacher
6	Venus	Wife, younger females, subordinate females in office
7	Saturn	Servants, workers at office, peon
8	*Rahu*	Paternal grandfather , lepers, maternal grand mother
9	*Ketu*	Paternal grandmother, son, dog, maternal grand father

87. How do you analyze *Karakas* in astrology?

Karaka is a very important planet for a

- — particular house,
- — particular person,
- — particular significances etc.

Its strength in the horoscope decides the potential and results of the above factors.

It is as important as house Lord, if not more.

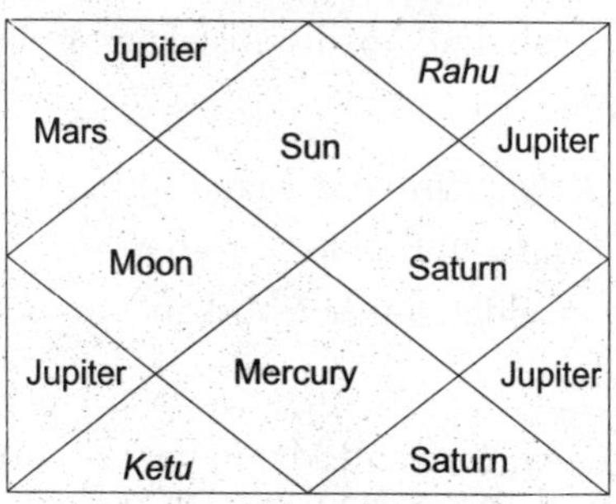

Karakas as per *Lal Kitab*

❑❑❑

ONE'S PERSONAL RELATIONSHIP WITH CERTAIN PERSONALITIES

88. Does the placement of planets in certain signs of *kaal purush kundli* of any use in studying your personal relationship with certain personalities?

Malefic (Saturn, *Rahu*, *Ketu* and Mars) in signs of *kaal purush* can give you dissatisfaction or non-cooperation of that live *Karaka*

Malefic (Saturn, *Rahu*, *Ketu* and Mars) in Aries/Scorpio (signs of Mars, the *Karaka* for younger brother) can lead to dissatisfaction from younger brother or non-cooperation of younger brothers.

Malefic (Saturn, *Rahu*, *Ketu* and Mars) in Taurus/Libra (signs of Venus, the *Karaka* for wife) can lead to dissatisfaction from wife or non-cooperation of wife.

Malefic (Saturn, *Rahu*, *Ketu* and Mars) in Gemini/Virgo (signs of Mercury, the *Karaka* for maternal relations)can lead to dissatisfaction from maternal relations or non-cooperation of maternal relations.

Malefic (Saturn, *Rahu*, *Ketu* and Mars) in Cancer (sign of Moon, the *Karaka* for mother)can lead to dissatisfaction from mother or non-cooperation of mother.

Malefic (Saturn, *Rahu*, *Ketu* and Mars) in Leo (sign of Sun, the *karaka* for father) can lead to dissatisfaction from father or non-cooperation of father.

Malefic (Saturn, *Rahu*, *Ketu* and Mars) in Sagittarius/Pisces (signs of Jupiter, the *karaka* for elder brother/husband) can lead to dissatisfaction from elder brother/husband or non-cooperation of elder brother/husband.

Malefic (Saturn, *Rahu*, *Ketu* and Mars) in Capricorn/Aquarius (signs of Saturn, the *Karaka* for servants) can lead to dissatisfaction from servants or non-cooperation of servants.

The above interpretation is based on the principle of Lord of signs and live *Karaka*s.

The role of separative planets is to be considered in this. The separative planets are Saturn, *Rahu*, *Ketu* and Mars.

89. Does the strength of a *Karaka* planet in transit of any use?

Strength of a *Karaka* planet in transit is of great use as it decides the delivery or end result of an event. Exalted planets in birth chart but getting debilitated in transit can reduce the positive results of the planet. For example, exalted Venus in a horoscope with a debilitated Venus in transit will affect the results of Venus during its *dasha* and the significance will get reduced. It can happen the other way round with debilitated in birth chart and exalted in transit giving a silver lining. This can act as silver lining in the dark at that time of *vimshotri dasha*.

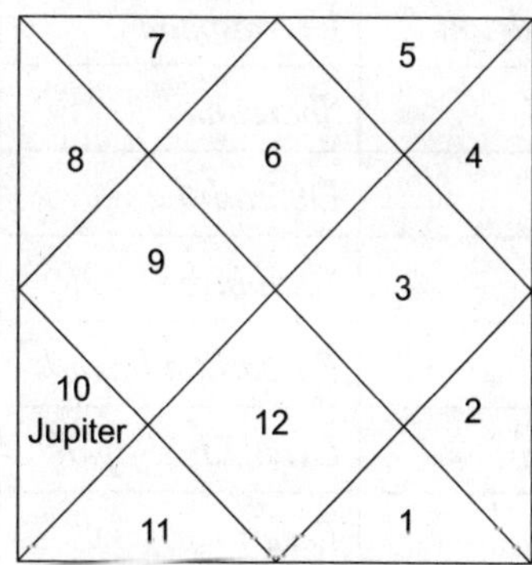

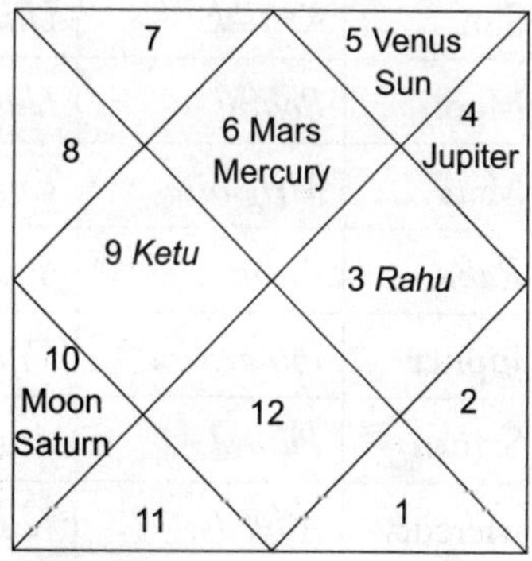

Jupiter exalted in birth chart getting debilitated in transit can mask the positive results of Jupiter at that time of *dasha*.

NAKSHATRAS AND THEIR USES IN PREDICTIONS

90. How many *nakshatras* are there?

There are 27 *nakshatras*. Over and above, there is the 28th *Nakshatra* known as *Abhijeet Nakshatra. Abhijeet Nakshatra* extends from 6 degree 40 minutes of Capricorn and ends at 10 degrees 53 minutes.

91. Name all the *nakshatras*.

Planet	*Nakshatra*	*Nakshatra*	*Nakshatra*
Ketu	*Ashwani*	*Magha*	*Moola*
Venus	*Bharni*	*Purva Phalguni*	*Purvashada*
Sun	*Kritikka*	*Uttar phalguni*	*Uttarashada*
Moon	*Rohini*	*Hast*	*Sharvana*
Mars	*Mrigshira*	*Chitra*	*Dhanishtha*
Rahu	*Ardra*	*Swati*	*Shatbhisha*
Jupiter	*Punarvasu*	*Vishakha*	*Purva Bhadrapad*
Saturn	*Pushya*	*Anuradha*	*Uttar Bhadrapad*
Mercury	*Ashlesha*	*Jyeshtha*	*Revati*

92. What are *nakshatras* and their use in astrological predictions?

Rashis or signs are further divided into *nakshatras*.

Each *Nakshatra* is of 13 degrees 20 minutes.

Each *Nakshatra* is further divided into four *charans* of 3 degrees 20 minutes each.

These are used when fine predictions are done.

A planet in the same sign will behave differently and will give different results as per the *nakshtra* Lord or star Lord.

A planet placed in Aries up to 13 degrees 20 minutes will have influence of *Ketu*.

Same planet placed between 13 degrees 20 minutes to 26 degrees 40 minutes will behave like Venus and same planet between 26 degrees 40 minutes to 30 degrees will behave like Sun.

In case of analysis of education and profession, the presence of maximum planets in *nakshatras* of natural malefics gives technical education and profession. The natural malefics are Saturn, Mars, *Rahu*, *Ketu* and afflicted Mercury.

The table below explains everything :—

SIGN	STAR	STAR	STAR
Aries	0 to 13-20 *Ketu*	13-20 to 26-40 Venus	26-40 to 30-00 Sun
Taurus	0 to 10-00 Sun	10-00 to 23-20 Moon	23-20 to 30-00 Mars
Gemini	0 to 6-40 Mars	6-40 to 20-00 *Rahu*	20-00 to 30-00 Jupiter
Cancer	0 to 3-20 Jupiter	3-20 to 16-40 Saturn	16-40 to 30-00 Mercury
Leo	0 to 13-20 *Ketu*	13-20 to 26-40 Venus	26-40 to 30-00 Sun
Virgo	0 to 10-00 Sun	10-00 to 23-20 Moon	23-20 to 30-00 Mars
Libra	0 to 6-40 Mars	6-40 to 20-00 *Rahu*	20-00 to 30-00 Jupiter
Scorpio	0 to 3-20 Jupiter	3-20 to 16-40 Saturn	16-40 to 30-00 Mercury
Sagittarius	0 to 13-20 *Ketu*	13-20 to 26-40 Venus	26-40 to 30-00 Sun
Capricorn	0 to 10-00 Sun	10-00 to 23-20 Moon	23-20 to 30-00 Mars
Aquarius	0 to 6-40 Mars	6-40 to 20-00 *Rahu*	20-00 to 30-00 Jupiter
Pisces	0 to 3-20 Jupiter	3-20 to 16-40 Saturn	16-40 to 30-00 Mercury

93. How do you see day and night birth in horoscope?

Astrologically, a day is of 24 hours starting from Sunrise to next Sunrise. If the average Sunrise time is taken as 6:00 am, then 24 hours is divided into 12 signs of 2 hours each. The movement of signs depends upon the position of the Sun at different times of a day e.g., Sun in 10th house means birth should be between 11a.m. and

1 p.m., if Sun is in 5th house the birth will be between 9 p.m. and 11 p.m. approximately.

S. NO.	SUN PLACED IN HOUSE	APPROXIMATE BIRTH TIME
1	FIRST	5 to 7 a.m.
2	SECOND	3 to 5 a.m.
3	THIRD	1 to 3 a.m.
4	FOURTH	11p.m. to 1 a.m.
5	FIFTH	9 to 11 p.m.
6	SIXTH	7 to 9 p.m.
7	SEVENTH	5 to 7 p.m.
8	EIGHTH	3 to 5 p.m.
9	NINTH	1 to 3 p.m.
10	TENTH	11 a.m. to 1 p.m.
11	ELEVENTH	9 to 11 a.m.
12	TWELFTH	7 to 9 a.m.

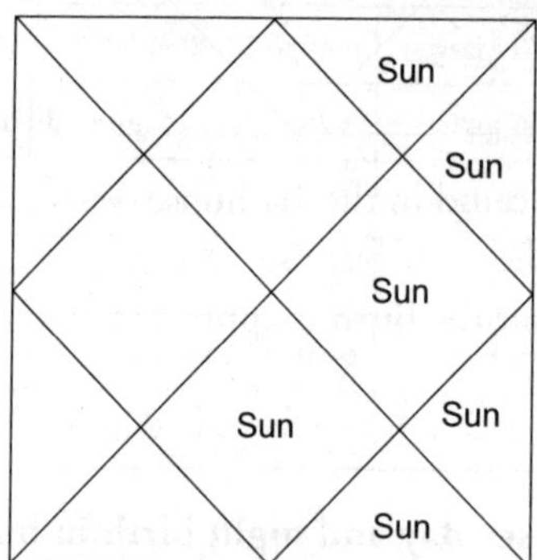

If you find in the horoscope, that Sun is placed somewhere from 7th to 12th houses, the time of birth is between Sunrise and Sunset or just around that. This can be used for confirming whether the horoscope is correct. Position of Sun is the main indicator, which distinguishes between day and night births.

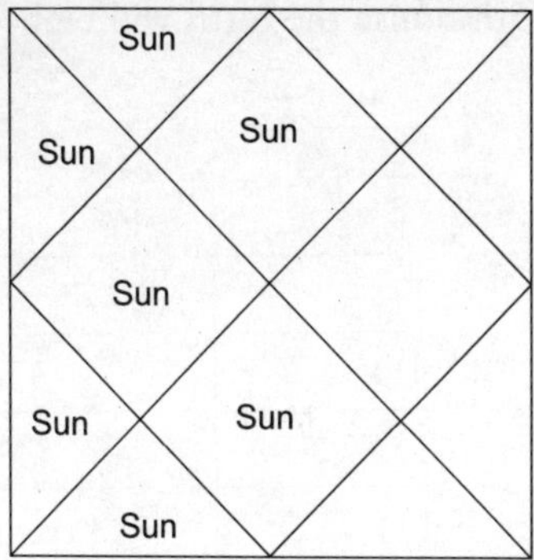

If the position of Sun is between 1st and 7th house that means the birth is between Sunset and just before Sunrise. These things would be helpful to confirm whether the horoscope is correct or not.

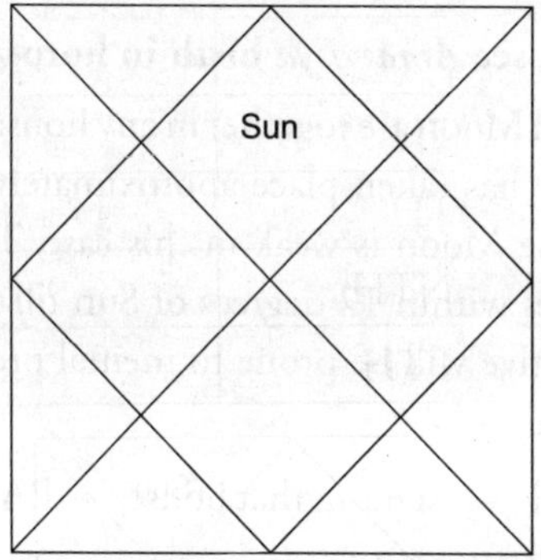

If position of Sun is found in the 1st house, it denotes that the birth is nearly around an hour of Sunrise. Whereas, the position of Sun in 7th house shows that the birth is approximately within an hour of Sunset.

94. How do you see *Pooranmashi* birth in a horoscope?

When Sun and Moon are found to be opposite to each other in the horoscope, the birth of the native would have taken place approximately around *Pooranmashi* (or+/- one *tithi*). Practically, this indicates that the Moon has strength, hence the native will be mentally strong. The final results depend upon the houses involved, sign in that house/P.A.C. of other planets.

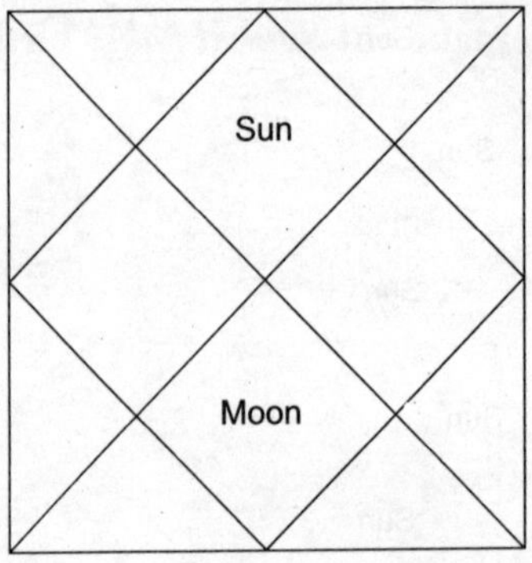

Moon has full strength on *Pooranmashi* day. This day is used in many religious *pujas* and ceremonies. In case of unknown *tithis* of death of females, *shradh* is done on *Pooranmashi* during the *shradhs*.

95. How do you see *Amavasya* birth in horoscope?

Whenever Sun and Moon are together in any house, this indicates that the birth of native has taken place approximately around *Amavasya* (+/- one *tithi*). The Moon is weak in this case. The *amavasya* starts when Moon comes within 12 degrees of Sun till it crosses Sun. As a result of it, the native will be prone to mental pressure. Final results will depend on the

— houses involved, — signs in that house, — P.A.C of other planets.

This day is very useful for donations and any kind of charity. In case of unknown *tithis* of death of males, *shradh* is done on *Amavasya* during the *shradhs*.

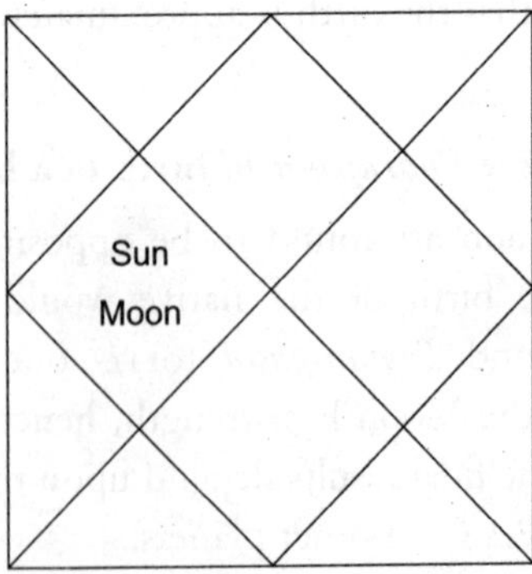

96. How do you make out *Shukal paksh* birth in horoscope and what are its significances?

Whenever you see the Moon's position is somewhere between 2nd to 7th house from Sun, this indicates that the Moon is going away from Sun (between *Amavasya* and *Pooranmashi.*) This is called as *Shukal paksh.*

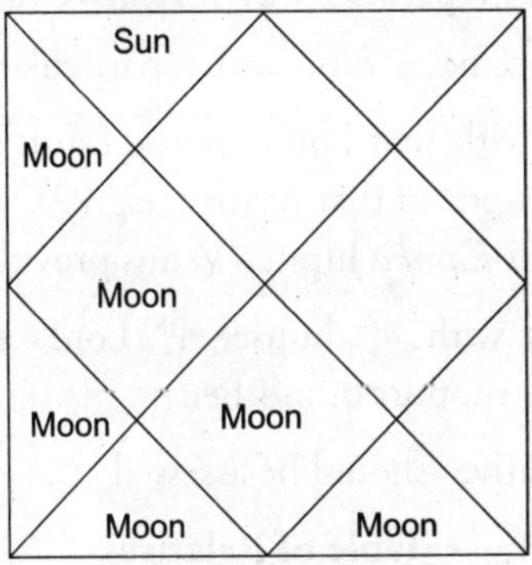

Significances of *Shukal paksh* are the strength of Moon which increases as it goes away from Sun. *Shukal paksh* is good for doing all positive activities. During these days all positive things can be promoted. This will be of great use when wearing gems, buying new things, beginning of auspicious events of life etc.

97. How do you make out *Krishan Paksh* birth in horoscope and what are its significances?

Whenever the Moon is placed somewhere between 7th to 12th houses from Sun, it indicates *Krishan Paksh.*

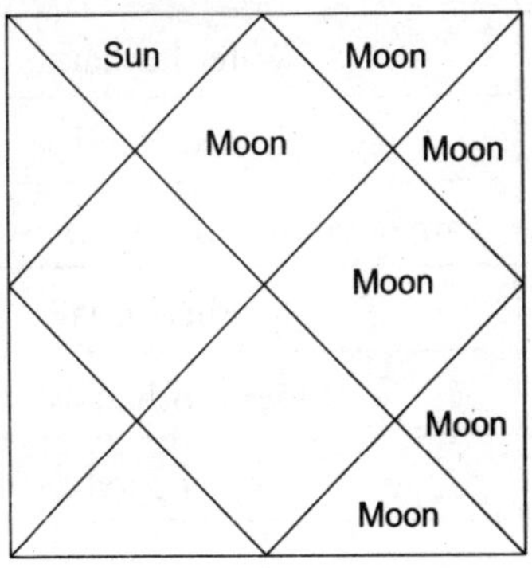

Significances of *Krishan Paksh* are the strength of Moon gradually decreases as it gets closer to Sun.

This *paksh* is good for all sorts of charitable activities, donations, remedial measures for past *karmas* like *pitar dosh*, *kaalsarp dosh* etc.

98. Which houses represent which relative in horoscope?

Every house has specific relation with a particular relative.

P.A.C. of benefics with that house, house Lord, and *Karaka* of that house provides strength to that relative. e.g PAC of benefics with 7th house, 7th Lord, and *Karaka* Jupiter/Venus provide good life partner.

P.A.C. of benefics with 4th house, 4th Lord, and *Karaka* Moon provides full strong support of mother.

Similarly, other relatives should be assessed.

Table of Relatives

House	Relative
1	Self
2	Family
3	Youngers, friends, father-in-law
4	Mother
5	1st child, elder brother/sister-in-law
6	Maternal uncle/aunt
7	Wife/ husband
8	In-laws family
9	Father, younger brother/sister-in-law
10	Mother-in-law
11	Elder brother/sister
12	Grand parents

99. How do you see debilitation in horoscope?

Debilitation in *Parashri* is based on *rashi* and can take place in any house. The interpretation will lead to different results

— as per-Lordship of the house of the planet,

— as per house placement of planet.

Debilitation of a planet leads to decrease in strength of that planet.

Benefics when debilitated lose their strength to shower positivity.

Debilitation of planets in different signs is shown below :-

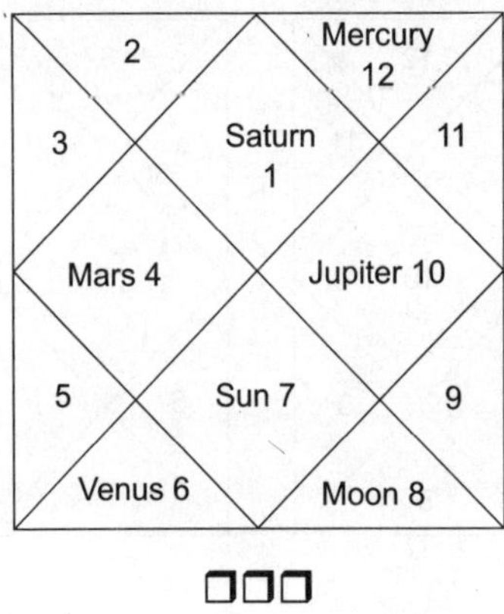

❑❑❑

YOGKARAKA PLANETS

100. What are *Yogkaraka* Planets?

When a planet's two signs occupy both *Kendra* and *Trines*, then it gives Yog *karaka* results. (Positive results and blessings of both *Vishnu* and *Laxmi ji*). Only Mars, Venus and Saturn can become Yog *karak*. Analyze yourself;

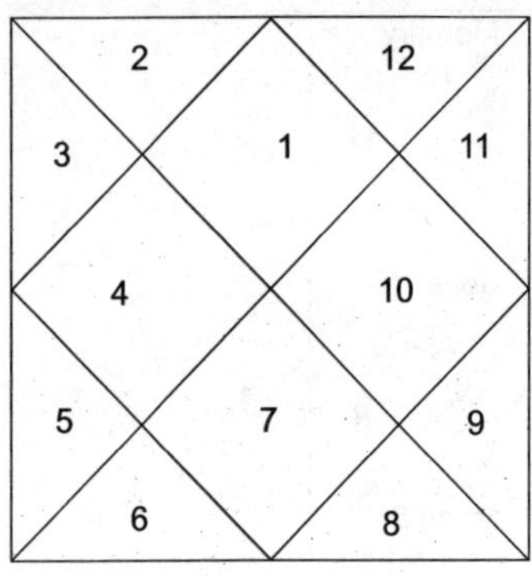

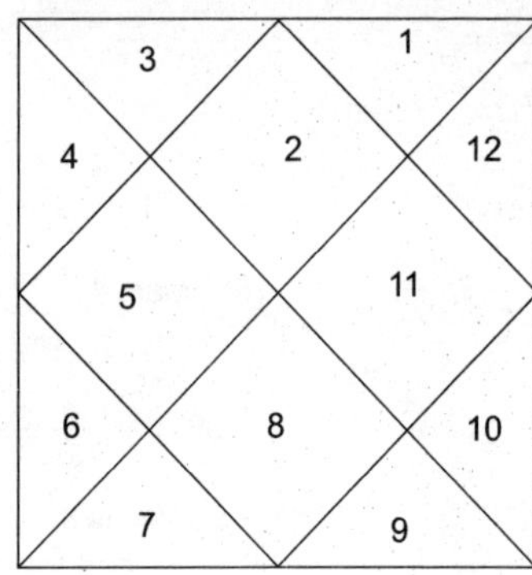

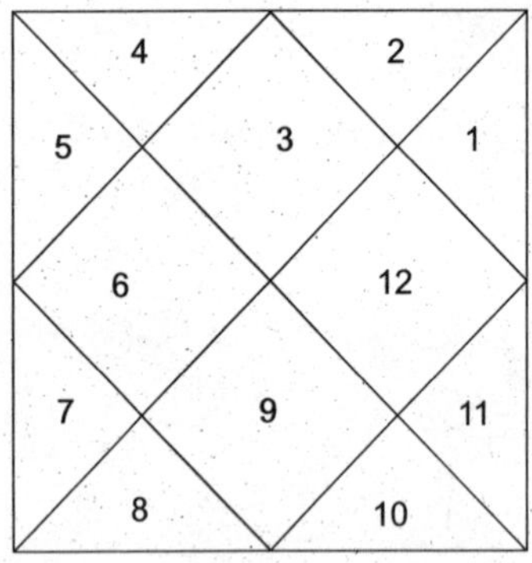

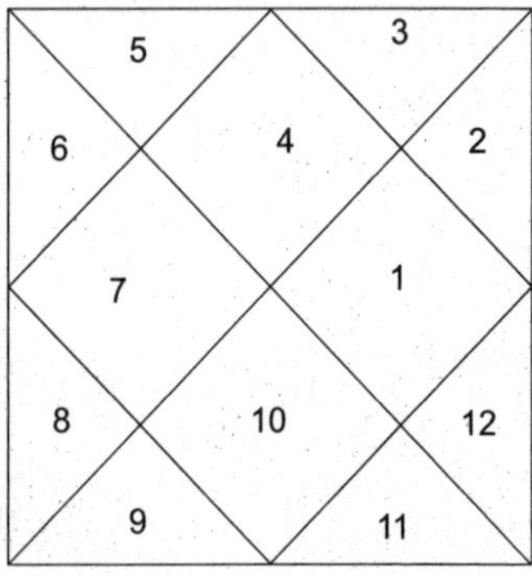

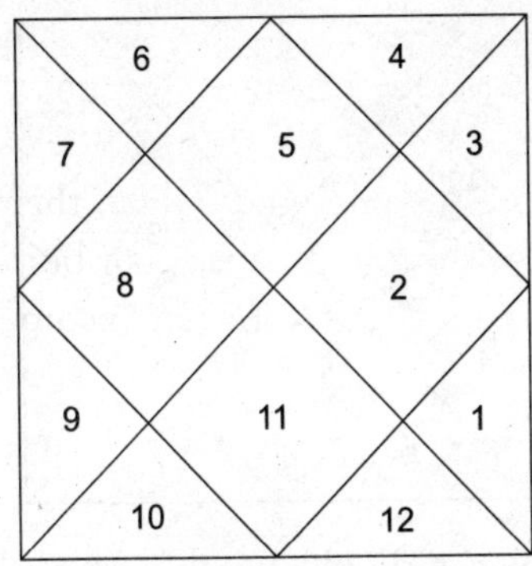
6
4
7
5
3
8
2
9
11
1
10
12

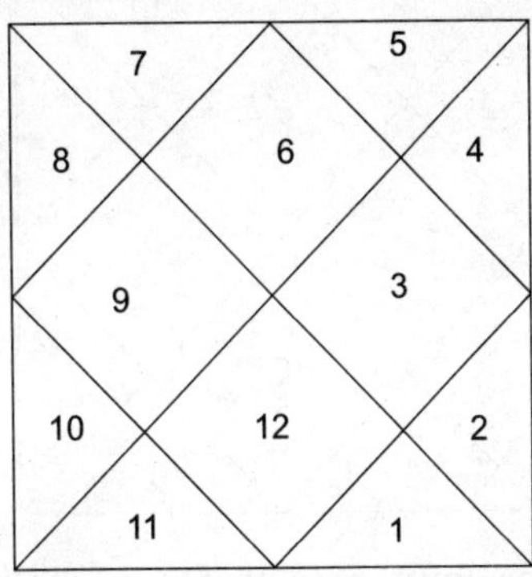
7
5
8
6
4
9
3
10
12
2
11
1

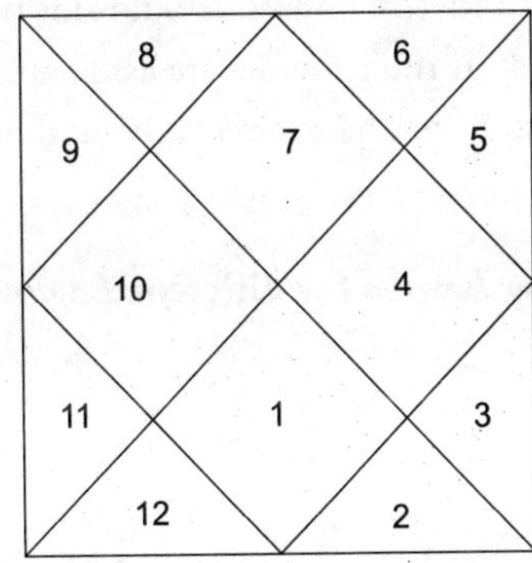
8
6
9
7
5
10
4
11
1
3
12
2

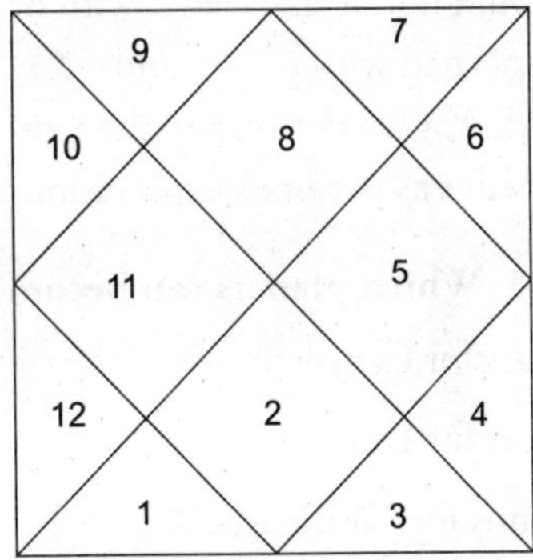
9
7
10
8
6
11
5
12
2
4
1
3

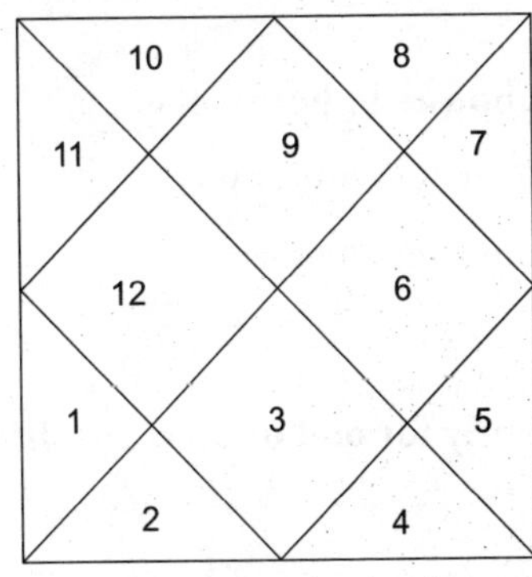
10
8
11
9
7
12
6
1
3
5
2
4

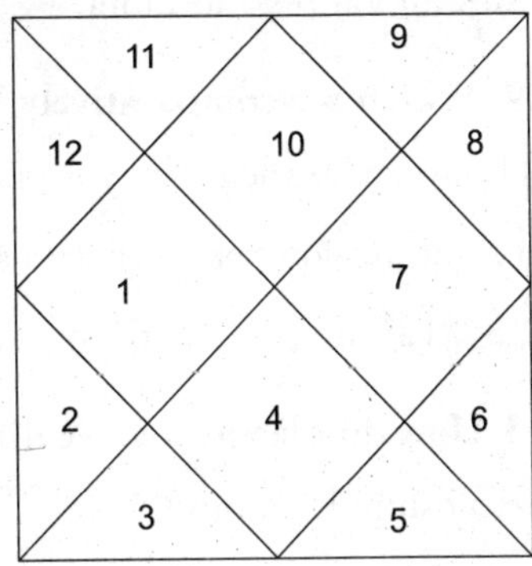
11
9
12
10
8
1
7
2
4
6
3
5

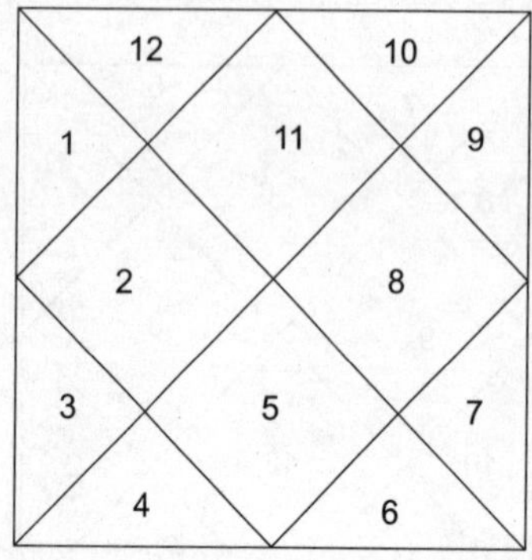

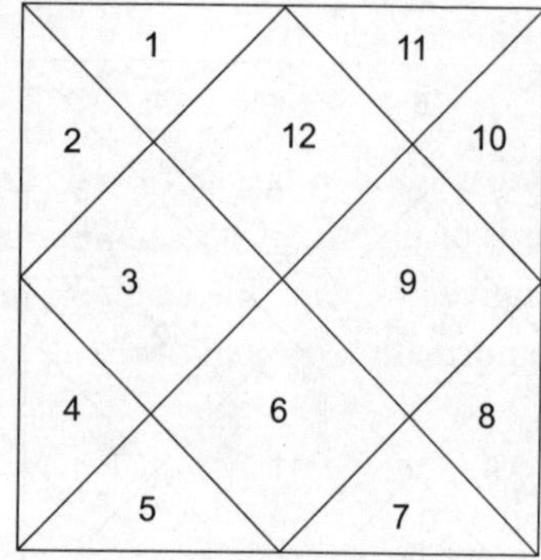

One must note that Yog *karaka* planet should not be afflicted. (It should not be in *Rahu-Ketu* axis, should not be retrograde, should not be associated with 6th, 8th and 12th houses, should not be associated with 6th, 8th and 12th Lords). If these factors are associated with Yog*karaka* planet then the results of the planet may not be positive as per one's expectations.

101. Which planets can become Yog *karaka* for different *Lagan*?

Mars for Cancer

Mars for Leo

Venus for Capricorn

Venus for Aquarius

Saturn for Taurus and Libra

102. Which are comparatively bad houses in horoscope?

All houses have their utility in the different events of life,

but some are comparatively bad as compared to others.

6th, 8th, 12th are comparatively bad houses.

103. How do planets behave differently for odd or even *lagans*?

F-friendship, E-enmity

For Aries/Gemini/Leo/Libra/Sagittarius/Aquarius *Lagans*.

4th Lord/5th Lord /8th Lord /9th Lord /12th Lords are friendly to *Lagan* Lord.

The point to be noted here is that only 6th Lord is inimical to *Lagan* Lord while 8th and 12th Lords are friends. So, the *dasha* of 8th/12th Lords or their P.A.C. with other house/house Lords and *Karaka*s may not give unfavourable results. The bad results may not be that bad as are normally expected of them.

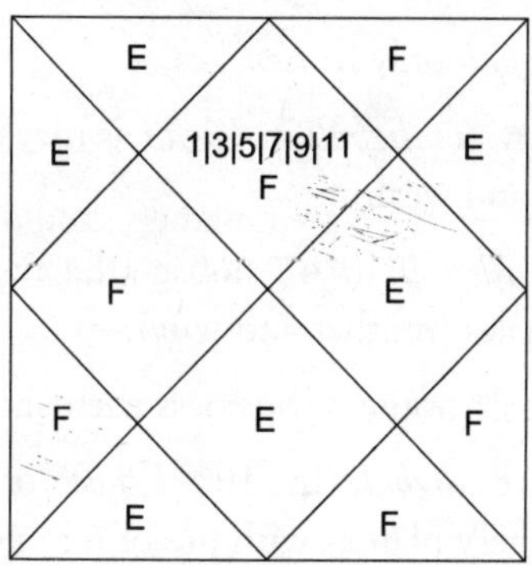

Taurus/Cancer/Virgo/Scorpio/Capricorn and Pisces *Lagans*.

2nd Lord/5th Lord/6th Lord/9th Lord/10th Lords are always friends

A notable point here is that out of the three *Dushtsthana*s (6th/8th/12th), only 8th and 12th are inimical to *Lagan* Lord, while 6th Lord is friend, so the *dasha* of 6th Lord or PAC (position, aspect, conjunction) of 6th Lord may not give unfavourable results. The bad results may not be that bad as are normally expected of them.

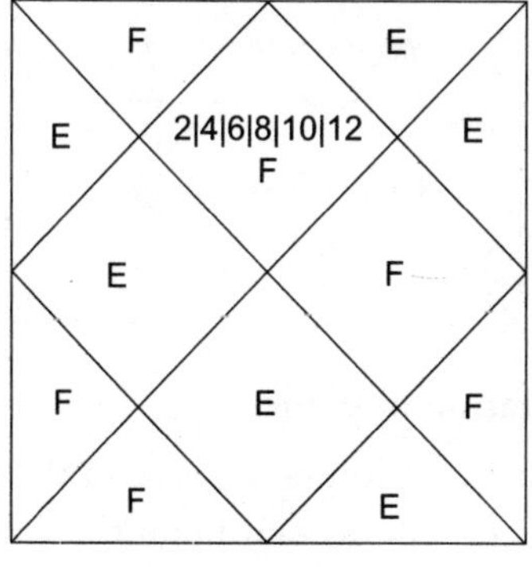

104. Are 6th, 8th, and 12th bad for everyone?

For odd *Lagans* 6th is worst while 8th and 12th may not be that bad.

For even *Lagans* 8th and 12th are worst while 6th may not be that bad.

(Note the friendship enmity charts given earlier)

105. What are digbali planets?

Digbali means extra strong in a particular direction.

Planets become *digbali* only in *Kendras*.

Jupiter and Mercury are *digbali* in *Lagan* as they are connected with brain, intelligence and wisdom.

Moon, Venus are *digbali* in 4th house (the residence) under the control of two females (mother and wife).

Saturn is *digbali* in 7th house of business partner.

Sun and Mars are *digbali* in 10th house of profession. Both commanding and fiery planets with fire of mid noon.

Digbali planets give the results of its optimum strength by being placed in particular positions as explained above. The planets give extra beneficial effects if they are in own sign/exalted/friendly signs and have P.A.C. of benefics.

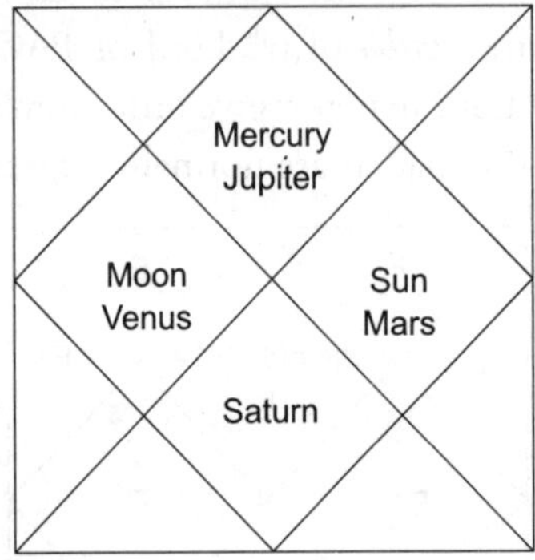

106. What is exaltation of planets?

As per *Parashri*, the exaltation takes place in the signs or *rashis*. The position or placement will depend upon the *Lagan*. The exaltation of the planet can take place in all twelve houses depending upon the *Lagan e.g.*, for Leo *Lagan* Sun exalts in 9th house, for Gemini *Lagan* Sun exalts in 11th house. The results will be quite different from each other for both the positions as the Lordship and placement are different. Exalted Sun as *Karaka* makes father's position strong and gives good status to the person as well. But its Lordship and placement gives results as per *Lagan*.

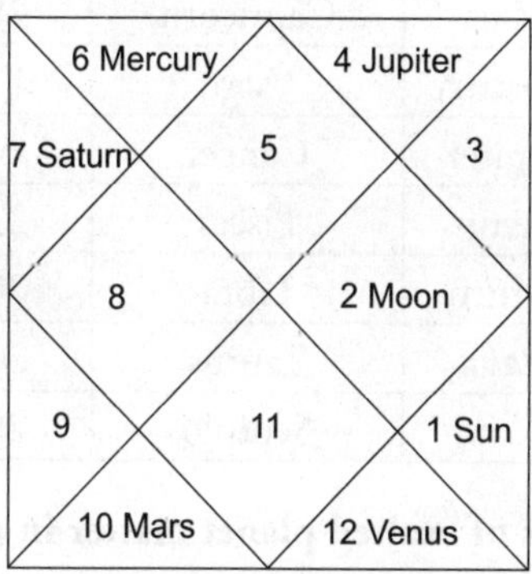

107. What does exaltation mean?

Exaltation of planet means it is placed at the most powerful degrees in a particular sign. The results of exalted planets should be analyzed under following categories:—

Whether the planet is:—

Natural benefic or malefic

Functional benefic or malefic

Lordship of house/houses of the planet

Placement of exalted planet with other planets

Conjunction of exalted planet with other planets

Aspect of other planets on the exalted planet.

The exaltation takes place in signs as per *Parashri*, while it takes place as per house in *Lal Kitab*.

108. What is extreme exaltation?

The table below shows extreme exaltation. Extreme exaltation takes place at a particular degree in a particular sign only.

Planet	Exaltation sign	Degree
Sun	Aries	10
Moon	Taurus	3
Mars	Capricorn	28
Mercury	Virgo	15
Jupiter	Cancer	5
Venus	Pisces	27
Saturn	Libra	20
Rahu	Taurus	20
Ketu	Scorpio	20

109. Does degrees of exalted planet matter in prediction?

Extreme exaltation takes place at a particular degree only as shown in table above and that is the most powerful position for the planet. Once the planet crosses that degree, the strength of planet starts decreasing.

110. What does debilitation mean?

Debilitation is 180 degrees opposite of exaltation point. The results again are analyzed under following categories:--

Whether the planet is—

Natural benefic or malefic

Functional benefic or malefic

Lordship of house/houses of the planet

Placement of debilitated planet with other planets

Conjunction of debilitated planet with other planets

Aspect of other planets on the debilitated planet.

The debilitation takes place in signs as per *Parashri*, while it takes place as per house in *Lal Kitab*.

111. What is extreme debilitation?

The table below shows extreme debilitation. Extreme debilitation takes place at a particular degree only.

Planet	Debilitation sign	Degree
Sun	Libra	10
Moon	Scorpio	3
Mars	Cancer	28
Mercury	Pisces	15
Jupiter	Capricorn	5
Venus	Virgo	27
Saturn	Aries	20
Rahu	Scorpio	20
Ketu	Taurus	20

112. Does degrees of debilitated planet matter in prediction?

Extreme debilitation takes place at a particular degree only as shown in the table above. This is the weakest position of the planets. Once the planet crosses that degree, the strength of planet starts increasing.

113. Name the *mool trikone* signs of planets.

Planet	Mool trikone sign	Degrees
Sun	Leo	1 to 20
Moon	Taurus	3 to 30
Mars	Aries	1 to 12
Mercury	Virgo	15 to 20
Jupiter	Sagittarius	0 to 10
Venus	Libra	0 to 15
Saturn	Aquarius	0 to 20

114. What do you understand by grading of planetary strength?

Different ways of grading the strength of planets are given in classical astrology, but the most commonly followed method is as below :—

Yog *karaka* (highest strength)

Exalted

Mool trikone sign

Own sign

Friends sign

Neutral sign

Inimical sign

Debilitated sign (least strength)

EXAMPLE :—

MARS

Yog *karaka*	For Cancer and Leo *Lagan*
Exalted	Capricorn 28 degrees
Mool trikone sign	Aries 01 to 12 degrees
Own signs	Aries, Scorpio
Friends sign	Cancer, Leo, Sagittarius, and Pisces
Neutral sign	Taurus, Libra
Inimical sign	Gemini, Virgo, Aquarius
Debilitated sign (least strength)	Cancer 28 degrees

115. How does a planet become strong?

The Following conditions make a planet strong as per *Parashri*.

1	Exalted
2	*Mool trikone*
3	Own house
4	Friendly house

5	Placed in *Trikones*
6	Lord of *Trikones*
7	Placed in *Kendra*
8	Associated with benefics
9	Conjunction with benefics
10	Aspect of benefics
11	*Shubh kartari* yoga
12	>4 points in *bhinashtakvarga*
13	>28 points in *sarvashtakvarga*
14	Improves in *navamsha* and other divisional charts
15	It is not debilitated
16	It is not combust
17	It is not in very beginning of a *rashi*
18	It is not in very end degree of a *rashi*
19	It is not in 6th ,8th ,12th houses
20	It is not associated with 6th, 8th, 12th Lords
21	It is not in inimical sign
22	It is not in *pap kartari* yoga
23	It is not in *mrityu* bhaga
24	It does not have P.A.C. with malefic
	Right *dasha* of a Right planet at the Right age makes the way for rich life at Right time. *Dasha* of exalted planets, *Dasha* of *Lagan* Lord, *Dasha* of 10th Lord etc., makes life progressive.

ANALYSIS OF A PLANET

116. How do you analyze a Planet?

Planet can be either a natural benefic or natural malefic. Natural benefic can be either functional benefic or functional malefic.

Functional benefic can be either strong or weak.

Functional malefic can be either strong or weak.

Strong or weak planet can be either well placed (*Kendras* or *Trikones*)

Strong or weak planet can be either ill placed. (in 6th, 8th, 12th house)

See the flow chart below to decide the quality and strength of planet.

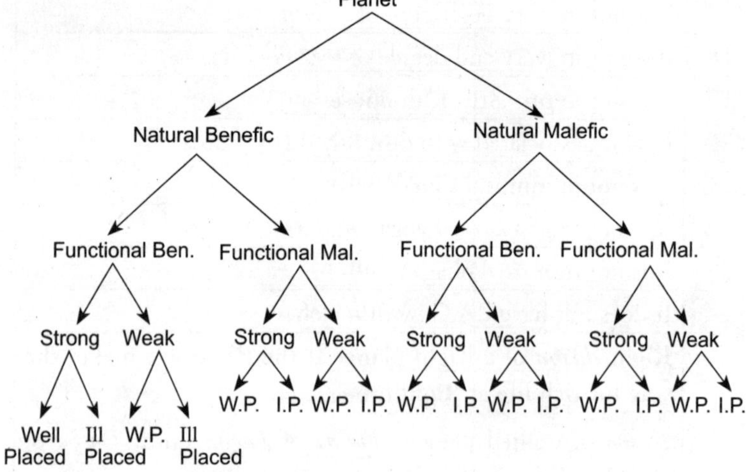

W.P. WELL Placed

I.P. ILL Placed

Natural benefic becoming a functional benefic with strength and well placed will give excellent results.

Natural malefic becoming a functional malefic with strength and ill placed will give worst results.

FUNCTIONAL BENEFICS SHOULD BE STRONG AND FUNCTIONAL MALEFICS SHOULD BE WEAK.

117. What are functional benefic planets?

All the planets change their role as per different *Lagan*s. A planet, which is favourable for a particular *Lagan* may be unfavourable for a different *Lagan*.

Even the natural malefic can become favourable while a natural benefic can become unfavourable.

Functional benefic planets are planets, which are comparatively beneficial for a particular *Lagan*. The table below gives functional benefics for different *Lagan*s.

Table of functional benefics

Lagan	Functional benefics
Aries	Mars, Sun, Jupiter
Taurus	Venus, Saturn, Mercury
Gemini	Mercury, Venus, Saturn
Cancer	Moon, Mars, Jupiter
Leo	Sun, Mars, Jupiter
Virgo	Merury, Venus, Saturn
Libra	Saturn, Mercury, Venus
Scorpio	Jupiter, Mars, Moon
Sagittarius	Jupiter, Sun, Mars
Capricorn	Saturn, Merury, Venus
Aquarius	Saturn, Venus, Mercury
Pisces	Jupiter, Mars, Moon

118. What are functional malefic planets?

All the planets change their role as per different *Lagan*s. A planet which is favourable for a particular *Lagan* may be unfavourable for a different *Lagan*.

Even the natural benefics can become unfavourable while a natural malefic can become favourable.

Functional malefic planets are planets which are comparatively unfavourable for a particular *Lagan*. The table below gives functional malefic for different *Lagan*s.

Table of functional malefics

Lagan	Functional malefic
Aries	Mercury, Saturn
Taurus	Moon, Jupiter, Venus
Gemini	Sun, Mars
Cancer	Mercury, Venus, Jupiter
Leo	Mercury,Venus,Saturn
Virgo	Moon, Mars, Saturn
Libra	Sun, Jupiter
Scorpio	Mercury, Saturn, Mars
Sagittarius	Venus, Saturn
Capricorn	Mercury, Mars, Jupiter
Aquarius	Moon, Mars, Jupiter
Pisces	Sun, Venus, Saturn

119. What is the difference between a natural benefic and functional benefic?

The natural benefics are Jupiter, Venus, Mercury (unafflicted), Moon (strong or *pakshbali*). This is the basic nature of planets but this can change as per *Lagan*, and the natural benefic can become functional malefic by getting the Lordship of bad houses. It can happen the other way round also when natural malefics like Mars, Saturn can become functional benefic by getting the Lordship of good house (*Trines* and *Kendras*).

The functional nature of a benefic or malefic planet is more important than natural benefic or malefic.

❑❑❑

DIFFERENT YOGAS

120. What is *Badhakpati*? Show *Badhakpatis* for Different Lagans.

Badhakpati (trouble creator) is a planet who creates trouble for the *jatak* during its *dasha*. *Badhak* means obstructive, creating hurdles, hindrances etc. *Badhakpati* planet is very important while analyzing health and its importance is crucial while analyzing death like situations. Role of *Badhak* is more important than *Marak* at the time of death. Approximate longevity should always be calculated before applying role of *Badhak*.

For moveable *Lagan* (1, 4, 7, and 10) 11th Lord is *Badhakpati*.

For fixed *Lagan* (2, 5, 8, 11) 9th Lord is *Badhakpati*.

For dual *Lagan* (3, 6, 9, 12) 7th Lord is *Badhakpati*.

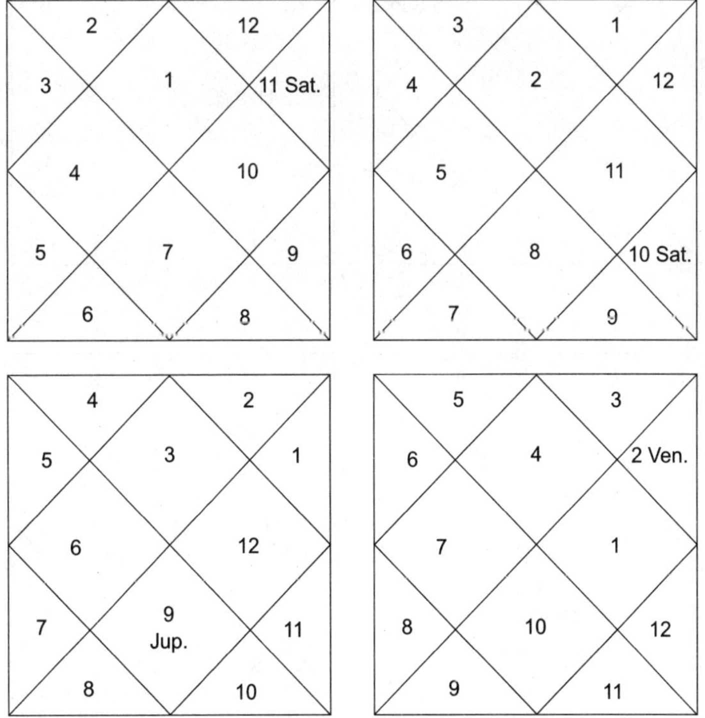

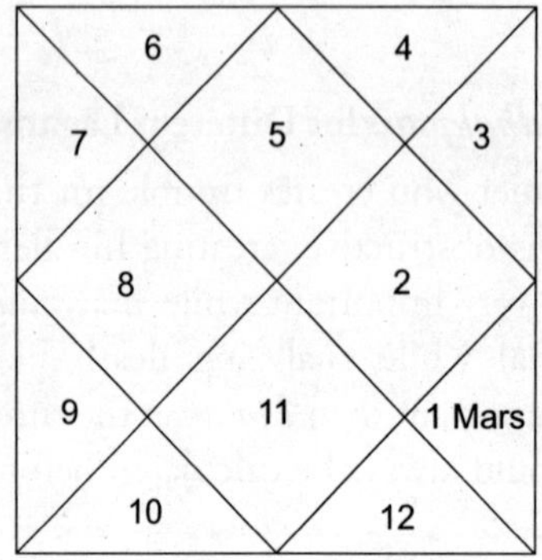
6
4
7
5
3
8
2
9
11
1 Mars
10
12

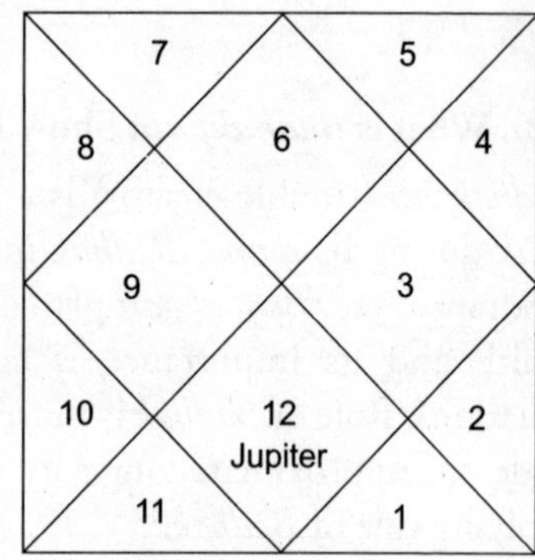
7
5
8
6
4
9
3
10
12
Jupiter
2
11
1

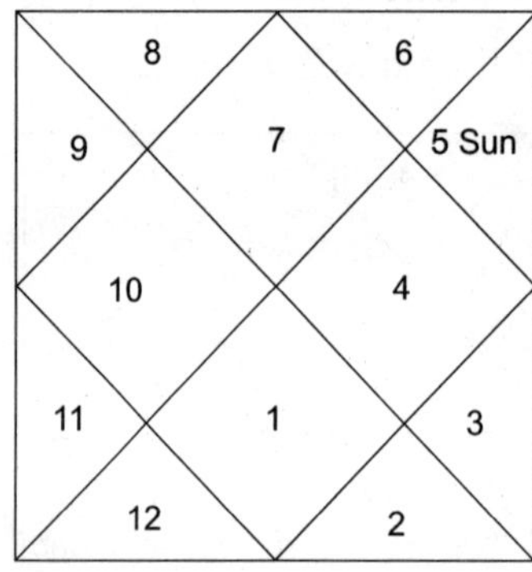
8
6
9
7
5 Sun
10
4
11
1
3
12
2

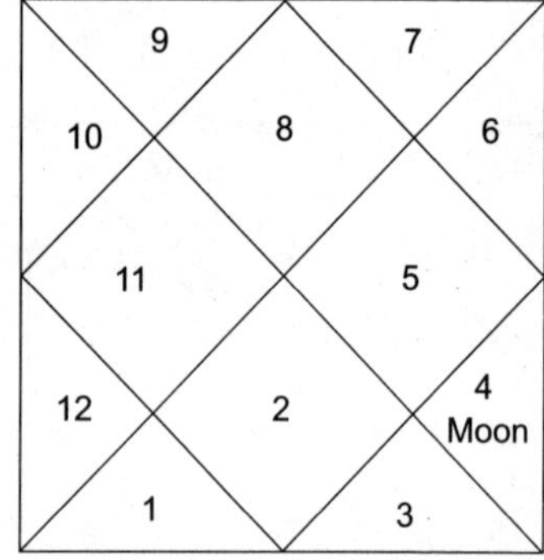
9
7
10
8
6
11
5
12
2
4
Moon
1
3

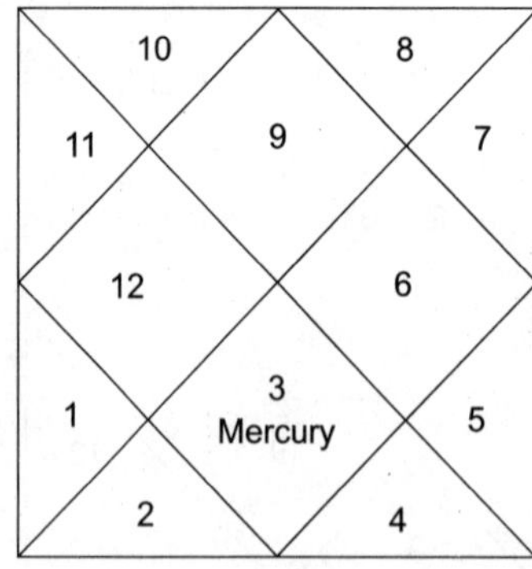
10
8
11
9
7
12
6
1
3
Mercury
5
2
4

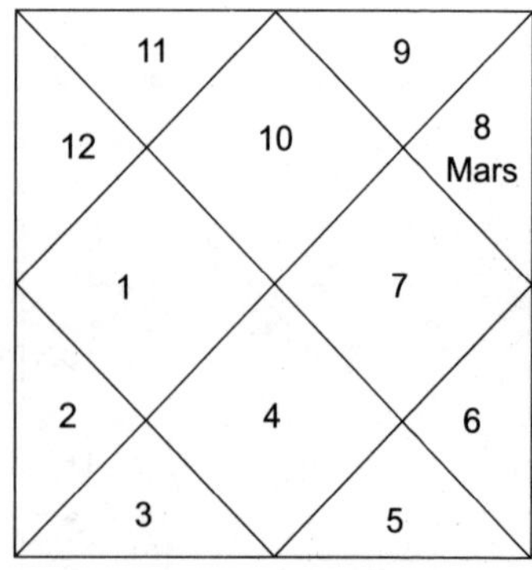
11
9
12
10
8
Mars
1
7
2
4
6
3
5

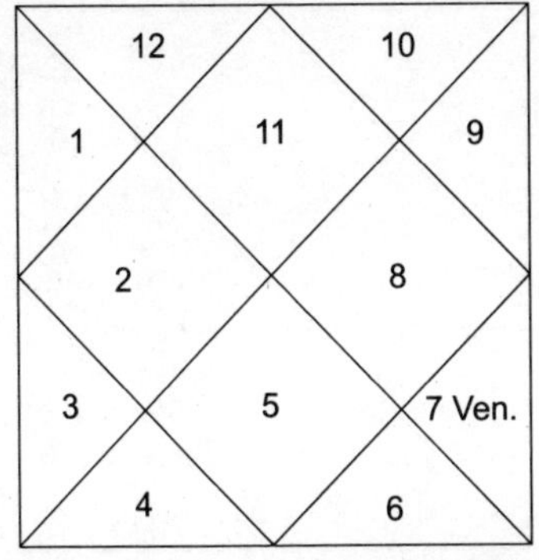

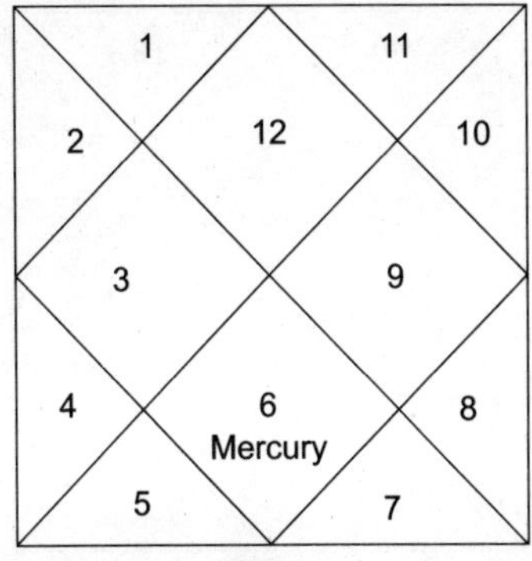

Moveable	*Badhak*	Fixed	*Badhak*	Dual	*Badhak*
Aries	Saturn	Taurus	Saturn	Gemini	Jupiter
Cancer	Venus	Leo	Mars	Virgo	Jupiter
Libra	Sun	Scorpio	Moon	Sagittarius	Mercury
Capricorn	Mars	Aquarius	Venus	Pisces	Mercury

121. What is *Kendrapati dosh*?

When a planet is Lord of two *Kendra*'s, it gets *Kendrapati* dosha. This can happen only for dual *Lagan*s (3, 6, 9, and 12). When Mercury *Lagans* are there, Jupiter gets *Kendrapati dosha*. When Jupiter *Lagans* are there, Mercury gets *Kendrapati* dosha.

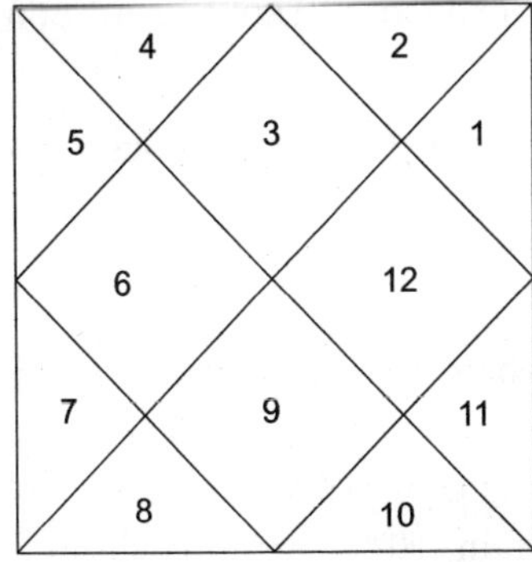

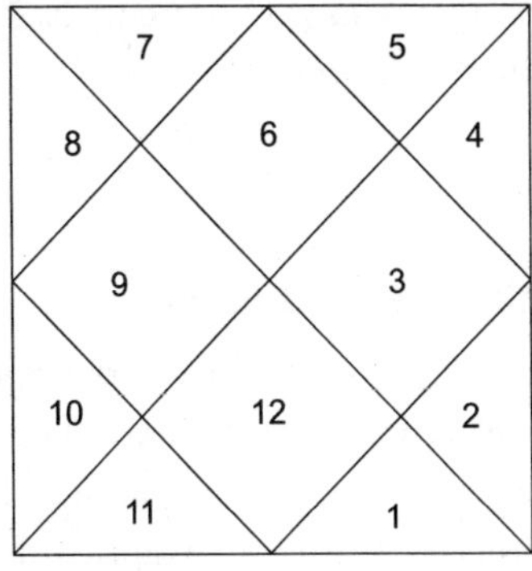

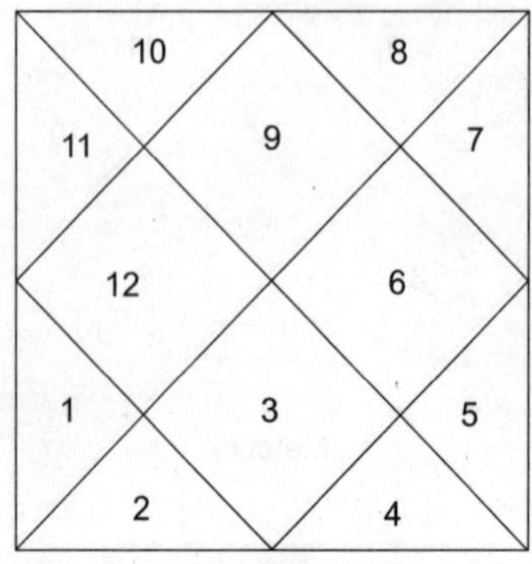

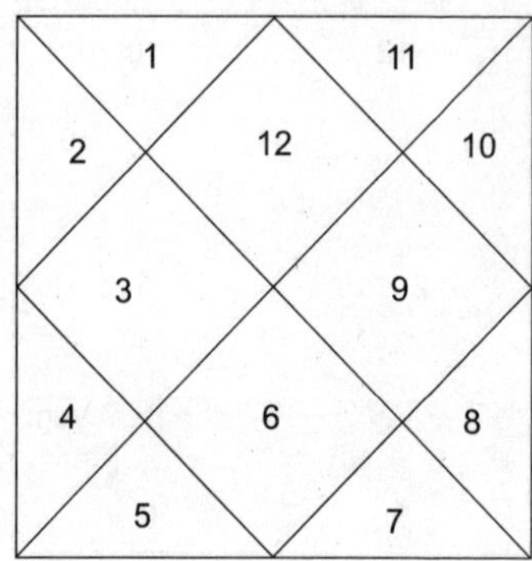

For Gemini *Lagan,* Jupiter is Lord of Sagittarius (Lord of 7th house which is *Kendra).*

For Gemini *Lagan,* Jupiter is Lord of Pisces (Lord of 10th house, which is *Kendra*).

For Virgo *Lagan,* Jupiter is Lord of Sagittarius (Lord of 4th house which is *Kendra*).

For Virgo *Lagan,* Jupiter is Lord of Pisces (Lord of 7th house which is *Kendra*).

For Sagittarius *Lagan,* Mercury is Lord of Gemini (Lord of 7th house which is *Kendra*).

For Sagittarius *Lagan,* Mercury is Lord of Virgo (Lord of 10th house which is *Kendra*).

For Pisces *Lagan,* Mercury is Lord of Gemini (Lord of 4th house which is *Kendra*).

For Pisces *Lagan,* Mercury is Lord of Virgo (Lord of 7th house which is *Kendra*).

122. What is Dispositer?

Dispositer – the Lord of the sign, where a planet is placed is called as dispositer of that planet. The strength of dispositer planet and its well-placed position promotes the results of planet. In the example, Venus is placed in Capricorn sign in 10th house. Its dispositer becomes Saturn, which is placed in 7th house in its exalted sign Libra.

As the dispositer of Venus is exalted and placed in *Kendra*, the results of 2nd house, 7th house and 10th house get promoted. Dispositer's role is very important because it decides the stability or instability of the planet. Strong and well-placed dispositor promotes the results of even a weaker planet. Weak and ill-placed dispositer can reduce the results of a strong favourable planet.

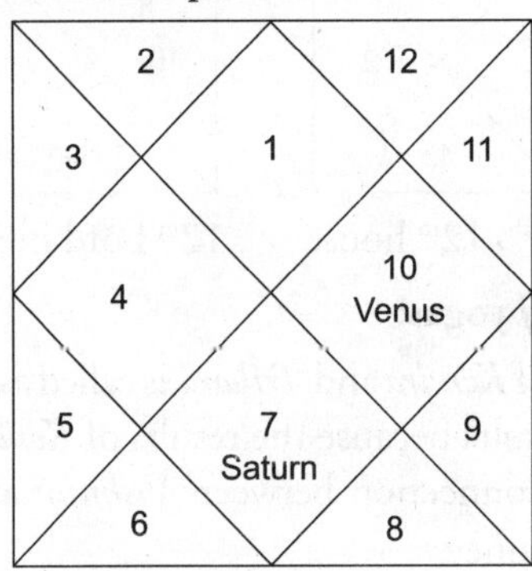

123. What is *Vipreet raj* yog?

Whenever Lord of *Dushtsthans* (6th, 8th, 12th house) goes to another *Dushtsthan*, it is called as *vipreet raj* yog. In my personal opinion, 3rd house should also be included into this. Such yogas give favourable results after initial struggles, obstructions, losses etc. The following combinations can take place :—

3rd Lord in 6th

3rd Lord in 8th

3rd Lord in 12th

6th Lord in 3rd

6th Lord in 8th

6th Lord in 12th

8th Lord in 3rd

8th Lord in 6th

8th Lord in 12th

12th Lord in 3rd, 6th and 8th

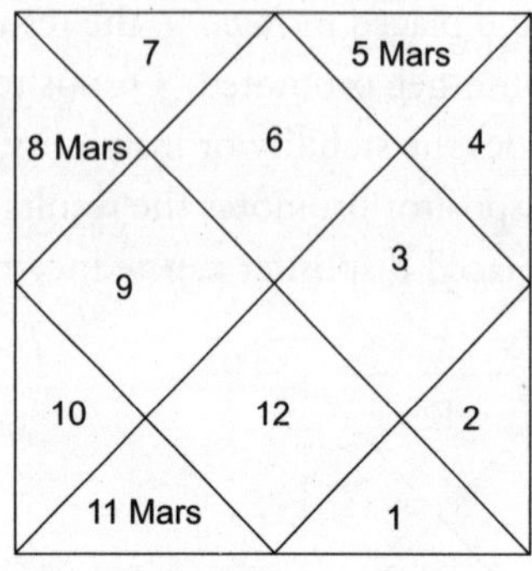

8th Lord in 3rd, 6th, 12th house

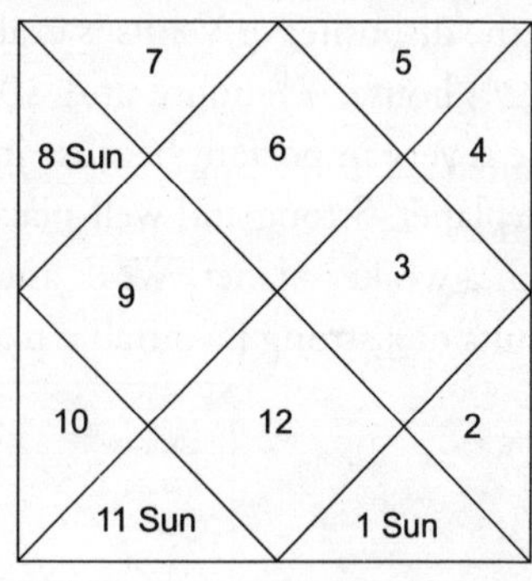

12th Lord in 3rd, 6th, 8th house

124. What are *Raj* yogas?

Any combination of *Kendra* and *Trikone* is called as rajyog. It normally gives favourable results because the results of *Kendra* and *Trikone* get interconnected. (Connection between *Vishnuji* and *Laxmi ji*). This gives status with money.

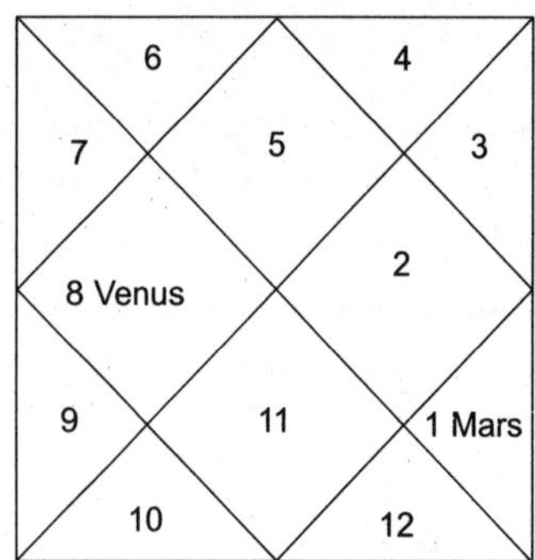

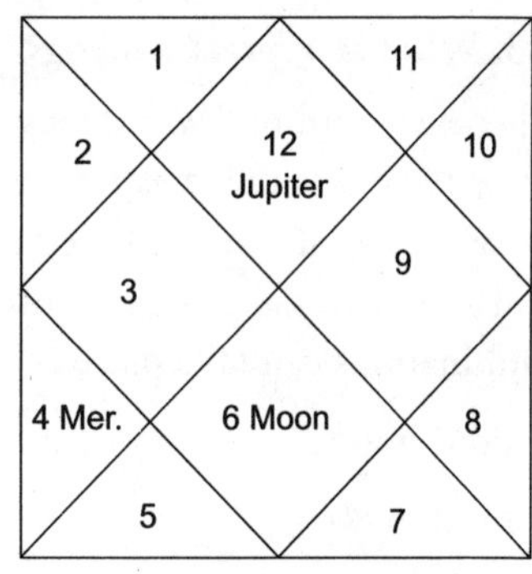

1, 5, 7 is combination of love affair and marriage

125. How do you see body parts in horoscope?

Parts of body or sections of body, if divided into twelve parts, then it is represented in the horoscope with representation of different parts as follows :—

1st house is head, 2nd house is face, 3rd house is arms and hands and so on till feet in 12th. (See the chart below)

If there is pac of malefics on

— a particular house. — house Lord — *Karaka* of house

Then these planets will affect that part of body during unfavourable *dasha* which has P.A.C. with above factors. P.A.C. of separative planets with 5th house, 5th Lord and *Karaka* Jupiter can give you stomach problems during *dasha* and unfavourable *gocher*.

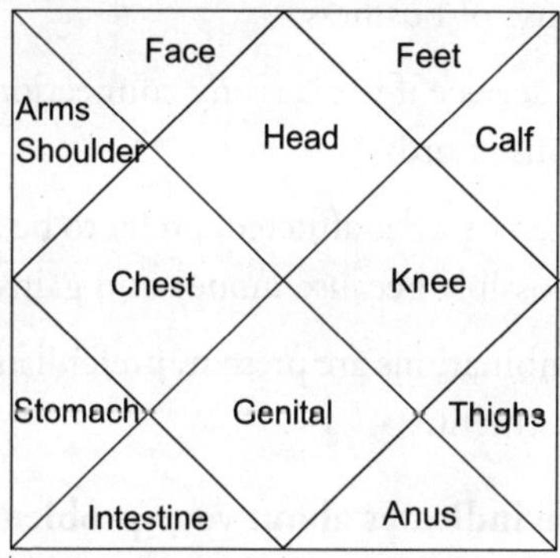

126. What are the effects of placement of *lagan* Lord in *dushtsthan*?

The effect of placement of *Lagan* Lord in *Dushtsthans* (6th /8th /12th house)

1st Lord in 6th house — health problem;

1st Lord in 8th – chronic health problems with medicines to be taken life long;

1st Lord in 12th — hospitalization;

If there is a P.A.C. of malefic planets — serious patient;

And if there is benefic P.A.C.; it gives recovery.

127. What are the effects of 5th Lord in 6th House?

5th Lord in 6th house leads to tussle between past *karmas* with diseases and disputes. This can lead to the following :-

1. Child problem
2. Not conceiving
3. Difficulty in delivery
4. Abnormal child
5. Disobedient child
6. Death of child

❑❑❑

PROFESSION AND GAINS

128. Which house indicates about your service or business?

7th house is the house of business.

One should prefer service if there is any connection between 6th and 10th house and house Lords.

When 11th is afflicted or 2nd is afflicted, prefer to be in a job and avoid business as far as possible because money and gains are affected.

If all the above combinations are present, prefer liaison work without your personal investment.

129. Which house indicates about your problems in profession?

Any affliction of 10th house, 10th Lord or affliction of *Karaka* Jupiter gives problems in profession.

Affliction of a house or house Lord or *Karaka* means its association with — separative planets

— Saturn, *Rahu*, *Ketu*, Mars, 12th Lord are the separative planets

— Association with 6th, 8th, 12th house

— Association with 6th, 8th, 12th Lords

Dasha of the above planets is the time of problem. *Gochar*/transit should also be considered.

130. What are the combinations for successful business man?

Combinations of wealth should be there in the horoscope.

2nd house of money and 11th house of gains should be strong.

More than 5 planets between 10th house and 3rd house.

Strong combination between *Kendra*s and *Trikones*.

Strong unafflicted Saturn makes you a business man.

If there is P.A.C. between 6th and 10th house one should remain in service

If Moon and Moon *Lagan* is weak, one is not able to bear fluctuations in business.

131. Which house indicates about your satisfaction or dissatisfaction in profession?

Any affliction of 10th house, 10th Lord, 11th house, 11th Lord or affliction of money *Karaka* Jupiter gives problems in profession.

Affliction of a house or house Lord or *Karaka* means its association with

— Separative planets (Saturn, *Rahu*, *Ketu*, Mars, 12th Lord)

— Association with 6th, 8th, 12th house

— Association with 6th, 8th, 12th Lords

The dissatisfaction in profession will be under the following conditions : —

Any affliction of 10th house by separative planets Saturn, *Rahu*, *Ketu*, Mars, 12th Lord,

Any affliction of 10th Lord by separative planets Saturn, *Rahu*, *Ketu*, Mars, 12th Lord,

Any affliction of *Karaka* Jupiter by separative planets Saturn, *Rahu*, *Ketu*, Mars, 12th Lord,

Any affliction of 10th house with 6th, 8th, 12th Lords

Any affliction of 10th Lord with 6th, 8th, 12th Lords

Any affliction of *Karaka* Jupiter with 6th, 8th, 12th Lords

Any association of 10th Lord with 6th, 8th, 12th houses

Any affliction of *Karaka* Jupiter with 6th, 8th, 12th houses

Any affliction of 11th house by separative planets Saturn, *Rahu*, *Ketu*, Mars, 12th Lord,

Any affliction of 11th Lord by separative planets Saturn, *Rahu*, *Ketu*, Mars, 12th Lord,

Any affliction of 11th house with 6th, 8th, 12th Lords

Any affliction of 11th Lord with 6th, 8th, 12th Lords.

The above factors should be analyzed from Moon horoscope also.

The *dashas* of the above factors between 20 years to 60 years is all the more important as that is the prime age for earning.

132. Which are money houses in astrology?

2nd, 5th, 9th, 11th houses are the money houses in astrology.

133. Which house indicates about your gains in life (money)?

11th house, 11th Lord and strength of Jupiter decides about your gains in life.

11th house and 11th Lord should be seen from Moon also.

11th house or 11th house Lord or *Karaka* Jupiter should not have any association with

— Seperative planets (Saturn, *Rahu*, *Ketu*, Mars, 12th Lord)

— Association with 6th, 8th, 12th house

— Association with 6, 8,12th Lords.

The above factors should be analyzed from Moon horoscope also.

134. Which house indicates about your wife/partner's profession?

7th house represents your life partner. Fifth from seventh (11th house) indicates education of partner while 10th from seventh, which means 4th house, represents your partners profession.

Regarding above significances. P.A.C. of benefics gives favourable results.

135. Which house indicates whether you have a working partner or housewife?

Any link of 7th house/7th Lord with your money houses (2nd, 5th, 9th, 11th) indicates a working partner.

136. How do you see short journeys/transfer?

Short journeys are seen from 3rd house. Short transfer is also seen from 3rd house. In today's context, office up to 50-60 kilometers with daily up down are under 3rd house.

137. How do you see long journeys and foreign trips?

Long or foreign journeys are seen from 7th, 9th and 12th houses and their Lords. If 4th house is badly afflicted, it can lead to settlement abroad.

138. How do you make out whether the person will come back to home land?

Placement of Jupiter in *Kendra*'s or *Trines* normally brings back the person to homeland or keeps him connected to the homeland after living abroad.

❑❑❑

THE HOUSES AND THEIR STRENGTH AND WEAKNESSES

139. How does a house become strong?

The Following conditions make a house strong as per *Parashri* :—

1	House which has its Lord in own house
2	House which is aspected by own Lord
3	House whose Lord is exalted
4	House whose Lord is in *mool trikone* sign
5	House whose Lord is in *trikone* (1st, 5th, 9th houses.)
6	House whose Lord is in *Kendra*'s (1st, 4th,7th and10th houses.)
7	House whose Lord is in friendly sign.
8	House whose Lord is associated with *trikone* Lords (1st, 5th, 9th house Lords)
9	House whose Lord is associated with *Kendra*'s Lord (1st, 4th, 7th, 10th houses.)
10	House whose Lord is not in (6th, 8th, 12th house.)
11	House whose Lord is not associated with 6th ,8th ,12th house Lords
12	House which is in *shubh kartari* (house which has benefics on both sides of the house)
13	House which is aspected by natural benefics.
14	House which is associated with natural benefics (P.A.C. of natural benefics with house)
15	House whose Lord is *vargottam* (planet which is placed in the same sign in birth and *navamsha* chart)
16	House whose Lord improves its position in *Vargas* especially D-9 (*navamsha*)
17	House which is associated with yog *Karka* planet
18	House whose Lord is "*arohi*" (moving towards its exaltation sign.)

19	House which is not in *Rahu Ketu* axis
20	House which is not associated with malefic or separaive planet like Saturn, Mars, Sun, *Rahu*, *Ketu*,12th Lord etc.
21	House which is strong in *ashtakvarga* (>30 points in *sarvashtakvarga* or > 4 points in *bhinastakvarga*)
22	House whose *Karaka* is well-placed in *Kendra* or *Trikones*
23	House whose *Karaka* is associated with benefics >> by conjunction >> by aspect
24	House whose *Karaka* is not associated with 6th /8th /12th houses
25	House whose *Karaka* is not associated with 6th /8th /12th house Lords
26	House whose *karaka* is not in *papkartari* (house which has melefics on both sides of the house).

140. What are benefic houses?

1st, 5th, 9th, 10th, 4th, 7th, 2nd, 11th are comparatively benefic houses.

141. What are malefic houses?

6th, 8th, 12th and 3rd are comparatively malefic houses.

142. How do you analyze a house?

Twelve houses of horoscope can be broadly divided into favourable and unfavourable houses.

Trikone (1, 5, 9) *Kendra*'s (1, 4, 7, 10) and money houses (2, 11) are favourable houses.

*Dushtsthan*s (6, 8, and 12) and *Trishadaya*y (3, 6, and 11) are comparatively unfavourable houses.

11th being common to both groups is favourable for finances but bad for health.

The results get affected by house Lord being natural benefic or natural malefic.

The results get modified by being functional benefic or functional malefic.

The diagram on the next page explains the house analysis.

A house can be either favourable or unfavourable.

The favourable houses are *Trikones, Kendras* and 2, 11.

The unfavourable houses are *dushtstans* and *Trishadayay*.

The favourable houses can have placement of functional benefics or natural benefics in them.

The unfavourable houses can have placement of functional benefics or natural benefics in them.

The favourable houses can have placement of functional melefics or natural melefics in them.

The unfavourable houses can have placement of functional melefics or natural melefics in them.

The favourable houses can have aspect of functional benefics or natural benefics in them.

The unfavourable houses can have aspect of functional benefics or natural benefics in them.

The favourable houses can have aspect of functional melefics or natural melefics in them.

The unfavourable houses can have aspect of functional melefics or natural melefics in them.

The favourable houses Lords can have placement of functional benefics or natural benefics with them.

The unfavourable houses Lords can have placement of functional benefics or natural benefics with them.

The favourable houses Lords can have aspect of functional melefics or natural melefics in them.

The unfavourable houses Lords can have aspect of functional melefics or natural melefics in them.

The favourable houses Lords can have conjunction of functional benefics or natural benefics with them.

The unfavourable houses Lords can have conjunction of functional benefics or natural benefics with them.

You should write further on your own as the placed planet can be either natural benefic or natural malefic.

You should write further on your own as the aspecting planet can be either natural benefic or natural malefic.

You should write further on your own as the conjunct planet can be either natural benefic or natural malefic.

To go further these natural benefic or natural melefics can be functional benefic or functional malefic.

You should write further on your own as the placed planet can be either functional benefic or functional malefic.

You should write further on your own as the aspecting planet can be either functional benefic or functional malefic.

You should write further on your own as the conjunct planet can be either functional benefic or functional malefic.

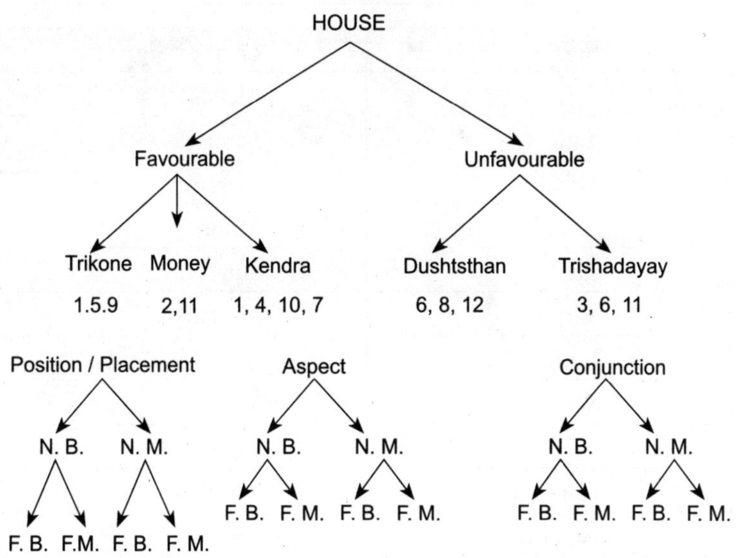

F.B. Functional Benefic **F.M.** Functional Malefic

N.B. Natural Benefic **N.M.** Natural Malefic

❒❒❒

QUALITIES OF SIGNS AND THEIR USES

143. Name the Lords of different signs.

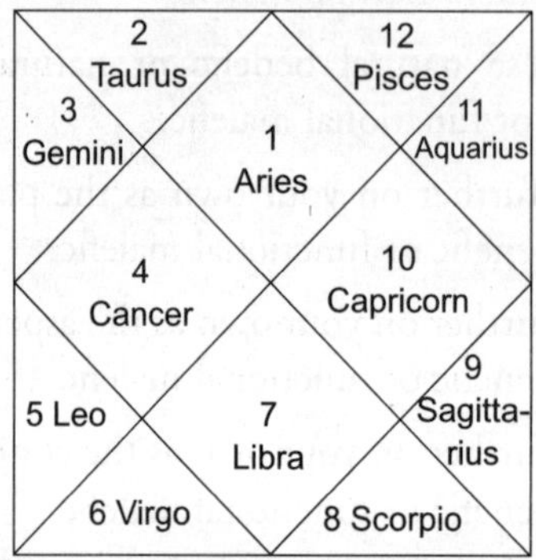

Sign	Lord of Sign
Aries	Mars
Taurus	Venus
Gemini	Mercury
Cancer	Moon
Leo	Sun
Virgo	Mercury
Libra	Venus
Scorpio	Mars
Sagittarius	Jupiter
Capricorn	Saturn
Aquarius	Saturn
Pisces	Jupiter

144. What are the qualities of signs and their uses?

Signs are the main feature of astrology, which determine the quality and quantity of different planets and houses. They influence the basic nature of planets as well as strength of planets. Any particular planet placed in a particular house will give different results as per the sign in the house. The sign will change the strength of planet which may vary from extreme exaltation (100%) to extreme debilitation (0%). Details in question number 145 onwards. Whenever analyzing qualities of signs, one should keep in mind the qualities and significances of the Lord of sign.

145. What are the qualities of Aries sign and its uses?

ARIES:

Lord	:	**Mars**
Nature of sign	:	Fiery, Moveable, Male, *Khastriya*
Planet exalts in this sign	:	Sun
Planet debilitates in this sign	:	Saturn
Direction of the sign	:	East
Stature of the sign	:	Short
Quality of sign	:	*Prishtodaya*
Part of the body	:	Head

Personality : The personality of this sign is short stature, fond of walking, sharp sight, eats sparingly and quickly, tough complexion.

Positive feature : The positive feature of this sign are frank, forceful, dynamic, creative, self-confident, adventurous, strong will power.

Negative feature : The negative feature of this sign are selfish, impatient, short tempered, fickle-minded, restless, stubborn and aggressive.

By knowing the above features, one can decide about the broader picture of the person. When person is born in Aries ascendant/*Lagan*, he will have the fiery, forceful characteristics of fiery planet Mars. He would like to dominate as per its nature of being a *Kshatriya* male. He or she would be a stout muscular person with energy of Mars. He or she would like to move further in life by taking quick decisions because of moveable nature.

The above features will get boosted when the sign Aries or its Lord Mars will have benefic P.A.C. of its friends and natural benefics like Jupiter, Moon etc.

The above features will get suppressed when the sign Aries or its Lord Mars will have malefic P.A.C. of its enemies. This can lead to headache, migraine etc.

146. What are the qualities of Taurus sign and its uses?

TAURUS :

Lord	:	**Venus**
Nature of sign	:	E*arthy*, Female, *Vaishya*
Planet exalts in this sign	:	Moon
Planet debilitates in this sign	:	Nil
Direction of the sign	:	South
Stature of the sign	:	Short
Quality of sign	:	*Prishtodaya*
Behaviour of sign	:	Fixed
Parts of the body	:	Face

Personality : The personality of this sign is having big face, large ears, darkish complexion, walks sportingly, good digestive system.

Positive feature : The positive feature of this sign is practical, trustworthy, careful, cautious, reliable, self-reliant and patient.

Negative feature : The negative feature of this sign is lazy, bit selfish, greedy, slow in action, materialistic, and possessive.

By knowing the above features, one can decide about the broader picture of the person. When person is born in Taurus ascendant/ *Lagan*, he will have the slow (fixed) and stable characteristics of e*arthy* nature. He would be more calculative and soft as per its nature of being a *vaishya*, female. He or she would be a soft, pleasing, attractive person with glamorous touch of Venus. He or she would like to move slowly with patience in life by taking decisions after taking due time because of fixed e*arthy* nature.

The above features will get boosted when the sign Taurus or its Lord Venus will have benefic P.A.C. of its friends.

The above features will get suppressed when the sign Taurus or its Lord Venus will have malefic P.A.C. of its enemies.

147. What are the qualities of Gemini sign and its uses?

GEMINI:

Lord	:	**Mercury**
Nature of sign	:	Airy, shudar, male, dual
Planet exalts in this sign	:	Nil
Planet debilitates in this sign	:	Nil
Direction of the sign	:	West
Stature of the sign	:	Medium
Quality of sign	:	*Shirshodaya*
Behaviour of sign	:	Dual

Personality : The personality of this sign is active, elevated nose, curly hair, thick neck, black eyes.

Positive feature : The positive feature of this sign is versatile, adaptable, witty, artistic, youthful, lively, and imaginative.

Negative feature : The negative feature of this sign is nervous, restless, gossipy, trickery and wavering mind.

By knowing the above features, one can decide about the broader picture of the person. When person is born in Gemini ascendant/ *Lagan*, he will have medium height and stature with airy, dual characteristics of airy planet Mercury. He would be intelligent, calculative and fluctuating as per the nature of its Lord Mercury. He or she would think many times before taking any decision but can back track because of dual nature.

The above features will get boosted, when the sign Gemini or its Lord Mercury will have benefic P.A.C. of its friends.

The above features will get suppressed, when the sign Gemini or its Lord Mercury will have malefic P.A.C. of its enemies.

148. What are the qualities of Cancer sign and its uses?

CANCER :

Lord	:	**Moon**
Nature of sign	:	Watery
Planet exalts in this sign	:	Jupiter
Planet debilitates in this sign	:	Mars
Direction of the sign	:	North
Stature of the sign	:	Medium
Quality of sign	:	*Prishtodaya*
Behaviour of sign	:	Movable

Personality : The personality of this sign is white complexion, long face, wide chest, long arms, broad waist, and fleshy neck.

Positive feature : The positive feature of this sign is intelligent, emotional, honest, self-reliant, intuitional mind and fond of music.

Negative feature : The negative feature of this sign is shy, lack of confidence, hypersensitive, unstable, stubborn, nervous and over emotional.

By knowing the above features, one can decide about the broader picture of the person. When person is born in Cancer ascendant/ *Lagan*, he will have the flexible, moderate, emotional characteristics of watery planet Moon. He would be of medium height, cool, moody, likes to take quick decisions because of moving nature.

The above features will get boosted, when the sign Cancer or its Lord Moon will have benefic P.A.C. of its friends and natural benefics like Jupiter.

The above features will get suppressed, when the sign Cancer or Lord Moon will have malefic P. A. C. of enemies and natural melefics like Saturn, *Rahu* etc., and is likely to suffer from chest diseases, *asthma*, emotional breakdown etc.

149. What are the qualities of Leo sign and what are its uses?

LEO :

Lord	**: Sun**
Nature of sign	: Fiery
Planet exalts in this sign	: Nil
Planet debilitates in this sign	: Nil
Direction of the sign	: East
Stature of the sign	: Tall
Quality of sign	: *Shirshodaya*
Behaviour of sign	: Fixed

Personality : The personality of this sign is broad shoulder, broad face, developed bones, reddish eyes and magnetic appearance.

Positive feature : The positive feature of this sign is active, creative, warm hearted, cheerful, truthful, adaptable and frank.

Negative feature : The negative feature of this sign is stubborn, arrogant and egoistic and gets angry over trifles.

By knowing the above features, one can decide about the broader picture of the person. When person is born in Leo ascendant/*Lagan*, he will have the slow (fixed), stable, characteristics of fixed nature. He would be more dominating, commanding, leading type nature. Being a *Kshatriya*, he or she would be a tough, strong, tall, arrogant person. He or she would like to move slowly but with aggression of fiery planet Sun.

The above features will get boosted, when the sign Leo or its Lord Sun will have benefic P.A.C. of its friends and natural benefics like Jupiter, Moon etc.

The above features will get suppressed, when the sign Aries or it's Lord Mars will have malefic P.A.C. of its enemies and natural melefics like Saturn, *Rahu* etc. and is likely to suffer from heart, bone, brain problems.

150. What are the qualities of Virgo sign and its uses?

VIRGO:

Lord	:	**Mercury**
Nature of sign	:	E*arthy*
Planet exalts in this sign	:	Mercury
Planet debilitates in this sign	:	Venus
Direction of the sign	:	South
Stature of the sign	:	Tall
Quality of sign	:	*Shirshodaya*
Behaviour of sign	:	Dual

Personality : The personality of this sign is handsome, attractive, broad face, fine eyes, massive cheek bones and slender body.

Positive feature : The positive feature of this sign is kind and truthful, loves music, diplomatic, analytical, intelligent, economical and precise.

Negative feature : The negative feature of this sign is finicky, lack of self-confidence, selfish, hyper critical and fussy.

By knowing the above features, one can decide about the broader picture of the person. When a person is born in Virgo ascendant/ *Lagan*, he will have tall height and stature with dual characteristics of airy planet Mercury. He would be intelligent, educated, and calculative and fluctuating as per the nature of its Lord Mercury. He or she would think many times before taking decisions but can back track because of dual nature. As compared to Gemini, the person with Virgo ascendant are more stable because of e*Arthy* nature.

The above features will get boosted when the sign Virgo or its Lord Mercury will have benefic P.A.C. of its friends.

The above features will get suppressed when the sign Virgo or its Lord Mercury will have malefic P.A.C. of its enemies.

151. What are the qualities of Libra sign and its uses?

LIBRA:

Lord	:	**Venus**
Nature of sign	:	Watery
Planet exalts in this sign	:	Saturn
Planet debilitates in this sign	:	Sun
Direction of the sign	:	West
Stature of the sign	:	Tall
Quality of sign	:	*Shirshodaya*
Behaviour of sign	:	Movable

Personality : The personality of this sign is tall, having fair complexion, fine eyes, handsome, prominent nose and curly hair.

Positive feature : The positive feature of this sign is romantic, idealistic, refined, diplomatic and humanitarian.

Negative feature: The negative features of this sign are being a slow worker, resentful, not realistic and building castles in air.

By knowing the above features, one can decide about the broader picture of the person. When person is born in Libra ascendant/ *Lagan*, he will be tall, move much faster, quick decision maker as compared to Taurus people, who have the slow (fixed) , stable characteristics of e*Arth*y nature. He would be more calculative and soft as per its nature female planet Venus. He or she would be a soft, pleasing, attractive person with glamorous touch of Venus. He or she would like to move faster in life by taking quick decisions because of moveable airy nature.

The above features will get boosted when the sign Libra or its Lord Venus will have benefic P.A.C. of it's friends.

The above features will get suppressed when the sign Libra or its Lord Venus will have malefic P.A.C. of its enemies.

152. What are the qualities of Scorpio sign and its uses?

SCORPIO :

Lord	**: Mars**
Nature of sign	: Watery
Planet exalts in this sign	: Nil
Planet debilitates in this sign	: Moon
Direction of the sign	: North
Stature of the sign	: Tall
Quality of sign	: *Shirshodaya*
Behaviour of sign	: Fixed

Personality : The personality of this sign is handsome, well developed bones, fearless eyes and round belly.

Positive feature : The positive features of this sign are being emotional, intelligent, determined, generous and sensual.

Negative feature : The negative feature of this sign is suspicious, jealous, vindictive and sarcastic.

By knowing the above features, one can decide about the broader picture of the person. When person is born in Scorpio ascendant/ *Lagan*, he will have the fixed, forceful characteristics of fiery planet Mars. He would like to dominate as per its nature of being a *Kshatriya*, male. He or she would be a tall, stout muscular person with energy of Mars. He or she would like to move further in life by taking slow but steady decisions because of fixed nature. The decisions are taken after lots of ifs and buts because of watery sign but with fiery Lord.

The above features will get boosted, when the sign Scorpio or its Lord Mars will have benefic P.A.C. of its friends and natural benefics like Jupiter, Moon etc.

The above features will get suppressed, when the sign Scorpio or its Lord Mars will have malefic P.A.C. of its enemies. This can lead to headache, migraine etc.

153. What are the qualities of Sagittarius sign and what are its uses?

SAGITTARIUS:

Lord	:	**Jupiter**
Nature of sign	:	Fiery
Planet exalts in this sign	:	Nil
Planet debilitates in this sign	:	Nil
Direction of the sign	:	East
Stature of the sign	:	Medium
Quality of sign	:	*Prishtodaya*
Behaviour of sign	:	Dual

Personality : The personality of this sign is large head and neck, well developed figure, fat thighs, and almond eyes and having good looks and good smile.

Positive feature : The positive feature of this sign is dynamic, sincere, honest, God fearing, energetic, humble and hating hypocrisy.

Negative feature : The negative feature of this sign is being restless, careless, tactless and irresponsible.

By knowing the above features, one can decide about the broader picture of the person. When person is born in Sagittarius ascendant/*Lagan*, he will have moderate, mature, educated, religious characteristics of planet Jupiter. He would like to dominate as per its nature of being a male planet with male sign. He or she would be a medium height person with wisdom of Jupiter. He or she would like to move further in life by taking quick decisions because of fiery moveable nature.

The above features will get boosted, when the sign Sagittarius or its Lord Jupiter will have benefic P.A.C. of its friends and natural benefics like Moon etc.

The above features will get suppressed when the sign Sagittarius or its Lord Jupiter will have benefic P.A.C. of its enemies and natural melefics like Saturn, *Rahu* etc.

154. What are the qualities of Capricorn sign and its uses?

CAPRICORN:

Lord	:	**Saturn**
Nature of sign	:	E*Arthy*
Planet exalts in this sign	:	Mars
Planet debilitates in this sign	:	Jupiter
Direction of the sign	:	South
Stature of the sign	:	Medium
Quality of sign	:	*Prishtodaya*
Behaviour of sign	:	Movable

Personality : The personality of this sign is lean, tall, having long hands, thin face, prominent nose and ears and weak lower limbs.

Positive feature : The positive features of this sign are being reliable, careful, determined, good stamina, sympathetic and with strong will power.

Negative feature: The negative features of this sign are being rigid, harsh, cruel, cunning and lazy nature.

By knowing the above features, one can decide about the broader picture of the person. When a person is born in Capricorn ascendant/ *Lagan*, he will have moderate, mature, elderly characteristics of planet Saturn. He would like to dominate as per its nature of being a male sign. He or she would be a medium height person with maturity, patience of Saturn. He or she would like to move further in life by taking quick decisions because of moveable sign.

The above features will get boosted, when the sign Capricorn or its Lord Saturn will have benefic P.A.C. of its friends and natural benefics like Venus, Mercury etc.

The above features will get suppressed when the sign Capricorn or its Lord Saturn will have benefic P.A.C. of its enemies and natural melefics like Mars.

155. What are the qualities of Aquarius sign and its uses?

AQUARIUS:

Lord	**:**	**Saturn**
Nature of sign	:	Airy
Planet exalts in this sign	:	Nil
Planet debilitates in this sign	:	Nil
Direction of the sign	:	West
Stature of the sign	:	short
Quality of sign	:	*Shirshodaya*
Behaviour of sign	:	Fixed

Personality : The personality of this sign is being handsome with prominent temples, fair looking, dark hair and body like a pitcher.

Positive feature : The positive feature of this sign is being independent, progressive, inventive, loyal, idealist and devoted to life partner.

Negative feature : The negative features of this sign are being rebellious, stubborn, tactless, eccentric and unpredictable.

By knowing the above features, one can decide about the broader picture of the person. When, person is born in Aquarius ascendant/ *Lagan*, he will have moderate, mature, elderly characteristics of planet Saturn. He would have fixed, adamant attitude as per its nature of being a fixed sign. He or she would be a short height person with maturity, patience of Saturn. He or she would like to move further in life by taking slow and steady decisions because of fixed sign.

The above features will get boosted when the sign Aquarius or its Lord Saturn will have benefic P.A.C. of its friends and natural benefics like Venus, Mercury etc.

The above features will get suppressed when the sign Aquarius or its Lord Saturn will have benefic P.A.C. of its enemies and natural melefics like Mars.

156. What are the qualities of Pisces sign and its uses?

PISCES:

Lord	**:**	**Jupiter**
Nature of sign	:	Watery
Planet exalts in this sign	:	Venus
Planet debilitates in this sign	:	Mercury
Direction of the sign	:	North
Stature of the sign	:	Short
Quality of sign	:	*Upbhodaya*
Behaviour of sign	:	Dual

Personality : The personality of this sign is being fair, stout, large head, beautiful eyes, plump figure and prominent nose.

Positive feature : The positive feature of this sign is being religious, superstitious, artistic, having kind nature, emotional, reserved and orthodox.

Negative feature : The negative feature of this sign is immoral, lack of self-confidence, nervous, confused, timid and stubborn.

By knowing the above features, one can decide about the broader picture of the person. When person is born in Pisces ascendant/ *Lagan*, he will have moderate, mature, educated, spiritual, charitable characteristics of planet Jupiter. He would like to dominate as per its nature of being a male planet. Pisces persons will be softer and accommodative as compared to Sagittarians because of dual, female and watery nature of Pisces as compared to fiery, male and moveable nature of Sagittarius. He or she would be a short height person with wisdom of Jupiter. He or she would like to move further in life by taking decisions after lots of ifs and buts because of dual, watery nature.

The above features will get boosted when the sign Pisces or its Lord Jupiter will have benefic P.A.C. of its friends and natural benefics like Moon etc.

The above features will get suppressed, when the sign Pisces or its Lord Jupiter will have benefic P.A.C. of its enemies and natural melefics like Saturn, *Rahu* etc.

157. How does the nature of planet changes as per nature of sign?

Fiery signs are Aries, Leo and Sagittarius (1, 5, and 9)

Earthy signs are Taurus, Virgo and Capricorn (2, 6, and 10)

Airy signs are Gemini, Libra and Aquarius (3, 7, and 11)

Watery signs are Cancer, Scorpio and Pisces (4, 8, and 12)

The placement of different planets in different signs influences the basic nature of planets. Fiery planets like Mars and Sun when placed in fiery sign become fierier. The relationship of such a planet with *Lagan*, *Lagan* Lord or Moon will make a person either hot or short tempered. This nature will further get modified as per moveable, fixed or dual nature.

Mars and Sun in fiery and moveable sign (Aries) will make the person rash in taking decisions.

Mars and Sun in fiery and fixed sign (Leo) will make the person more rash and adamant in taking decisions.

Mars and Sun in fiery and dual sign (Sagittarius) will make the person fluctuate in rash decisions.

Mars in own fiery sign Aries will be more energetic and rash as compared to Mars in own sign Scorpio, because Scorpio is a watery sign (cool and unstable).

So, it is the nature or effect of signs, which changes or modifies the nature, quality and results of a planet.

158. How many types of signs are there?

Signs have been divided into different categories for different purposes.

Different classifications of signs are as follows :—

A. Fiery, *earthy*, airy and watery

B. Odd (male) and even (female)

C. *Shirshodya*, *Prishtodaya* and *upbodhaya*

D. Moveable, fixed and dual

E. Short and long assertion etc.

159. What is a sign Lord?

The Lord of a sign or *rashi* is called the sign Lord or *rashi* Lord. The placement of a planet in a particular *rashi* gets affected by the relationship it has with the *rashi* Lord. Mars placed in Leo/Sagittarius/Pisces etc., will be more comfortable as the *rashi* Lords are friends of Mars. The placement of Mars in Gemini/Virgo/Capricorn or Aquarius will make Mars uncomfortable as the Lords are inimical to Mars.

160. What is the difference between sign Lord and house Lord?

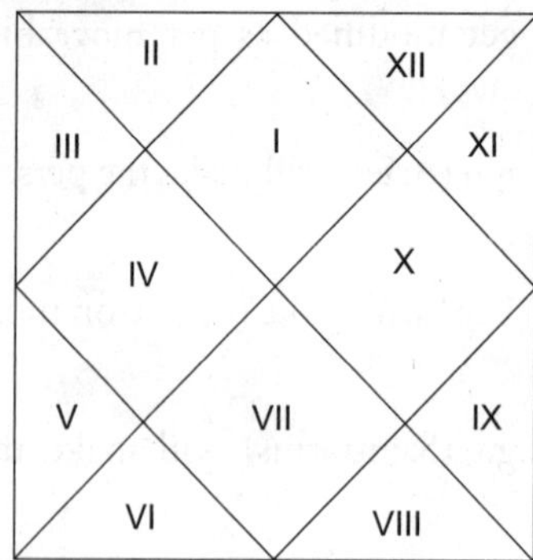

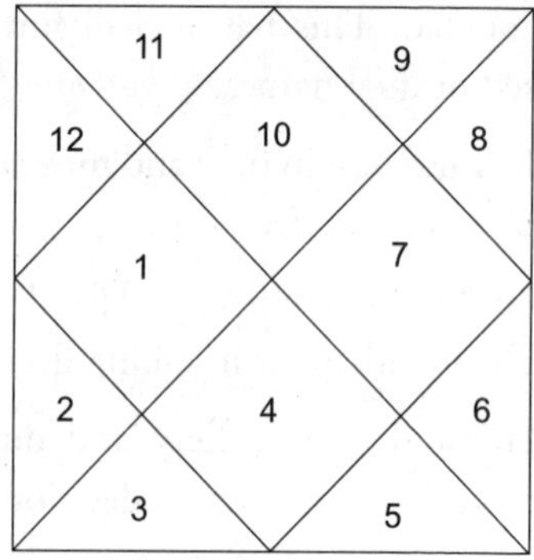

Houses are fixed in astrology as per their significances. The sign in a house change the qualities of the significances of the house.

If you have Capricorn *Lagan* the house Lord is Saturn, if Taurus the house Lord is Venus.

If Cancer sign is there in *Lagan*, then house Lord is Moon. So, the house Lord changes as per sign in house, while the sign Lord never changes.

Taurus will always be represented by Venus irrespective whether Taurus comes in 4th/5th/8th or any house.

161. What are moveable signs and their uses?

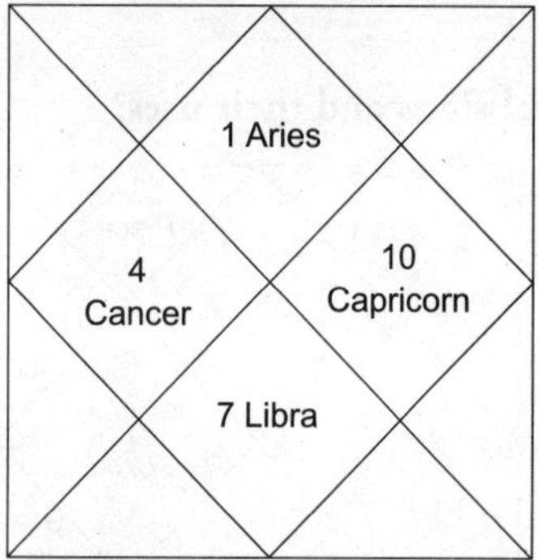

Moveable signs are Aries, Cancer, Libra and Capricorn (1, 4, 7, and 10). The placement of more planets in moveable signs makes a person more mobile, energetic, opting for changes, frequent transfers, quick decision takers etc. Presence of Moon in moveable sign makes a person ever willing to change, take quick decisions etc. Presence of moveable *Lagan* in *prashan kundli* shows change, transfer, movement etc.

162. What are fixed signs and their uses?

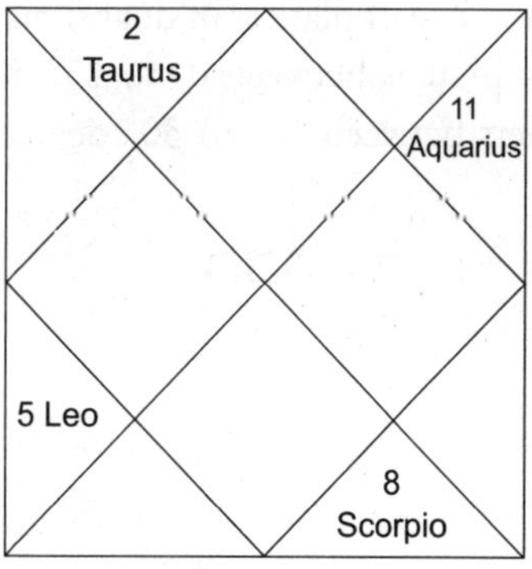

Fixed signs are Taurus, Leo, Scorpio, Aquarius (2, 5, 8, and 11). The placement of more planets in fixed signs makes a person more stable, adamant, likes to stay put at one place etc. Presence of Moon in fixed sign makes a person never willing to change. He never takes quick decisions etc. Presence of fixed *Lagan* in *prashan kundli* shows stability, no change, no sale, no transfer, no death in case of death *hora*ry etc.

163. What are dual signs and their uses?

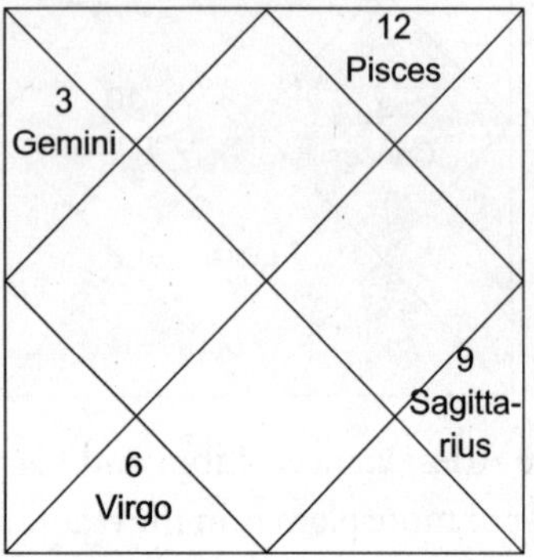

Dual signs are Gemini, Virgo, Sagittarius, and Pisces (3, 6, 9 and 12). The placement of more planets in dual signs makes a person more fragile, indecisive, unable to take firm decisions etc. Presence of Moon in dual sign keeps a person always in a dilemma. He is fluctuating type, postpones decisions, flexible etc. Presence of dual *Lagan* in *prashan kundli* shows indecisive query, may or may not change, etc. The presence of planets in dual signs give their results as per their degrees— planets between 0° to 15° degrees behave more like fixed and planets between 16° to 30° degrees behave more like moveable.

HOW TO SEE SHORT, MEDIUM AND LONG ASSERTION IN A HOROSCOPE?

164. How do you see Short, Medium and Long Assertion in a Horoscope?

The sign in *Lagan* helps in deciding the correct *Lagan* in case of doubt of birth time. The height of person is divided into three categories as per sign in *Lagan*. These are short, medium and long.

Short : birth *Lagan* 11, 12, 1, 2 (Aquarius, Pisces, Aries, Taurus)

Medium : birth *Lagan* 3, 4, 9, 10 (Gemini, Cancer, Sagittarius. Capricorn)

Tall : birth *Lagan* 5, 6, 7, 8, (Leo, Virgo, Libra, and Scorpio)

e.g. Leo, Virgo, Libra, Scorpio sign in *Lagan* makes one comparatively tall as compared to other *Lagans*. This should be analyzed keeping in mind the *desh*, *kaal*, *patar*. (The family background should be kept in mind). These are used in verifying the *Lagan* in case of doubt in time (*Lagan* at the beginning or end degrees).

				5	6	7	8				
				T	A	L	L				
		3	4					9	10		
		M E	D	-	-	-	-	IU	M		
1	2									11	12
S	H									O	RT

165. How do you analyze different significances?

For analyzing any significance,

— One should try to note the house representing that significance.

— the house Lord of the significant house.

— the *Karaka* of the significant item.

— All these three factors should be seen from Moon horoscope also.

— for superfine tuning, analyze concerned divisional chart.

Brief table below gives the important significant items and the factors to be considered.

S.No.	Significance	Factors to be seen
1	Body	*Lagan*, *Lagan* Lord ,Sun, dispositer of Sun
2	Wealth	2nd house, 2nd Lord , Jupiter
3	Self-efforts	3rd house, 3rd Lord, Mars, *Lagan*, *Lagan* Lord
4	Younger brother	3rd house, 3rd Lord, Mars
5	Property	4th house, 4th Lord,
6	Plot	4th house, 4th Lord, Mars
7	Apartment	4th house, 4th Lord, Venus
8	House (old)	4th house, 4th Lord, Saturn
9	Mother	4th house, 4th Lord, Moon
10	Vehicles	4th house, 4th Lord, Venus
11	Education	2nd house, 2nd Lord, 4th house, 4th Lord, Mercury, Jupiter.
12	Basic (primary)	2nd house, 2nd Lord, 4th house, 4th Lord, Mercury, Jupiter
13	Higher education	2nd house, 2nd Lord, 4th house, 4th Lord, 5th house, 5th Lord, Mercury, Jupiter, 5th house and 5th Lord from Moon
14	Graduation	2nd house, 2nd Lord, 4th house, 4th Lord, 5th house, 5th Lord, Mercury, Jupiter, 5th house and 5th Lord from Moon

15	Post-graduation	2nd house, 2nd Lord, 4th house, 4th Lord, 5th house, 5th Lord, 9th house, 9th Lord Mercury, Jupiter, 9th house and 9th Lord from Moon
16	Research	2nd house, 2nd Lord, 4th house, 4th Lord, 5th house, 5th Lord, 8th house, 8th Lord, 9th house, 9th Lord Mercury, Jupiter, 8th house and 8th Lord from Moon
17	Spiritual education	2nd house, 2nd Lord, 4th house, 4th Lord, 5th house, 5th Lord, 8th house, 8th Lord, 9th house, 9th Lord, 12th house, 12th Lord, Mercury, Jupiter, 12th house and 12th Lord from Moon
18	Children	5th house, 5th Lord, Jupiter, along with Venus in males
19	Speculation	5th house, 5th Lord, Mercury, Jupiter
20	Legal matters	6th house, 6th Lord, Jupiter, Saturn, Mars
21	Competition	6th house, 6th Lord, Jupiter, *Rahu*
22	Loans	6th house, 6th Lord, Jupiter, Mercury
23	Partner	7th house, 7th Lord, Jupiter
24	Life partner	7th house, 7th Lord, Jupiter along with Venus in males
25	Business partner	7th house, 7th Lord, Jupiter along with *dhan* yogas
26	Longevity	8th house, 8th Lord, Saturn, 3rd house, 3rd Lord
27	Obstructions in life	8th house, 8th Lord, *Rahu*, *Ketu*
28	Father	9th house, 9th Lord, Sun

29	Fortune	9th house, 9th Lord, Jupiter
30	Profession	10th house, 10th Lord, Saturn, Sun, Mercury, Jupiter
31	Government job	10th house, 10th Lord, Sun
32	Consultancy	10th house,10th Lord, Jupiter
33	Business	10th house, 10th Lord, Mercury
34	Politician	10th house, 10th Lord, Sun, Saturn
35	Laborious Jobs	10th house, 10th Lord, Saturn
36	Gains	11th house, 11th Lord, Jupiter, no PAC of 6th, 8th, 12th houses or Lord
37	Elder brother	11th house,11th Lord, Jupiter
38	Expenses	12th house,12th Lord, Jupiter
39	Hospitalization	12th house,12th Lord, Saturn
40	Jail	12th house, 12th Lord, Mars
41	*Moksh*a	12th house,12th Lord, *Ketu*
42	Foreign	12th house, 12th Lord, 9th house, 9th Lord, 7th house, 7th Lord, *Rahu*
43	Donations	12th house,12th Lord, Jupiter
44	Enjoyment and pleasure	12th house, 12th Lord, Venus and *Rahu*
45	Short travels	3rd house, 3rd Lord
46	Long travels	7th house, 7th Lord, 9th house, 9th Lord, 12th house,12th Lord

The above table should be used very carefully. One must:-

Recognize the event first.

Will I have wealth in life?

Will I have gains in life?

For analyzing wealth, your stress should be more on 2nd house, 2nd Lord and *Karaka* Jupiter.

For analyzing gains, your stress should be more on 11th house, 11th Lord and *Karaka* Jupiter.

166. What is the difference between sign and house?

Signs or *rashis* have certain significances and some fixed qualities. The significances of houses are fixed. The houses in a horoscope are fixed while the signs in different houses are different based on the sign in *Lagan*. The position of planets in different signs effects the strength of a planet *e.g.*

— Sun in Aries makes Sun exalted and gives excellent results.

— Sun in Leo makes Sun in own house and gives very good results.

— Sun in Libra makes Sun debilitated and gives bad results.

One must understand that the above results are indicative of comparative strengths of planet.

Note :

Houses are fixed.

Signs change as per *Lagan*.

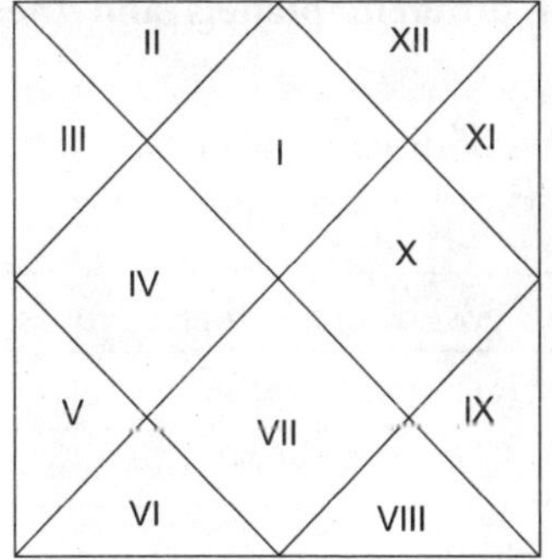

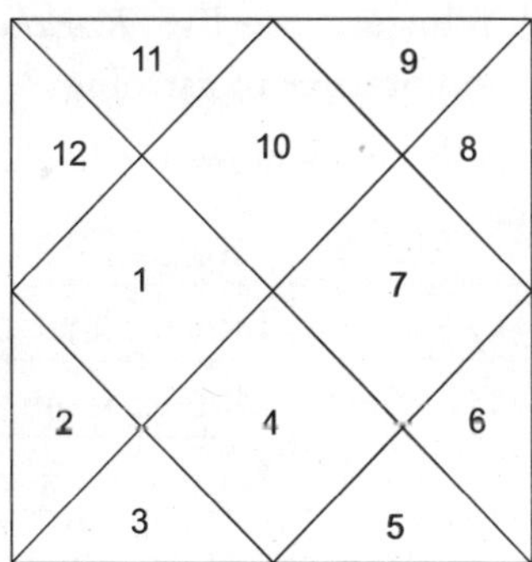

167. What is the importance of degree of planets?

The degrees of a planet can vary between 0°to 30°. The strength, *avastha* of planets varies with the variation of degrees of planets. The results also change when the *avastha* and strength changes as per degrees of planets. Change in degrees of Moon can change the whole *dasha* pattern. The change of degrees of planets can change their *nakshatras*. The change in degrees can change the divisional charts and the placement of planets in different houses.

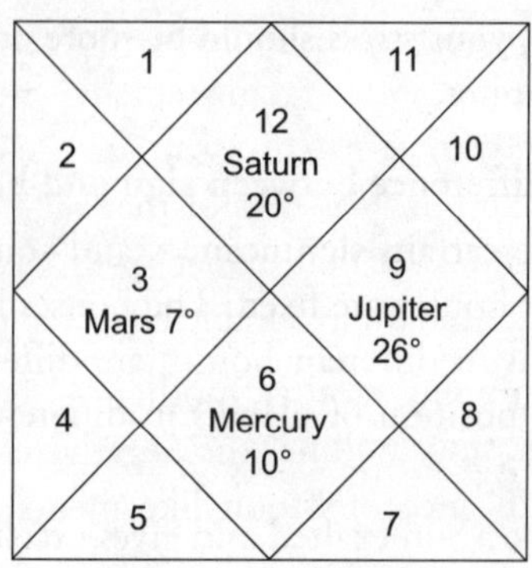

168. Does degree of *lagan* and degree of planets have any combined use in astrology?

The degrees of *Lagan* decide the divisional charts and the degrees of planets decide the placement of planets in different houses. This can lead to lots of variation of results. With the change of degrees of planets, the *Nakshatra* changes and the internal influence of planet also changes leading to total variation of results.

169. Who are the live *Karakas* of different planets and their importance in astrology?

The table below shows the live *Karaka*s of different planets.

S.NO.	Planet	Live *Karakas*
1	Sun	Father, father-in-law, government officials, boss
2	Moon	Mother, mother-in-law , elderly ladies
3	Mars	Younger brother
4	Mercury	Younger sister, mother's sister
5	Jupiter	Elder brother, priest, teacher
6	Venus	Wife, younger females, subordinate females in office
7	Saturn	Servants, workers at office, peon
8	*Rahu*	Paternal grandfather, lepers
9	*Ketu*	Paternal grandmother, son, dog

The table above is very useful in taking remedial measures of troubling planets. Whenever your work or event or activity gets struck in life, try to take maximum blessings of that relative by obeying and worshipping the *mantras* of that planet. Your good cordial relations with everyone dilutes the unfavourable effects of different planets.

Obeying and worshipping mother, mother-in-law and elderly ladies and taking their blessings nullifies the negative effects of Moon and promotes the significance of Moon like mental peace, happiness, peace at home etc.

Obeying and worshipping father, father-in-law, boss or seniors in office by taking their blessings nullifies the negative effects of Sun and promotes the significance of Sun like spiritual health, brain development, command, dominance, leadership and general health etc.

Obeying younger brother, sister and helping and supporting them nullifies the negative effects of Mars and promotes the significance of Mars like muscle power, general health, peace at home, conceiving in females as it represents uterus etc.

Obeying and worshipping mother's sisters or brothers and taking their blessings nullifies the negative effects of Mercury and promotes the significance of Mercury like intelligence, education,nerve power, business sense, mathematical knowledge, communication skills, speech etc.

Obeying and worshipping elder brother, elder sister, teachers, gurus and taking their blessings nullifies the negative effects of Jupiter and promotes the significances of Jupiter like applied knowledge, money, healthy body, happiness, harmony and peace at home etc.

Taking care of your wife, female subordinates, maids etc. nullifies the negative effects of Venus and promotes the significance of Venus like luxuries of life, sexual power, happiness, physical beauty etc.

Obeying and worshipping elderly persons and taking good care of servants and subordinates nullifies the negative effects of Saturn and promotes the significances of Saturn like patience, relief from pains, stability, happiness, peace at home etc.

Obeying and worshipping paternal grandfather, maternal grandmother and taking their blessings nullifies the negative effects of *Rahu* and promotes the significance of *Rahu* like cleverness, diplomacy, research etc.

Obeying and worshipping paternal grandmother, maternal grandfather and taking their blessings nullifies the negative effects of *Ketu* and promotes the significance of *Ketu* like spiritual knowledge, mystical powers, path to *Moksh*a etc.

THE AVASTHAS OF PLANETS AND THEIR EFFECTS ON THE RESULTS OF PLANETS

170. What are the *avasthas* of planets and their effects on the results of planets?

Different types of *avasthas* have been explained in classics. One of the *avasthas* depending on degrees of planets and the placement in odd or even sign is explained below.

The table shows *avastha* and its effects for odd *Lagans* and as per degrees of planets.

Degrees of Planet in Odd signs	*Avastha* of planet	Results of Planet
0-6	*Balavastha*	25%
6-12	*Kumaravastha*	50%
12-18	*Yuvavastha*	100%
18-24	*Vridhavastha*	Very little
24-30	*Mritavastha*	No benefic results

The table shows *avastha* and its effects for even *lagnas* and as per degrees of planets.

Degrees of Planet in Even signs	Avastha of planet	Results of Planet
24-30	*Balavastha*	25%
18-24	*Kumaravastha*	50%
12-18	*Yuvavastha*	100%
6-12	*Vridhavastha*	Very little
0-6	*Mritavastha*	No benefic results

171. What are separative planets?

Saturn, Mars, *Rahu*, *Ketu*, Sun (natural malefic) along with 12th Lord act as separative planets. Involvement of these planets with a house, house Lord and/or a planet as *Karaka* always creates trouble.

172. What is the role of separative planet?

Separative planets are Saturn, *Rahu*, *Ketu*, Mars and 12th Lord.

The separative planets spoil the results of the house, with whom they get connected by P.A.C. (position, aspect, conjunction).

The separative planets spoil the results of the planet, with whom they get connected by P.A.C. (position, aspect, conjunction).

The separative planets spoil the results of the *Karaka*, with whom they get connected by P.A.C. (position, aspect, conjunction).

The results are variable.

When only one separative planet has P.A.C. :– problem goes unnoticed

When two separative planet have P.A.C. :– problem cannot be ignored.

When three separative planet have P.A.C. :– problem gets more serious

When four separative planet have P.A.C. :– problem gets worse

When five separative planet have P.A.C. :– problem will be almost death like, disastrous, total loss etc.

Total loss position is when more than three seperative planets have P.A.C. with house, house Lord and *Karaka* without any P.A.C. of natural benefics.

173. Name the exaltation, debilitation and mool trikone signs of planets?

The exaltation of planet is the most powerful position of planet. This is followed by *mooltrikone* position and so on. The least powerful position of a planet is the debilitation. This is very useful in deciding the quality as well as quantity of results as per *desh*, *kaal* and *patar*.

The table on the next page shows the exaltation, debilitation and *mool trikone* signs of planets.

Planet	Exaltation	Debilitation	*Mool trikone*
Sun	Aries	Libra	Leo
Moon	Taurus	Scorpio	Taurus
Mars	Capricorn	Cancer	Aries
Mercury	Virgo	Pisces	Virgo
Jupiter	Cancer	Capricorn	Sagittarius
Venus	Pisces	Virgo	Libra
Saturn	Libra	Aries	Aquarius

174. How to use planets/houses and signs together?

Planets have fixed qualities, houses have fixed qualities, while signs have the power to change qualities of the planets and houses. It is the sign which makes a planet exalted or debilitated. It is the sign which makes a planet in own sign, *mool trikone* sign, exalted, debilitated, inimical sign, friendly sign etc. These variations can give lots of different results of planets in the same house. Let us take an example of Sun in 4th house in different signs.

175. What are *Shirshodaya*, *Pirshodaya* and *Upbhodaya* signs?

Shirshodaya signs are — 3, 5, 6, 7, 8, 11

Pirsodaya signs are — 1, 2, 4, 9, 10

Upbhodhaya signs are — 12

176. What are the uses of *Shirshodaya*, *Pirshodaya* and *Upbhodaya* signs?

Shirshodaya signs rising as *Lagan* at the time of *prashna* give favourable, positive healthy and progressive results.

Pirshodaya signs normally give negative, unfavourable, unhealthy results and loss.

Upbhodaya signs give result in consequences which are delayed and can be positive or negative.

But one must remember that this is just one of the parameters of *prashna kundli.* Other factors like P.A.C. of benefics and melefics should be analyzed before taking any decision.

177. How to give strength to the house in the horoscope?

You can provide strength to a house by maintaining *satwik* attitude and not annoying any of the live *Karaka*s of the house Lord. Rather one should take blessings of the live *Karaka*s as much as possible. In earlier times, people used to touch the feet of elders and take their blessings. This used to help a lot in diluting the ill effects of many planets.

Taking blessings of paternal grandfather by touching his feet used to rectify ill effects of *Rahu.*

Taking blessings of paternal grandmother by touching her feet used to rectify ill effects of *Ketu.*

Taking blessings of maternal grandfather by touching his feet used to rectify ill effects of *Ketu.*

Taking blessings of maternal grandmother by touching her feet used to rectify ill effects of *Rahu.*

Taking blessings of maternal uncles and aunts by touching their feet used to rectify ill effects of Mercury.

Taking blessings of eunuch at the time of birth and other important auspicious functions used to rectify ill effects of Mercury.

Taking blessings of father by touching his feet used to rectify ill effects of Sun.

Taking blessings of father-in-law by touching his feet used to rectify ill effects of Sun.

Taking blessings of mother-in-law by touching her feet used to rectify ill effects of Moon.

Taking blessings of mother by touching her feet used to rectify ill effects of Moon.

Taking blessings of elderly persons by touching their feet used to rectify ill effects of Saturn.

Taking blessings of teachers, priests etc. by touching their feet used to rectify ill effects of Jupiter.

Respecting and taking care of younger siblings used to rectify ill effects of Mars.

Respecting and taking care of wife used to rectify ill effects of Venus.

Forgetting the values of live *Karaka*s and not respecting other persons is a major cause of troubles in our life in today's world.

IMPORTANT FACTORS IN PREDICTING AN EVENT

178. What are the important factors in predicting an event?

There are two important factors in predicting an event—

1. Static promise of an event.
2. Dynamic fulfilment of an event.

Static factors are :–

Strength of planets

Strength of houses

Strength in *shadbal*

Strength in *ashtakvarga*

Strength in divisional charts etc.

Dynamic factors are :–

Dasha of *mahadasha* Lord

Dasha of *antardasha* Lord

Dasha of *pratyanterdasha* Lord etc.

Double transit of Saturn and Jupiter

Desh kaal patar

For predicating any event in any natal chart, we have to study *dasha-antardsahas* of planets and transit of planets particularly double transit of Saturn/Jupiter.

The static strength of planets, houses, *Karaka*s etc. will remain the same throughout life irrespective of age, *desh*, *kaal*, *patar*. This shows the potential of the horoscope as per our *karmas*. One can try to dilute the bad or unfavourable effects by different remedies but can never deny the whole effects.

The dynamic factors are more important as they are the ones who deliver the results, which can be favourable or unfavourable depending upon the strength of planets and house etc. In earlier days, our grandparents used to consult the priest or astrologer and used to take remedial measures for static problems like *pitar dosha*, *gand mool*, *grahans* etc. This used to help in diluting the ill effects of bad static combinations thereby helping in a better dynamic effects in times to come.

179. What are odd *lagans* and how do they affect the nature of a person?

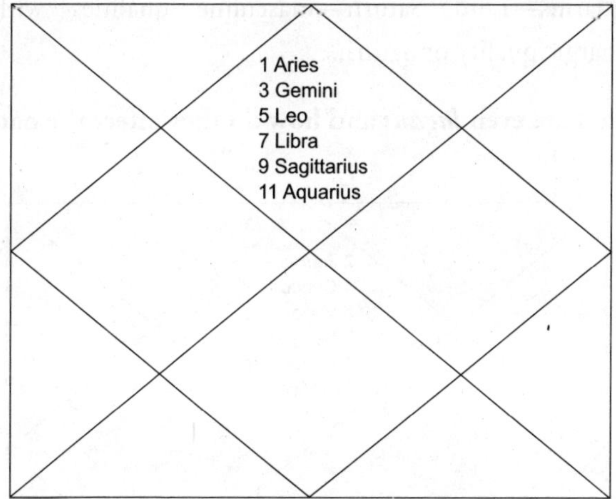

Odd signs are 1, 3, 5, 7, 9 and 11. These are also known as male signs.

Odd signs/*rashi* in *Lagan*:-

Odd sign *Lagan* persons are supposed to be more dominating, positive, and active with masculine qualities. But this further gets modified by

— the nature of sign.

— nature of Lord of sign *e.g.*

1. **Aries**—Lord Mars—masculine qualities with aggression of Mars.

3. Gemini —Lord Mercury—masculine qualities with intelligence of Mercury.

5. Leo — Lord Sun–masculine qualities with status and dominance of Sun.

7. Libra—Lord Venus—masculine qualities with beauty of Venus.

9. Sagittarius—Lord Jupiter—masculine qualities with God fearing qualities of Jupiter.

11. Aquarius—Lord Saturn—masculine qualities with slow, lethargic quality of Saturn.

180. What are even *lagans* and how do they affect the nature of a person?

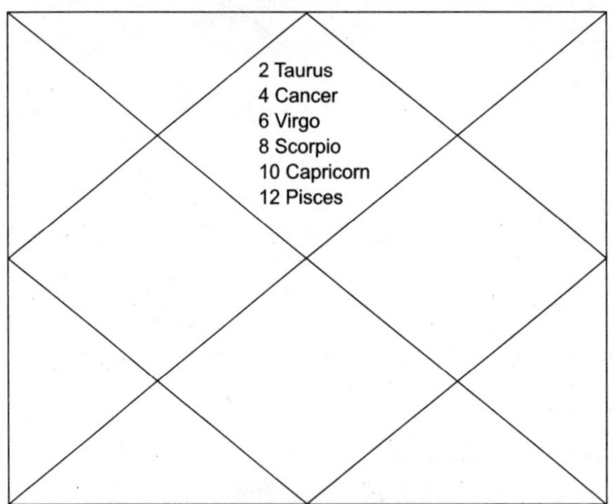

Even signs are 2, 4, 6, 8, 10 and 12. These are also known as female signs.

Even sign *Lagan* are supposed to be less active, pessimistic, suppressive etc. with mainly feminine qualities.

But this gets further modified by—

— nature of sign.

— nature of Lord of sign etc.

2. **Taurus** —Lord Venus– feminine qualities with beauty of Venus.
4. **Cancer**—Lord Moon–feminine qualities with emotional motherly touch of Moon.
6. Virgo—Lord Mercury–feminine qualities with intelligence of Mercury.
8. **Scorpio**—Lord Mars–feminine qualities with aggression of Mars.
10. **Capricorn**—Lord Saturn–feminine qualities with slow, lethargic qualities of Saturn
12. **Pisces**—Lord Jupiter–feminine qualities with God fearing charitable qualities of Jupiter.

181. What are the effect of own sign Sun placed in 4th house?

Own sign Sun in fourth house makes Sun strong. Sun as 4th Lord gives positive results of 4th house. Sun as malefic Lord of *Kendra* sheds its malefic effects and does not give unfavourable results. This provides a house,vehicle, happiness and support from mother, good education up to higher secondary level etc.

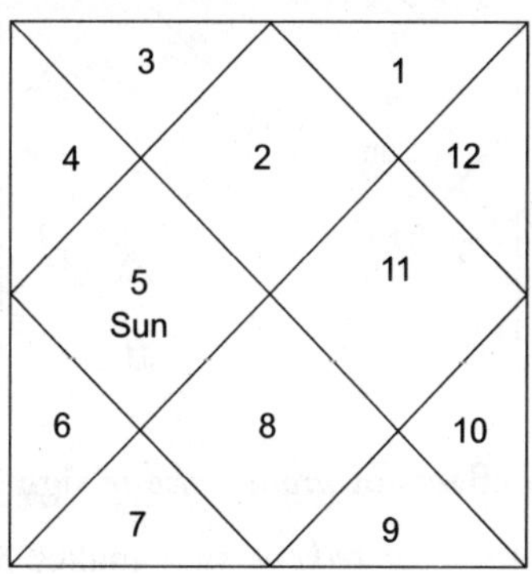

182. What are the effects of exalted sign Sun in 4th house?

Sun exalted in 4th house gives positive results of Sun. Sun as Lord of 8th house of longevity gives long life by getting exalted and placed in *Kendra* but simultaneously affecting the atmosphere of home with its aggression and obstructions as 8th Lord.

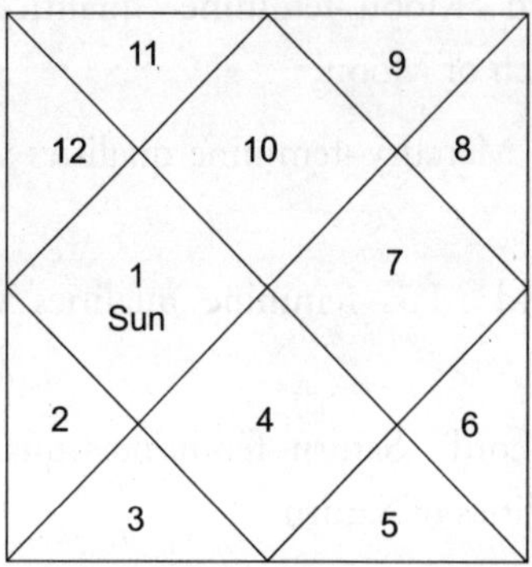

183. What are the effects of debilitated sign Sun in 4th house?

Sun debilitated in 4th house makes the atmosphere at home very fiery, argumentative, and unpleasant. Money being spent on property without enjoyment or peace. (Sun as 2nd Lord of money house going to 4th house of property.)

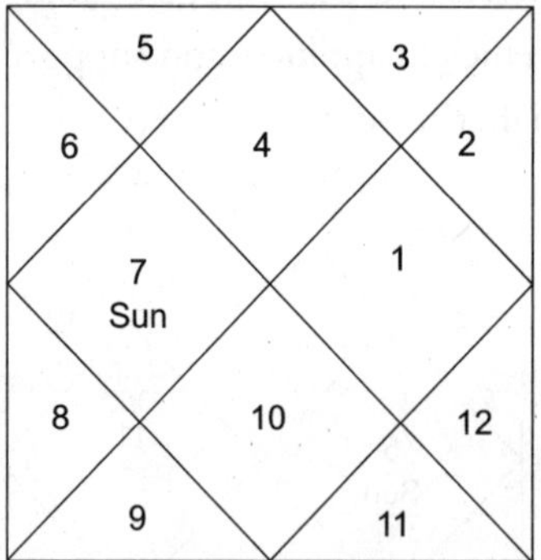

184. What are the effects of *mool trikone* sign Sun in 4th house?

Own sign Sun in its *mool trikone* sign makes Sun strong. Sun as

4th Lord gives positive results of 4th house. Sun as malefic Lord of *Kendra* sheds its malefic effects and does not give unfavourable results.

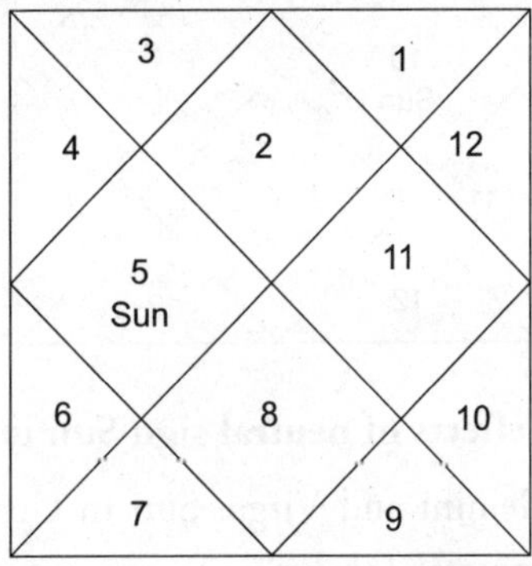

185. What are the effects of friendly sign Sun in 4th house?

Sun in friendly sign Sagittarius gives favourable results. Sun as 12th Lord makes person to spend on vehicles or properties. Sun is friendly in Aries, Cancer, Scorpio, Pisces signs. The results will vary according to its Lordship depending upon the *Lagan* sign.

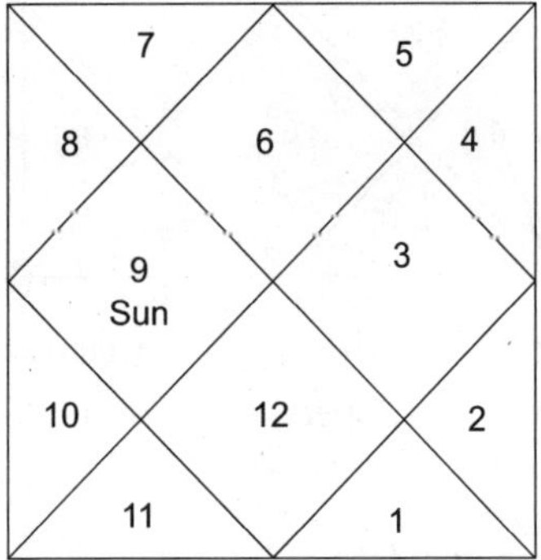

186. What are the effects of inimical sign Sun in 4th house?

Sun in inimical sign Capricorn reduces its results of gains as eleventh Lord. Sun's inimical signs are Taurus, Libra, Capricorn and Aquarius. The results will depend on its Lordship of particular house.

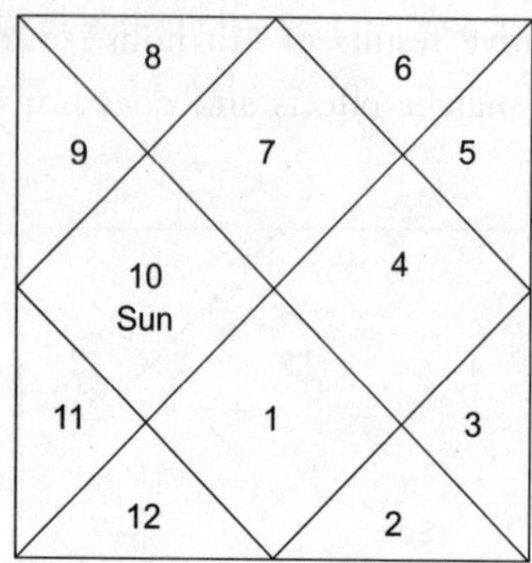

187. What are the effects of neutral sign Sun in 4th house?

Sun is neutral in Gemini and Virgo. Sun in Gemini in 4th house brings the significances of 6th house to property, vehicles etc. This leads to loans, disputes, differences, accidents etc.

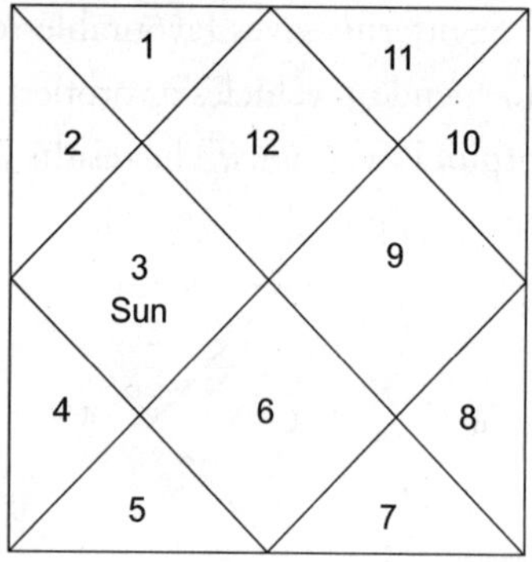

Note: Before giving final prediction, other factors and role of other planets by P.A.C. (Position, Aspect, and Conjunction) should always be considered.

These above placements of Sun in different positions is just an example to show the highly variable results of Sun just by variation of its placement in different signs. It is the sign which changes the position and potential of a planet in spite of being placed in same 4th house.

SADESATI AND ITS EFFECTS

188. What is *sadesati*?

Sadesati takes place when transit Saturn comes in

– 12th house to birth Moon

– Over birth Moon

– 2nd house from birth Moon

The position of transit Saturn approximately make a period of seven and half years. This period gives results depending upon the sign and *Nakshatra* of birth Moon.

Normally the results depend on the

— age of person

— *desh, kaal, patar*.

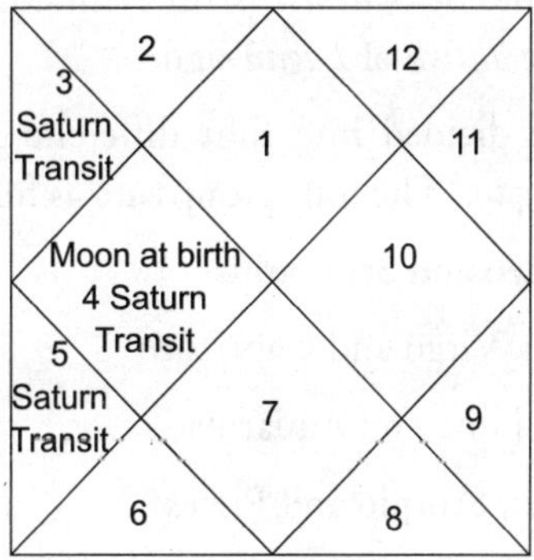

189. What are the effects of *sadesati*?

As Moon and Saturn have inimical relationship with each other, this period normally makes a person mentally uncomfortable. People generally believe that *Sadesati* results are not good but it may not be true as it depends upon multiple factors like :—

Moon sign

Lordship of Moon

Lordship of Saturn

Nakshatras of different signs

Degrees of Moon etc.

190. What is the role of Moon sign in *sadesati*?

The placement of Moon in a particular sign decides the three signs in which *Sadesati* will happen. The friendship and enmity of these sign Lords with Saturn plays a major role in deciding the favourable and unfavourable results of *Sadesati*.

191. Does *nakshatra* play any role in analysis of *sadesati*?

Yes, the role of *Nakshatra* Lords of *Sadesati* signs play a very important role. Friendship between *Nakshatra* Lord and Saturn gives favourable results, while enmity between *Nakshatra* Lord and Saturn increases unfavourable results.

192. Do *tatwa* play any role in *sadesati*?

Yes they do. The role of *Sadesati* is different for different *Lagan*s depending upon the *Tatwa* of *Lagan* sign.

The *Lagan*s can be divided into four different groups depending upon the sign in *Lagan*. The four groups are as follows :—

Fiery signs: Aries, Leo and Sagittarius

Earthy signs: Taurus, Virgo and Capricorn

Airy signs: Gemini, Libra and Aquarius

Watery signs: Cancer, Scorpio and Pisces

Depending upon the sign in *Lagan*, the Lordship of Saturn and Moon get changed. When Saturn gets Lordship of *trikone* (5th house, 9th house) or becomes yog *karaka*, (Taurus and Libra *Lagan*), the *Sadesati* can be rather favourable provided it is not afflicted.

193. Does degree of Moon play any role in *sadesati*?

Results of *Sadesati* are dependent on degrees of Moon. As per great astrologer Shri Karve, the results of *Sadesati* are felt within 45 degrees on either side of degrees of Moon. For example, if Moon is at 20 degrees in Taurus ,the results of *Sadesati* will start when Saturn comes at 5 degrees in Aries and will last till Saturn reaches 5 degrees of Cancer. (45 degrees on either side of birth Moon's degree).

194. What is the importance of lagan degree in the horoscope?

The degrees of *Lagan* is very important, as that decides the *Nakshatra*, *charan* etc. For example Moon at Leo 5° degrees will be under the *Nakshatra* of *Ketu*, at 17° degrees will be in *Nakshatra* of Venus and at 28° degrees will be in the *Nakshatra* of Sun. The effects and results of all the three situations will be different. Besides this, different divisional charts get changed with variation of degrees of *Lagan*. Once the *Lagan* of divisional chart changes, all the placements of different planets also change. This fact is of great use while analyzing horoscopes of twins.

DINMAAN, RAHU KAAL AND MAHURAT

195. What is *dinmaan*?

Dinmaan is the time duration from Sunrise to Sunset.

It is calculated as follows : Sunset time — Sunrise time = *dinmaan.*

This is very important for calculating exact *hora* chart.

This is very important for calculating exact *Abhijeet mahurat.*

This is the time when majority of the *Lal Kitab* remedies should be performed.

Ratrimaan is the time duration from Sunset to next day Sunrise.

Ratrimaan is calculated as follows : Sunrise time of next day — Sunset time of today = *ratrimaan.*

This is very important for calculating *hora* chart.

This is very important for calculating *Abhijeet mahurat.*

This is the time when majority of the *Tamsik* or tantric remedies are performed.

196. What is *Rahu kalam* and its effects?

Rahu kalam is a particular time period everyday which should be avoided during any auspicious activity or *mahurat.*

RAHU KAAL

DAY	TIME
MONDAY	7:30 A.M. TO 9:00 A.M.
TUESDAY	3:00 P.M. TO 4:30 P.M.
WEDNESDAY	12 NOON TO 1:30 P.M.
THURSDAY	1:30 P.M. TO 3:00 P.M.
FRIDAY	10:30 A.M. TO 12 NOON
SATURDAY	9:00 A.M. TO 10:30 A.M.
SUNDAY	4:30 P.M. TO 6:00 P.M.

197. What is *mahurat* and its importance in donations?

Mahurat is the moment when any particular activity or event is started. "Well begun is half done", this holds very true in *mahurat* of astrology. Any event started after considering the different favourable factors of *Panchang* gets completed with least of troubles or hurdles.

"Well begun is half done"

Whenever a particular activity is started at a particular time after considering the favourable *vaar*, *tithi*, *Nakshatra*, yog and *karan* as per the nature of activity, it gives very quick favourable results. If it is done in a particular *Lagan* with placement of certain planets in certain houses and signs, the work gets fulfilled on its own.

Role of *Mahurat* in Donations

Donations done in *krishan paksh* give results faster.

Donations on particular days of planet also gives faster favourable results.

Donations at particular time of planet also gives faster favourable results. (for *Rahu*, Saturn around sunset)

Donations at particular *hora* of planet also gives faster favourable results.

Donations on particular days like *Amavasya*, *Surya Grahan*, *Chander Grahan*, *Sankranti* etc. gives faster favourable results.

198. What is *Gaudhuli mahurat* and its use?

Gaudhuli mahurat is again very important as *Abhijeet mahurat* is. Whenever you do not have an auspicious *mahurat*, but still you want to perform the activity, *Gaudhuli mahurat* can be used. It is especially useful in case of marriage ceremonies.

199. What is *Abhijeet mahurat*?

Abhijeet mahurat is a time of 48 minutes around mid-noon as well as mid-night. The exact time should be calculated by taking midpoint of *dinmaan*/*ratrimaan*. Twenty-four minutes should be taken on either side of this time. *e.g.*

Sunset time – Sunrise time 2

If Sunset time is 18:40 IST

If Sunrise time is 5:40 IST

18:40 – 5:40 = 13:00 hrs. (*Dinmaan*)

Dinmaan divided by 2 = midpoint of day (13hrs divided by 2 = 6hrs 30 minutes).

Mid-day will be Sunrise (05:40 + 6hrs 30 minutes =12:10hrs)

Abhijeet mahurat time 12:10 minus 24 minutes =11:46 a.m.

Abhijeet mahurat time 12:10 plus 24 minutes = 12:34 p.m.

Total *Abhijeet mahurat* time 11:46 a.m. to 12:34 p.m.

NOTE : Please avoid *Abhijeet Mahurat* on Wednesday as it clashes with *Rahu Kaalam* as explained on the next page.

PANCHANG AND ITS IMPORTANCE

200. What is *Panchang* and its importance?

Panchang consists of five factors (*Paanchang*). These five factors are day (*vaar*), *tithi*,*Nakshatra*, yog and *karan*. They all are very useful in Astrology especially in *mahurat* and *prashan kundli*.

We have seven days starting from Sunday, Monday, Tuesday, Wednesday, Thursday, Friday and Saturday. They all have their own importance in *mahurat*. Out of the seven days, comparatively Thursday, Friday, Monday and Wednesday are more benefic for auspicious activities.

Everyday has a specific planet as its Lord. The Lord of the day has certain jurisdictions under his control. The characteristics of the day Lord decides the type of activity during that day.

Sunday .... fixed and constant work, coronation, gold, starting medical treatment, fire related rituals, work of wood, purchase of cow, woollen clothes, weapon related work, leather.

Monday .... silver, ornaments, pearls, water related activities, sexual indulgence, agriculture, food, flower, song and music, milk, garment, beauty parlour.

Tuesday .... surgery, weapon, fire-related activities, deeds of cruelty, theft, electricity, destruction related activities, cheat someone.

Wednesday .... writing, compilation, learning, marriage, welfare, dance, music, arguments, alchemy, art-craft related work, debate.

Thursday .... religious activities, auspicious acts, vehicle, travelling, medication, ornaments, new clothes, medicines.

Friday .... entertainment, shopping, land deals, sexual indulgence, dance, music, bed making, garments, fine arts.

Saturday .... house building, shifting into a new house, and spiritual, long lasting work, steel, servant, service.

Tithis are formed by the distance between moon and sun. We have total 30 *tithis.* Fifteen in *Shukal paksh* and fifteen in *kishan paksh.* These *tithis* are further divided into five categories:—*nanda*, *bhadra*; *jaya*, *rikta* and *poorna*. They all have their utility in astrology especially in day-to-day *mahurat* and *prashna kundli.*

There are twenty-seven *nakshatras* of 13 degrees and 20 minutes each. They all have their utility in astrology in day to day *mahurat* and *prashna kundli*. The *nakshatras* are the fine factors of astrology. The nature of a planet in a sign gets diversified, when we note the *nakshatras* in which it is placed *e.g.*,

Sun in Aries from 0 to 13 degree 20 minutes will be influenced by *Ketu*

Sun in Aries from 13-20 to 26-40 degrees will be influenced by Venus

Sun in Aries from 26-40 to 30 degree will be influenced by sun.

The results of Sun will vary accordingly. The finer results will be based as per the nature of *nakshtra* Lord.

There are twenty-seven yogas, which all have their utility in astrology

In day-to-day *mahurat* and *prashna kundli*, the nature of yoga as per specific activity either promotes or denies that activity.

The results of different yogas in brief is as follows :—

Vishkumbha	**Bad**
Preeti	Good
Ayushman	Good
Saubhagya	Good
Shobhana	Good
Atiganda	**Bad**
SuKarma	Good
Vajra	**Bad**
Vyatipata	**Bad**

Dhriti	Good
Shoola	Good
Ganda	**Bad**
Vriddhi	Good
Dhruva	Good
Vyaghata	Good
Harsh	Good
Siddhi	Good
Variyana	Good

Parigha	**Bad**
Siddha	Good
Shubh	Good
Brahma	Good
Vaidhriti	**Bad**

Shiva	Good
Sadhya	Good
Shukal	Good
Indra	Good

Half of a *tithi* is called as *karan*. They all have their utility in Astrology, day-to-day *mahurat* and *prashna kundli*. The results of different *karan*s in brief is as follows:---

If the person is born in good *karan* then no problem and if one is born in bad *karan*, then the problem will increase. Good yoga and *karan* are used for auspicious activities and bad yogas are avoided. The *karan* on a particular day also affects the results of activity to a great extent.

1.	बव	इन्द्र	बालक की तरह काम करने वाला, चंचलता
2.	बालव	ब्रहमा	सादी पोशाक, विनम्रता, गम्भीर, राजा द्वारा सम्मान
3.	कौलव	सूर्य	वाहन सुख, राजा द्वारा सम्मानित, सुंदर
4.	तैतिल	सूर्य	मधुर वाणी, चतुर, परोपकारी
5.	गर	पृथ्वी	गम्भीर, प्रतापी, युद्ध जीतने वाला
6.	वणिज	लक्ष्मी	चतुर, धनी, दूसरों के सुख में दखल देने वाला
7.	विष्टी	यम	विरोध करने वाला, बदनाम
8.	शकुनि	कलियुग	ज्योतिषी, समय को जानने वाला, कठिनाइयों में पड़ने वाला
9.	चतुष्पद	रूद्र	चारों तरफ का जानकार
10.	नाग	सर्प	तेजस्वी, वाचाल, फुर्तीला, अभिमानी
11.	किंष्तुघन	वायु	मजबूर, दूसरों के अधीन काम करने वाला

THE MOST POPULAR *DASHA* SYSTEM USED BY ASTROLOGERS

201. Which is the Most Popular *Dasha* System Used by Astrologers?

Vimshotri dasha is the most popular *dasha* being used. Calculations up to 120 years can be done very easily and *dasha* pattern can give a visual picture of your life activities on a broader basis. The dynamic astrology is mainly dependent on *dasha* and *gocher*. The final results which may be favourable or unfavourable are delivered only during the *dasha*. The favourable planets for *Lagan* will give favourable results during their *dasha* depending upon the strength of *dasha* Lord. The unfavourable planets for *Lagan* will give unfavourable results during their *dasha* depending upon the strength of *dasha* Lord. These factors have to have correlation with *gocher* also.

202. Give the *dasha* pattern of *vimshotri dasha*?

Dasha pattern of *vimshotri* is as follows: ---

PLANET	DURATION OF *DASHA* IN YEARS
Ketu	7
VENUS	20
SUN	6
MOON	10
MARS	7
Rahu	18
JUPITER	16
SATURN	19
MERCURY	17

Dasha at birth depends upon the degree of Moon at birth. The pattern of *dasha* is fixed. It is the starting point, which is calculated as per degrees of Moon at birth.

203. What are the uses of *dasha*?

You have heard the famous Hindi song

Waqt kee har shaih gulam

Waqt kaa har shaih pai naam

Waqt hai phullon kee saiz

Waqt hai kanton kaa taaz.

EVERYBODY IS A SLAVE OF TIME

EVERYTHING IN THIS WORLD HAS A PREDESTINED NAME AS PER TIME

TIME CAN BE A BED OF ROSES

TIME CAN BE A BED OF THORNS

The words of this song are fully applicable to the *dasha* of different planets as per *dasha* pattern.

God through *dasha* pattern and *gochar* makes you realize the value of time.

Dasha analysis guides us to know the timing of an event.

Dasha analysis tells us about the quality and quantity of the results.

Dasha guides us towards the right direction provided *dasha* Lord is favourable and strong.

Dasha analysis can help us in deciding whether to go for preventive measures or promotional measures. One must try to analyse all three consecutive *dashas* for better prediction. The present *dasha* will tell present followed by future of next *dasha*. The previous one will tell about your position from where you are proceeding.

204. What are the sub-divisions of *dasha*?

- Each *mahadasha* is again divided into 9 sub-periods ruled by 9 planets. These sub-periods in *mahadashas* are called as *antardsahas*. (a.d.)

The nine sub-periods in *antardasha* are called praty *antardashas.* (p.d.)

The nine sub-periods in praty *antardashas* are called sookshma *dasha.* (s.d.)

The nine sub-periods in sookshma *dashas* are called *prana dasha.* (pr.d.)

Therefore, it is very important that we understand the method of analyzing the *dasha* (main period) and *bhukti* (*antar dasha*) results etc.

205. How do you calculate *vimshotari dasha* in detail?

- *Dasha* is calculated as per placement and degrees of Moon at the time of birth.
- Note the placement of Moon in a sign, degrees of Moon and *Nakshatra* of Moon.
- Calculate the remaining degrees of the *Nakshatra* yet to be covered by Moon.
- First *dasha* will belong to the Lord of the *Nakshatra.*
- Calculate the *dasha* pattern as mentioned earlier in 120 years of *dasha.*
- *Dasha* at birth was Mars. *Dasha* to follow are as given below.
- Moon at birth in Capricorn
- Degrees of Moon at birth : 24:01:56
- As per *Nakshatra* table given on page number 33, *Nakshatra* of Mars starts at 23:20:00 in Capricorn and ends at 6:40:00 in Aquarius.
- This total of 13 degrees and 20 minutes of Mars *dasha* is equal to 7 years of *vimshotri dasha.* Each *Nakshatra* is of 13 degrees and twenty minutes

  (13×60 =780 +20 =800 minutes).

  Moon still has to travel 12:38:04(13:20:00 – 00:41:56 =12:38:04 or 12×60=720+38=758minutes 04 seconds.)

  800 minutes=7years of Mars *dasha.*

758minutes will be equal to = 7×758/800 = 6years 7months and 15days.

This balance of *dasha* should be added to the date of birth of person. Where this period ends, the next *dasha* would start followed by the pattern of *vimshotri dasha.*

Dasha	Starting of *dasha*	Ending of *dasha*	Age of person
MARS	2-9-1963	17-4-1970	1-7 years
Rahu	18-4-1970	17-4-1988	7-25 years
JUPITER	18-4-1988	17-4-2004	25-41 years
SATURN	18-4-2004	17-4-2023	41-60 years
MERCURY	18-4-2023	17-4-2040	60-77 years
Ketu	18-4-2040	17-4-2047	77-84 years
VENUS	18-4-2047	17-4-2067	84-104 years
SUN	18-4-2067	17-4-2073	104-110 years
MOON	18-4-2073	17-4-2083	110-120 years

206. How do you calculate *antardasha*?

Each *mahadasha* is divided into 9 *antardashas.* Note the planet ruling the *mahadasha.*

First *antardasha* will always belong to the same planet and *antardashas* go in the same sequence as *dasha* pattern of *vimshotri dasha* as mentioned above.

During the major period of each planet all other planets share periods proportionate to their period in the *vimshotari dasha.*

207. How do planets give their results during *dasha* and antardasha etc.?

Each planet gives the results as per its strength and P.A.C. during its *dasha* and *antardasha.* The strength of planets is very important in deciding the quantity of results. The functional position of a planet as a functional benefic or functional malefic decides the quality of results. The functional benefics will give benefic results and functional malefics will give unfavourable results.

208. How do you find out the timing of events through *vimshotari dasha*?

The birth chart of any native is the negative picture of his life which gets unfolded as per *dasha* and transit. The horoscope only indicates the static promise. The colour of life picture to come depends upon the benefic and malefic *dasha* at different stages of life.

The time when promise will fructify depends upon *dasha* and transit of planets. The planetary *dasha* operative at a particular time of life will give its results as per planet's natural significations, Lordship of houses, planet's placements, aspects and strength.

209. How do you find out the timing of events through transit of planets?

Whenever, any important event is happening in the life of a native, the transit of planets play very important role, particularly the double transit of Saturn and Jupiter.

When Saturn and Jupiter both influence a house, house Lord, *Karaka* then activities related to that house/*Karaka* starts happening.

— the activity or event can get fructified within 2 years 6 months as per transit of Saturn on above factors.

— 12 to 13th months as per transit of Jupiter.

— 6 months as per transit of Mars.

— 1 month as per transit of Sun.

— 1 week as per transit of Moon.

In transit, Sun indicates the month of event and the Moon indicate the week/day of event. In other words, we can say once Saturn approves and Jupiter blesses the concerned factors for the event, the fructification of the concerned event starts. The results will depend upon whether the *dasha* is favourable or unfavourable.

210. What are the important factors in predicting an event?

For predicting any event in any natal chart, we have to study the static factors along with dynamic factors. The static factors are the strength of planets, houses, house Lords, *Karaka*s etc. The dynamic factors are *dasha*, *antardashas* of planets and transit of planets particularly transit of Saturn/Jupiter.

211. Name the favourable *dashas* in astrology.

Favourable *dashas* are

Dasha of functional benefics.

Dasha of planet placed in Trines.

Dasha of planet placed in *Kendra.*

Dasha of planet placed in exaltation.

Dasha of planet placed in *mool trikone.*

Dasha of planet placed in own house.

Dasha of planet placed in fast friend house.

Dasha of planet which is not combust.

Dasha of planet, which is not placed in 6th, 8th, 12th houses.

Dasha of planet which is not conjunct with 6th, 8th, 12th Lords.

Dasha of planet, which is not in beginning of a sign.

Dasha of planet, which is not in end of a sign.

Dasha of planet, which is not enemy of *Lagan* Lord.

Dasha of planet, which is strong in *shadbal.*

Dasha of planet, which is Lord of a good house and
placed in good house from Moon *Lagan.*

Dasha of planet, which is Lord of a good house and
placed in good house from Sun *Lagan.*

Dasha of planet, which is not in 6th, 8th, 12th houses from its own signs.

Dasha of *Rahu* and *Ketu* if placed in *Kendra* or Trines and associated with *Kendra* or Trines Lord.

Dasha of a planet if it has more than 4 points in its bhinashtak Vargas.

Dasha of a planet if it has more than 28 points in its sarvashtak Varga.

*Antar*dsahas of planets, who are 4:10, 3:11, and 5:9 relative position from *mahadasha* Lord.

Dasha of planet which gains strength in divisional charts.

Dasha of planet which has natural benefics placed in its signs.

Dasha is favourable when the dispositer is benefic and well-placed with strength.

Dasha of planet which gains in sarvashtak in its signs in navamsha chart.

Dasha of a planet when it gains strength in *navmansha.*

P.A.C. of natural benefics and yog*Karka* improves the results of planet and house.

IMPORTANT PRINCIPLES TO STUDY RESULTS OF *DASHA* AND GOCHAR

212. What are important principles to study results of *dasha* and *gochar*?

Mahadasha and *Antardasha* Lords should be assessed separately

Mahadasha and *Antardasha* Lords should be friends of *Lagan* Lord

Mahadasha and *Antardasha* Lords should be friends of each other

Mahadasha and *Antardasha* Lords should be natural benefics and unafflicted

Mahadasha and *Antardasha* Lords should be placed in 4:10, 3:11, and 5:9 from each other.

Strong *mahadasha* and strong *antardasha* .... very good results.

Strong *mahadasha* and weak *antardasha* .... less good effects.

Weak *mahadasha* and strong *antardasha* .... some good results.

Weak *mahadasha* and weak *antardasha* .... very bad results.

Malefic *mahadasha* and malefic *antardasha* .... very bad results.

Example:

Rahu/Mars, Mars/Saturn etc.

Mahadasha of functional malefic and *antardasha* of functional malefic .... very bad results

Mahadasha of functional malefic and *antardasha* of functional benefic .... mixed results.

213. Does *dasha* of blood relatives play any role in life of a person?

The results of *dasha* gets modified by the *dasha* of close blood relatives.

As we all have heard, *"apna khoon apna hee hota hai"*. Destiny of real blood relatives is definitely connected with each other. The real blood relatives to be considered are mother, father, real brothers, real sisters, sons, daughters only. The horoscopes and *dasha* pattern of the above relations is very important in verifying an event especially of life and death situations.

214. What are the effects of *dasha* when planet is Lord of Trines and *dushtsthan*?

The Lordship of Trines (1, 5, and 9) prevails when *dasha* Lord is Lord of 6/8/12 also, but the results of 6/8/12 *sthaan* will also be there. Out of the *dushtshtanas*, we must note which planet is worst, bad or neutral for that *Lagan* as per friendship enemity with *Lagan* Lord.

215. What are the important aspects of *dasha*?

Important points

Dasha affects the personality of a person

Dasha Lord shows both its effects of

— natural benefic/natural malefic

— functional benefic/functional malefic

Dasha results are dependent on transit also

Dasha results vary as per *desh kaal paatr*.

216. Is there any method to improve the *dasha* results?

Try to respect the planets before they teach you the hard way

Try to respect and take blessings of natural live *Karaka*s of *dasha* Lord planets to prevent unfavourable results and simultaneously promote favourable results.

217. Does *dasha* pattern play any role in life?

The results of *dasha* pattern affect the life of everyone. Persons with *dasha* pattern of *Trikones* and *Kendra*s have a comparatively better life pattern, provided the planets are strong and unafflicted.

Persons with *dasha* pattern of *trik* houses have a hard life pattern. But on close observation you will realize that *dasha* pattern of *Trikones* and *Kendras* only is not possible. Make horoscopes of all twelve *lagnas* and try to apply *dasha* pattern starting with *Trikone* or *Kendra*.

Make sheets of 12 *lagnas* and try to analyse as per Lordship, placement and other P.A.C. factors.

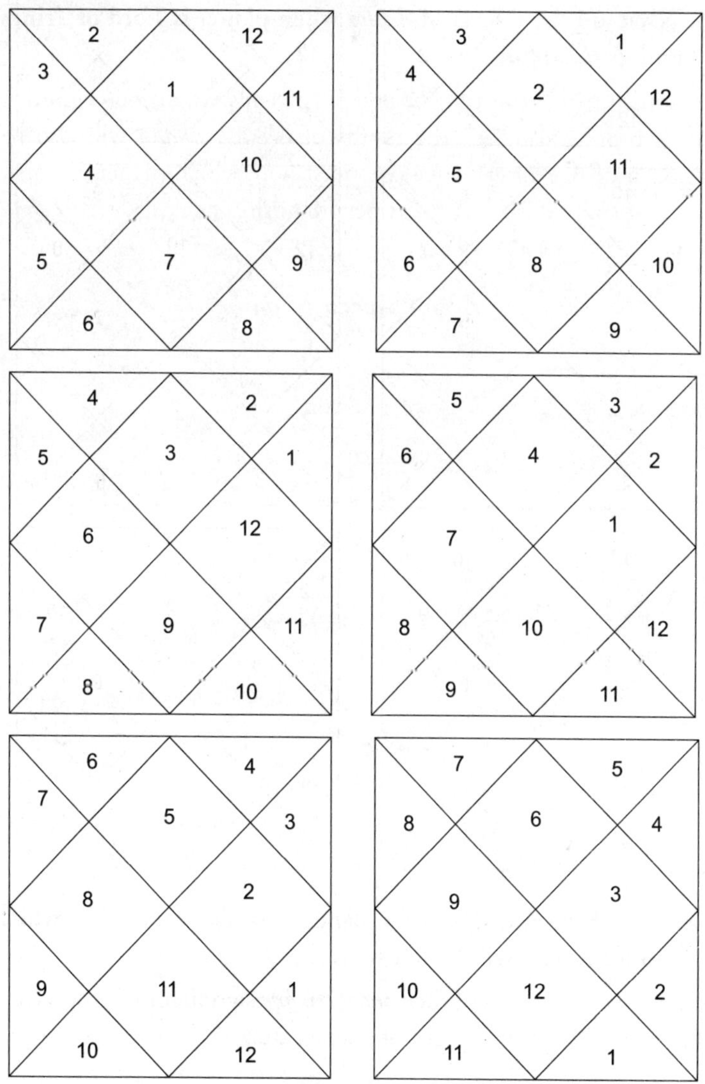

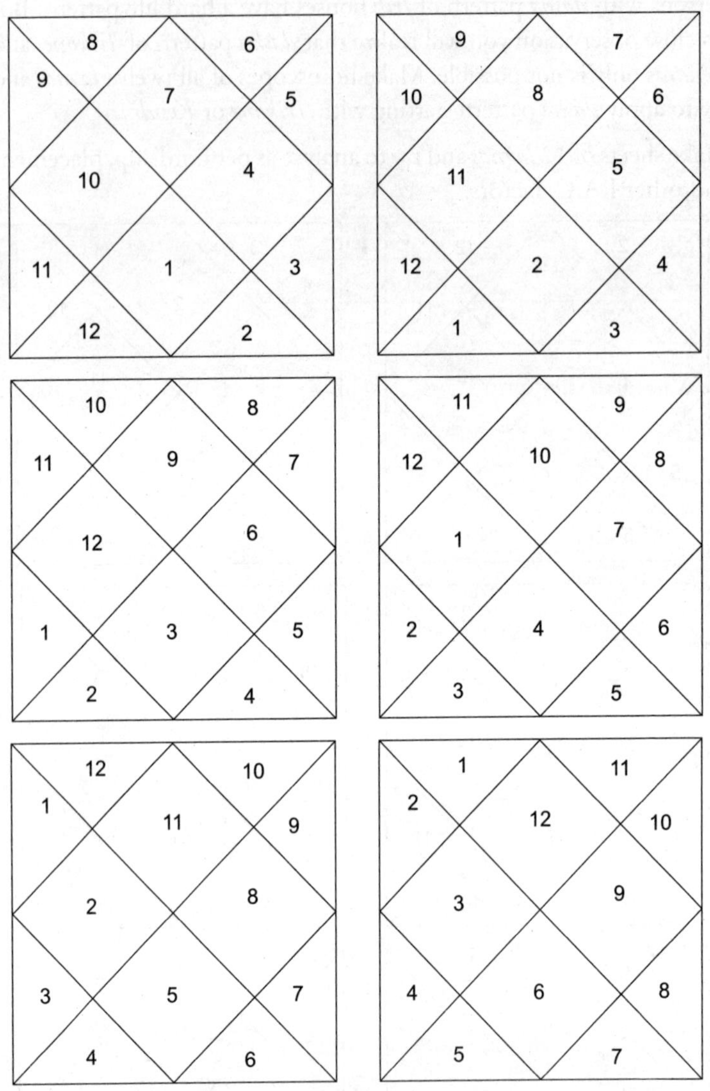

218. Out of the two signs of a planet, how do you decide, which house results will be felt first?

Planets give the results of their *mool trikone* sign first followed by the other sign. *Mool trikone* signs of planets are :—

Planet	*Mool trikone* sign of the planets
Sun	Leo
Moon	Taurus
Mars	Aries
Mercury	Virgo
Jupiter	Sagittarius
Venus	Libra
Saturn	Aquarius

219. What are the main ways by which a planet can give results?

Dasha of a planet gives results in four ways:

1. As Lord of different houses
2. As a benefic or malefic
3. As a natural *Karaka*
4. As Lord of permanent houses of *Kaal purush kundli*

1. As Lord of different houses :— Mars will give results of 4th house and 9th house for Leo *Lagan*. The Lordship varies as per rising *Lagan*.
2. As a benefic or malefic :—

   This is further divided into :—

   Natural benefic or natural malefic

   Functional benefic or functional malefic
3. As a natural *Karaka* (the results of planet give its results as a *Karaka* also which are very important.)
4. As Lord of permanent houses of *kaal purush kundli*. (Mars will give results of 1st and 8th house also as it is permanent Lord of these two houses (Aries and Scorpio in *kaal purush kundli*)

   No planet will shed its basic nature in spite of getting modified by sign, Lordship, *Lagan*, its strength etc.

One cannot change either the basic horoscope or the *dasha* pattern of life but still variations occur depending upon the — *desh kaal paatr*

(The role of planet gets modified by *desh, kaal, paatr. Manglik dosh* is not considered in childhood but is fully considered in adulthood at the time of marriage. The results will depend upon the strength of planet and strength of houses).

— event at a particular time and age (transit of different planets at that time)

— *raja* yoga and other favourable yogas also will be of no use if they are without strength and their *dasha* does not operate in your life-time at the right moment.

Right *Dasha* of Right Planet at Right Age Makes Everything Right.

220. Name the basics of *dasha* analysis?

Basic points of *dasha* analyses

See the relationship of *dasha* Lord with *Lagan* Lord

Whether the *dasha* Lord is natural benefic or malefic

Whether the *dasha* Lord is functional benefic or functional malefic

Strength of *maha dasha* Lord

Strength of *antar dasha* Lord

Strength of praty*antar dasha* Lord

Relationship of *maha dasha* Lord with *Lagan* Lord

Relationship of *antar dasha* Lord with *Lagan* Lord

Relationship of praty*antar dasha* Lord with *Lagan* Lord

The relative position of *mahadasha* and *antar dasha* Lord

The relative position of *mahadasha* and *antar dasha* Lord from their own signs

The strength and position of *mahadasha* and *antar dasha* Lord

The strength and relative position of *mahadasha*, *antar dasha* Lord in divisional charts

Full P.A.C. of *mahadasha*, *antardasha* and praty*antar dasha* Lords

Strength of *mahadasha*, *antardasha* and praty*antar dasha* Lords as per *shadbal*

Strength of *mahadasha*, *antardasha* and praty *antar dasha* Lords as per *ashtakvarga*

Desh kaal paatr as per country/age and personality along with event of life.

The role and effects of transit especially of Saturn and Jupiter

Thc role and effects of transit especially of *Karaka* planet e.g., Venus/ Jupiter for marriage, Mars for lands etc.

The role and effects of transit especially of planet, whose *dasha* is running at that time.

The *dasha* pattern should be applied in Moon *kundli* also.

Strength of *dasha* Lords should be studied in *navamash*a chart.

The event to be analyzed should be co related with *karaka*.

TRANSIT OF PLANETS AND THEIR EFFECTS

221. What is *gochar* or transit?

Gochar or transit is the position of different planets at any moment. It keeps on changing every moment. The position of different planets of *gochar* carries lots of meaning with it.

Giving any prediction without combining the transit with *dasha* and other factors is a blunder. The results of an exalted planet get reduced if the planet is debilitated or weak in transit.

222. What is double transit and its importance in predictions?

Double transit is simultaneous transit of Saturn along with Jupiter on a house, house Lord, sign, sign Lord and different planets.

Clearance by double transit of Saturn followed by Jupiter is a must before any activity concerning a house, house Lord, *Karaka* takes place. If you want to buy plot, the double transit of Saturn and Jupiter on 4th house/4th Lord or *Karaka* Mars is a must. The 4th house and 4th Lord are to be seen both in birth chart as well as in Moon horoscope. Double transit promises fulfillment within one year provided the *dasha* is favourable and the horoscope has a promise for the event.

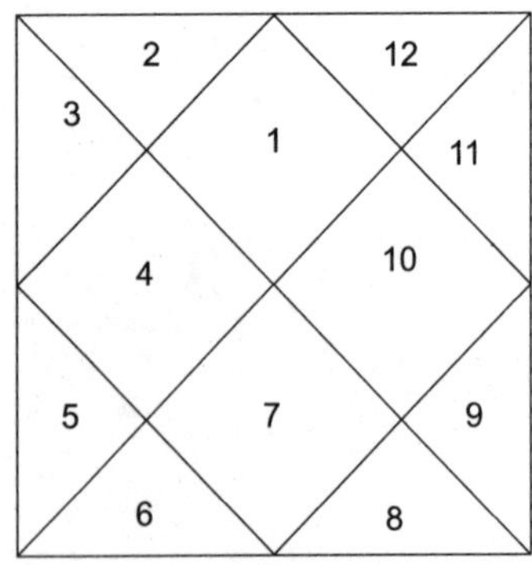

Transit Saturn is in Scorpio thereby activating Scorpio, Capricorn, Taurus and Leo signs by its placement and 3rd, 7th and 10th aspects respectively.

Transit Jupiter is in Leo thereby activating Leo, Sagittarius, Aquarius and Aries by its placement and 5th, 7th and 9th aspects respectively.

So, the double transit effect is on Leo sign in 6th house.

This will activate the 6th house thereby precipitating loans, diseases, disputes etc.

223. What is the role of Mars in transit timings?

The activities promised by double transit (of Saturn and Jupiter) to be fulfilled within one year get cut short to six months by transit of Mars.

224. What is the role of Sun in transit timings?

The activities promised by double transit to be fulfilled within one year get reduced to one month with the transit of Sun.

225. What is the role of Moon in transit timings?

The activities promised by double transit to be fulfilled within one year get further reduced to one week with the transit of Moon within the one month, which has been cleared by transit of Sun.

226. Can transit supersede birth chart (d-1)?

Transit cannot supersede birth chart. It can be helpful in certain cases.

227. How the strength of the transit planet useful in astrology?

Transit of planet is useful in day-to-day *mahurat* for everything. Exaltation of Venus in transit will promote sale of cars, luxury items etc. You can buy luxurious items like car, jewellery, dresses, glamour items etc. during this period. The principle is that the significances of a planet get promoted when that planet gains strength in transit.

228. Does the strength of a transit planet affect the *mahadasha/ antardasha* of your horoscope?

The strength of planets in transit do affect the results of *dasha* Lord

Favourable *dasha* and favourable transit—fully favourable

Favourable *dasha* and unfavourable transit—favourable results get reduced

Unfavourable *dasha* and favourable transit—silver lining in a dark period

Unfavourable *dasha* and unfavourable transit—totally unfavourable

229. Does the weakness of a transit planet affect the results of *mahadasha/antardasha* of your horoscope?

The weakness of *dasha* Lords in transit reduces the favourable results of planet.

230. Does the strength of a Karaka planet in transit is of any use?

Strength of a *Karaka* planet in transit is of great use as it decides the delivery or end result of an event. Exalted Venus in a horoscope with a debilitated Venus in transit will affect the results of Venus during its *dasha* and the significances will get reduced. It can happen the other way round with debilitated in birth chart and exalted in transit giving a silver lining.

231. Do planets give immediate results, when they enter a sign during transit?

This depends upon the planet. The time of planetary effects is different for different planets.

Sun and Mars (fiery planets) give the effects as soon as they enter a sign (0° to 10° degrees).

Jupiter and Venus give results from 10° to 20° degrees.

Moon and Saturn give results in the last ten degrees (20° to 30° degrees).

Mercury and *Rahu* give their results throughout the sign (0° to 30° degrees).

232. Which is the single most important principle to analyze health?

Self or body is signified by the first house, while diseases or ill health is signified by 6th house. If the owner of first house is stronger than the owner of sixth house, good health is assured very fast after any disease or the person will recover.

233. Which is the single most important principle to analyze wealth?

Self is signified by the first house and gains by 11th house while expenses are signified by 12th house. If the owner of first and eleventh houses are stronger than the owner of 12th house then gains are assured in life. Strong 2nd house indicates good cash in hand.

P.A.C. of benefics with 2nd, 11th houses promotes positive flow of money during their *dashas*.

P.A.C. of melefics with 2nd, 11th houses prevents positive flow of money during their *dashas*.

P.A.C. of 6th, 8th, 12th Lords with 2nd, 11th houses prevents positive flow of money during their *dashas*.

P.A.C. of 1st, 5th, 9th Lords with 2nd, 11th houses promores positive flow of money during their *dashas*.

All the above factors are the static factors which indicate about potential of money and wealth. It is the *dasha* pattern along with transit which really decides the flow of money and wealth. The ups and downs are also decided by *dasha*, transit and *desh*, *kaal*, *paatr*.

IMPORTANT QUESTIONS RELATING TO STUDYING A HOROSCOPE

234. How can you know about your past *karmas* by planets in your horoscope?

The planets in a horoscope get placed as per past *karmas* and *renanbandhan.*

Table of past *karmas* and possible position of planet in this birth

Planet	Exalted or Strong	Debilitated or weak
Sun	Served father, government, led *satwik* life	Insulted father, father-in-law, government
Moon	Served mother, elderly ladies, *satwik* life	Insulted mother, mother-in-law, elderly ladies
Mars	Respected youngsters	Insulted youngsters,
Mercury	Respected *behan, bua, beti.* Did fair business deals	Insulted *behan, bua, beti*
Jupiter	Followed religion, respected father, elders	Insulted priest, *peepal,* elders of the family
Venus	Respected wife, young female subordinates	Insulted wife, female servants
Saturn	Helped servants, served elders	Insulted servants, elders
Rahu	Helped lepers, served grand-parents	Killed snakes, insulted grand-parents
Ketu	Served at religious places, served dogs	Killed dogs, insulted grand-parents

235. Does a natural malefic sheds its total maleficence by becoming a functional benefic?

No, no planet whether malefic or benefic ever loses its basic nature. The natural malefic becoming a functional benefic gives positive results of the houses it owns and the house where it is placed. It even tries to improve the results of houses and planets it aspects.

236. Does a natural benefic sheds its total beneficence by becoming a functional malefic?

No, no planet whether malefic or benefic ever loses its basic nature. The natural benefic becoming a functional malefic gives unfavourable results of the houses it owns and the house where it is placed. It even tries to influence the results of houses and planets it aspects.

237. What is the importance of *mool trikone* signs? Name the *mool trikone* signs of all the planets?

Except Sun and Moon, all planets have Lordship over two signs. One of these two signs is marked as *mool trikone* sign. The planets normally give the results of its *mool trikone* sign first followed by results of other sign.

Planet	Lordship of signs	*Mool trikone* sign
Sun	Leo	Leo
Moon	Cancer	Taurus
Mars	Aries, Scorpio	Aries
Mercury	Gemini, Virgo	Virgo
Jupiter	Sagitarius, Pisces	Sagittarius
Venus	Taurus, Libra	Libra
Saturn	Capricorn. Aquarius	Aquarius

238. How are *panchmahapurush* yogas formed?

In formation of *panch* (5) *mahapurush* yogas, only Mars, Mercury, Jupiter, Venus and Saturn are considered.

Placement of these planets in *Kendra* and in their own signs or in exaltation sign from *Lagan* or Moon *Lagan* forms the yoga.

Name the *panch mahapurush* yogas.

Yoga forming planet	Name of yoga	Position of planet in own signs	Position of planet in exaltation sign	Position of planets in houses from lagan	Position of planets in houses from Moon
Mars	*Ruchak*	1, 8	10	*Kendra*	*Kendra*
Mercury	*Bhadar*	3, 6	6	*Kendra*	*Kendra*
Jupiter	*Hans*	9,12	4	*Kendra*	*Kendra*
Venus	*Malaya*	2, 7	12	*Kendra*	*Kendra*
Saturn	*Shash*	10, 11	7	*Kendra*	*Kendra*

Venus 7
5
8
6 Sun
Mercury
4
9 *Rahu*
3 *Ketu*
Sat 10
Moon
12
Jupiter
2
11
1 Mars

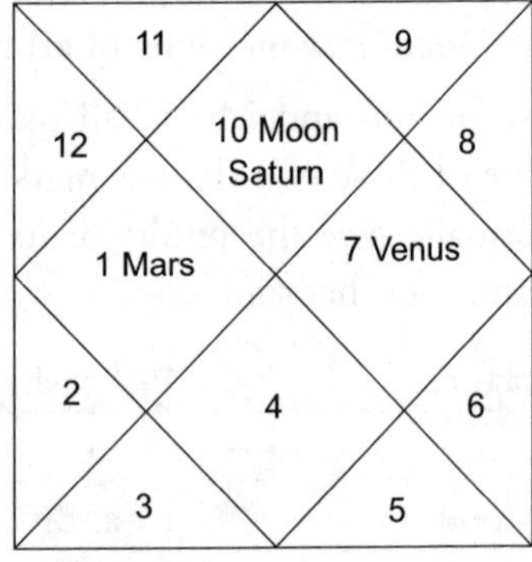

In the horoscope above, all five *panch mahapurush* yogas are getting formed :—

1. *Bhadra yoga formed by Mercury (Mercury in Kendra and exalted*)
2. *Hansa* yoga formed by Jupiter (Jupiter in *Kendra* and in own sign)
3. *Shasha* yoga is formed (Saturn in *Kendra* from Moon and in own sign)
4. *Ruchak* yoga is formed (Mars in *Kendra* from Moon and in own sign)

5. *Malaya* yoga is formed (Venus in *Kendra* from Moon and in own sign)

239. What are the results of *panchmahapurush* yogas?

Panchmahapurush yogas are the extra powerful position of planets. The planet forming *panchmahapurush* yoga gives excellent results as per its significance. The results are more apparent during the *dasha* of planet.

240. Can one mix more than one system while analyzing a horoscope?

There are many ways of analysis of horoscope as per different methods prescribed by our *Rishis*. You can make analysis by any method or system provided you do not mix up the principles of two systems together. One should analyze a horoscope as per one system and should try to complement and confirm the findings as per other system.

241. What are the basic parameters for analyzing a horoscope as per *Parashri* system?

Analysis by *Parashri* method:

After making sure that the horoscope is correct, proceed as mentioned below :—

→ See the strength of *Lagan* and *Lagan* Lord. (Body)

→ See the strength of Moon. (Mind)

→ See the strength of Sun. (Soul)

→ See the placement of planets in *Kendras* (Status)

→ See the placement of planets in *Trikones* (Money)

→ See the placement of malefic in 3, 6, 11(longevity and self-efforts)

→ See the strength of planets (power to fulfill an event during *dasha*)

→ See the strength of houses (potential or promise of significances)

→ See the strength of *karakas* (power to fulfill particular significance)

→ See *panchmahapurush* yogas and other benefic yogas as *gaj-kesari* etc.

→ See the *dasha* pattern from birth onwards (*dashas* of *Kendras* and *Trikones* for overall growth, prosperity, status, honours etc.

→ See the role of functional benefics and functional malefic.

→ See the co-relation as per age with *dasha* pattern.

→ See the *gochar* (double transit) of slow moving planets especially of Saturn (*karmas*) and Jupiter (*jeev*).

→ See the circumstances of person(*paatr*),

Time (*kaal*) and place (*desh*).

→ Decide the remedy as per *dasha*, *gochar*, activity etc.

THE BASIC PARAMETERS FOR ANALYZING A HOROSCOPE AS PER LAL KITAB SYSTEM

242. What are the basic parameters for analyzing a horoscope as per *Lal Kitab* system?

→ Convert the horoscope of *Parashri* to *Lal Kitab kundli* by removing the signs in houses and presuming first house as Aries.

→ See the placement of planets as per *kaal-purush kundli.*

→ See the exaltations, debilitations, own house as per houses.

→ See the position of *Karaka*s in the horoscope.

→ See the relationship between planet placed in a house and the house Lord.

→ See the relationship between planet placed in a house and *Karaka* of house.

→ Note the *dasha* of a planet as per age of person (35 years cycle).

→ Note the *dasha* Lord's position in *varshphals* for that age.

→ Note the position of planets in different *varshphals.*

→ Note the placement of planets in 8th, 6th, 12th houses.

→ Note the placement of planets in *Kendra*s especially *Lagan.*

→ Note the placement of *Karaka*s in 6th, 8th, and 12th houses.

→ Note the placement of *Karaka*s in *Kendra*'s, *Trikones.*

→ Note the different *rins* in the horoscope.

→ Note the *grahan*'s of Sun and Moon.

→ Note the *rini* planets (planet which has to pay the *rin*) as per *Lagan kundli*

→ Note *rini* planets (planet which has to pay the *rin*) as per *varshphal* charts.

→ Study the position of planets placed in 6th, 8th, and 12th in next year's *varshphals* also for seeing the relief or continuity of problem.

→ Do the remedy as prescribed in a proper manner with full faith and devotion.

→ Repeat the remedies like *grahan* etc. throughout life.

→ Maintain a good moral character throughout life.

→ Be charitable and try to lift downtrodden, poor, needy persons of society.

→ Repay the *rins* before wearing the gem of a planet.

(*Pahlay rin chukao fir rattan apnao*)

→ Please remember that *"Samay Se Pehle Aur Muqqadar Se Adhik Kisi Ko Nahin Milta."* One cannot get anything more or before the destined time and fortune.

→ Remedies give you grace period for recovery by over draft, which can be repayed later in form of

.... donations

.... *mantras*

.... social service

.... good moral character.

.... good *aacharan* etc.

(More details in my book on *Lal Kitab*.)

243. Can one club *Parashri* and *Lal Kitab* systems together?

Yes. One should analyze a horoscope as per one system and should try to complement and confirm the findings as per other system. My personal opinion is to diagnose or analyze by *Parashri* system and confirm by *Lal Kitab* system. *Lal Kitab* will be more useful for remedial part.

244. What are the special guidelines one should remember before giving any prediction or advising anyone with a remedial measure?

– never give prediction on the basis of a single principle

– synthesize all factors before making final decision

– analyze the horoscope in a systematic way

First see *rins* and repay

Note *grahan*s and do remedy

Note weak house

Make *varshphal* and note the weakness repeated

Do remedy for that weak planet in that year

Try to maintain the factors mentioned under *aacharan*

Keep the preventions and limitations of remedy rules in mind.

245. What are the rules to be kept in mind?

Try to do the remedies with full faith

Involve yourself physically as far as possible like serving food with your own hands, worshiping on your own, *kar sewa* with own hands etc.

Have patience before rejecting or selecting a new remedy

That Astrology also has its limitations should always be borne in mind

Do not be selfish, pray for others, so that others can pray for your well-being

Always do good *karmas* to secure a permanent favourable future.

246. What are the most important principle of astrology?

Note the P.A.C. of separative planets with any house /

Note the P.A.C. of separative planets with house Lord or

Note the P.A.C. of separative planets with *Karaka*.

Separative planets are Saturn, Mars, *Rahu*, twelfth Lord.

Whenever a house suffers by association of separative planets the significances of house suffers.

Whenever a house Lord suffers by association of separative planets the significances of house suffers.

Whenever a *Karaka* of a house suffers by association of separative planets, the live significances of house suffers.

The above predictions can be a certainty :—

If there is no P.A.C. of natural benefics on house, house Lord or *Karaka*.

The above predictions can be a certainty :—

If there is no P.A.C. of functional benefics

On house, house Lord or *karaka*

The above predictions can be a certainty :—

If there is no P.A.C. of *trikone* Lords on house, house Lord or *Karaka*

Event takes place in *antardasha* of a planet.

Event is precipitated by double transit of Saturn and Jupiter.

247. What do you understand by the physical and functional results of a planet?

Physical results of planets should be associated with different parts of body or organs, besides the live personalities. The functional results are when things like money, property, and other assets are affected.

DIVISIONAL CHARTS AND THEIR EFFECTS

248. What are divisional charts?

Divisional charts are the sub-divisions of birth chart into different charts as per the activity or matters of life of *jatak*. The 30 degrees of birth chart are sub divided into different sub divisions of 15 degrees, 10 degrees, 2 degree 30 minutes etc. for different divisional charts.

249. How many divisional charts are used in astrology and what is the relative numerical value of different charts?

There are sixteen main divisional charts.

S. NO.	DIVISION NO.	NAME	POWER
1	D-1	BIRTH	3.5
2	D-2	*HORA*	1
3	D-3	*DREKANNA*	1
4	D-4	*CHATURTHAMSHA*	0.5
5	D-7	*SAPTAMSHA*	0.5
6	D-9	*NAVAMSHA*	3.0
7	D-10	*DASHAMSHA*	0.5
8	D-12	*DWADAMSHA*	0.5
9	D-16	*SHODAMSHA*	2.0
10	D-20	*VIMSHAMSHA*	0.5
11	D-24	*CHATURVIMSHAMSHA*	0.5
12	D-27	*SAPTAVIMSHAMSHA*	1.0
13	D-30	*TRIMSHAMSHA*	1.5
14	D-40	*KHAVEDAMSHA*	0.5
15	D-45	*AKSHVEDAMSHA*	0.5
16	D-60	*SHASTIAMSHA*	5

250. What are the different significances of sixteen divisional charts?

The significances of the divisional charts is as shown below in the table.

S. NO.	NUMBER	NAME OF DIVISIONAL CHART	SIGNIFICANCES OF DIVISIONAL CHART
1.	D-1	BIRTH/*LAGNA*/*RASHI*	EVERYTHING
2.	D-2	*HORA*	MONEY, WEALTH, FAMILY, SPEECH
3.	D-3	*DREKKANA*	YOUNGERS, SELF EFFORTS, COURAGE
4.	D-4	*CHATURAMSHA*	MOTHER, FIXED ASSETS, PROPERTY
5.	D-7	*SAPTAMSHA*	CHILDREN
6.	D-9	*NAVAMSHA*	LIFE PARTNER, MARRIED LIFE, DESTINY
7.	D-10	*DASHAMSHA*	PROFESSION, STATUS
8.	D-12	*DWADASMSHA*	PARENTS
9.	D-16	*SHODAMSHA*	MOVEABLE ASSESTS, VEHICLES
10.	D-20	*VIMSHAMSHA*	SPIRITUAL LIFE
11.	D-24	*CHATURVIMSHAMSHA*	KNOWLEDGE, ACADEMIC ACHIEVEMENT
12.	D-27	*SAPTAVIMSHAMSHA*	STRENGTH, STAMINA

13.	D-30	*TRISHAMSHA*	MISERIES, MISFORTUNES, ILLNESS
14.	D-40	*KHAVEDAMSHA*	AUSPICIOUSNESS IN LIFE
15.	D-45	*AKSHVEDAMSA*	GENERAL FEATURES OF LIFE
16.	D-60	*SHASHTIAMSA*	GENERAL ASPECTS OF LIFE

251. How do you use divisional charts for the prediction?

A particular chart is chosen as per the activity of life *e.g.*, for profession, note

— The strength of *Lagan* of birth chart

— The strength of 10th Lord of birth chart

— The strength of *Lagan* of *dashamsha* chart

— The strength of 10th Lord of *dashamsha* chart

— note the strength of *Lagan* Lord of birth chart in *dashamsha* chart

— note the strength of 10th Lord of birth chart in *dashamsha* chart

Combining above factors, real potential of your professional life can be predicted.

252. What is the importance of divisional charts?

Divisional charts are the secret, hidden parts of basic chart. As a house is divided into drawing room, *puja* room, bath room, kitchen, study room etc. for different activities, in the same way sixteen different divisions are made to study different aspects of a person's life. These can be related to money, health, diseases, property, parents, wife, profession etc. The same planets of basic chart can behave in different manner in different divisional charts.

EFFECTS OF NATURAL BENEFICS AND MALEFICS IN DIFFERENT HOUSES

253. What are the results when natural benefics are placed in *Trines*?

This is one of the most powerful and benefic position for a planet. The results will be tenfold when the planet is a functional benefic also.

254. What are the results when natural benefics are placed in *Kendras*?

This is one of the most powerful and benefic position for a planet. The results will be fivefold, when the planet is a functional benefic also.

255. What are the results when natural benefics are placed in $6^{th}/8^{th}/12^{th}$ house?

This is one of the worst position for a planet. The results will be even more bad when the planet is a functional benefic also. These positions are the sheer wastage of benefics.

256. What are the results when natural benefics are placed in 3rd, 6th, 10th, and 11th house?

This is one of the powerful and benefic position for a planet provided the *jatak* has the strong will power to fulfill his efforts. The results will be proportionate to the efforts if the planet is a functional benefic also.

257. What are the results when natural malefic are placed in 2nd /11th house?

The natural malefic in 2nd and 11th houses makes a person miser. He or she does not share his money with anyone. Malefic in 11th can give money by unlawful means. Planets in eleventh house can give health problems.

258. What are the results when natural malefic are placed in *Trines*?

Natural malefic gain strength when placed in Trines but they spoil the significances of the Trine houses. They give stronger results of the houses under their Lordship.

259. What are the results when natural malefic are placed in *Kendras*?

Natural malefic gain strength when placed in *Kendra* but they spoil the significances of the *Kendra* houses. They give stronger results of the houses under their Lordship.

260. What are the results when natural malefic are placed in 6th/8th/12th house?

Natural malefic when placed in 6th, 8th and 12th houses are better than in Trines or *Kendra*'s. They spoil the significances of the 6th, 8th and 12th houses. By spoiling the negative effects of the 6th, 8th and 12th houses they give favourable results.

261. What are the results when functional benefics are placed in 3rd, 6th, 10th, and 11th houses?

When functional benefics are placed in 3rd, 6th, 10th, 11th houses, they give favourable results only after lots of efforts. The results are assured when they are aspected by benefics.

262. What are the results when functional benefics are placed in 2nd/11th house?

When functional benefics are placed in 2nd, 11th houses, they give favourable results with lots of money and gains. The results are assured and manyfold, when they are aspected by benefics.

263. What are the results, when functional benefics are placed in *Trines*?

This is one of the most powerful and benefic position for a planet. The results will be tenfold, when the planet is a natural benefic also.

264. What are the results when functional benefics are placed in *Kendras*?

This is one of the powerful and benefic position for a planet. The results will be 5 fold when the planet is a natural benefic also.

265. What are the results when functional malefic are placed in 6th/8th/12th house?

This is one of the powerful and benefic position for a planet. The results will be favourable regarding the 6th, 8th, 12th house significances only. Bad planet going to bad place. Problems followed by recovery.

266. What are the results when functional malefic are placed in 3rd, 6th, 10th, 11th houses?

The results will be available only after lots of self-efforts and struggles. The results are better, when aspected by natural benefic also.

267. What are the results when functional malefic are placed in 2nd/11th?

The natural malefic in 2nd and 11th houses makes a person miser. He or she does not share his money with anyone. Malefic in 11th can give money by unlawful means. It can give health problems.

268. Should functional benefics be strong?

Yes, stronger the better. They should not be afflicted.

269. Should functional malefic be strong?

No, they should be weak. This prevents the planet to give unfavourable results, so the intensity of unfavourable results gets reduced.

IMPORTANCE OF MOON IN ASTROLOGY

270. What is the importance of Moon *Lagan*?

Moon is one of the *Lagan*s and is very important in astrology. It gives the mental picture of the *jatak*.

When date of birth is known but time is not known, Moon *kundli* can give you lots of information about life of a person. The transit results are more accurate from Moon *Lagan*.

271. What are the uses of Moon?

For name keeping(*naamkaran*)

For birth sign based on moon *Lagan*

Dasha calculation for dynamic analysis

Gold/silver/bronze *payaa* (fraction)

Gand mool calculation

Matching of horoscopes

Moon *Lagan* for analysis where birth time not known

Results of transit

Special yogas like *gaj kesari*

Balarishth calculation

Special importance in festivals like

Karva chauth, Eid, Diwali etc.

Sadesati calculations

272. What are the uses of *janam rashi* (birth moon sign)?

Birthday celebration

Mundan

Religious ceremonies

Sadesati calculations

Coronation ceremonies

Marriage ceremonies

Mantra sidhis

Donations

273. What are the uses of *prachalit* name (popular or legal name)?

Foundation laying

Entry into house

Professional activities

Public dealings

Official works

Legal matters

Remarriage

274. What is the importance of Sun *lagan*?

Sun is one of the *Lagans* and is very important in astrology. It shows the dominance in life and the spiritual side of person. It is *Karaka* for brain, bones, heart etc., and most important parts of body.

275. What is the importance of *Sudershan Chakra*?

Sudershan chakra is the combined chart, where *Lagan*, Moon *Lagan* and Sun *Lagan* are combined in ascendant. This gives the combined picture of body, mind and soul.

276. What are the factors which should be considered before giving results?

The predictions should be made after synthesizing:

1. The strength of planets,

2. Strength of house
3. Strength of *Karaka* and
4. Running *dasha* at that time etc.
5. Transit of Saturn and Jupiter
6. Transit of *dasha* Lords
7. Transit of *Karaka* for the event
8. *Desh kaal paatr*

First of all, the position of the *Lagan* and Lord of *Lagan* should be seen.

If the Moon is strong and has P.A.C. of favourable Mercury and Jupiter (*Karukas* for intelligence and applied knowledge), the native can make best use of opportunities available to him.

If the Sun is strong and has P.A.C. of favourable Mercury and Jupiter, the native gets good status, position in life.

If all these factors i.e. the ascendant, the Moon, the Sun, are strong, the native would get good opportunities for advancement in life with happiness and position.

The P.A.C. of any house/house Lord/*Karaka* decides the quality and quantity of an event in life. The results finally unfold depending upon *dasha* and *desh, kaal, paatr.*

After the horoscope has been cast properly with divisional charts, identify the functional nature of the planets from the ascendant.

Note the functional benefics and functional malefic planets. Find out the strength of planets.

Find out the current operating *dashas* (the *mahadasha/antardasha/ pratyantar dasha* Lords).

Find out the transits on the date in question.

Find out the natal and transit strength of the *mahadasha* and *antardasha* Lords.

277. What are the important factors in predicting an event?

There are two important factors in predicting an event:—

i. Static promise of an event

ii. Dynamic fulfilment of an event

Static factors are :—

Strength of planets

Strength of houses

Strength in *shadbal*

Strength in *ashtakvarga*

Strength in divisional charts etc.

Dynamic factors are :—

Dasha of *mahadasha* Lord

Dasha of *antardasha* Lord

Dasha of *pratyanterdasha* Lord etc.

Double transit of Saturn and Jupiter

Desh kaal paatr

For predicating any event in any natal chart, we have to study *mahadasha/antar*dsahas of planets and transit of planets particularly double transit of Saturn/Jupiter.

278. What does *Rahu* represent?

Rahu represents suddenness, enjoyment, entertainment, illusion, glamour, diplomacy, cunningness, cleverness, addiction, sexual acts etc. *Rahu* acts like Saturn.

Whenever *Rahu* has P.A.C. with 9th house/9th Lord/Jupiter, then it gives lots of religious trips. P.A.C. of Jupiter with *Rahu* gives you more results of *amrit* (positive results).

279. What does *Ketu* represent?

Ketu represents *Moksh*, mystery, research, meditation etc. During the *dasha* of *Ketu* a proper diagnosis can never be done. Proper time of meditation is before sunrise, because that is the perfect time of *Ketu*. *Ketu* acts like Mars. Association of Jupiter with *Ketu* pacifies the negative effects of *Ketu*.

280. What is eclipse?

Eclipse is a situation, when the light of Sun or Moon is unable to reach e*arth*.

A solar eclipse occurs in the day time at new Moon, when the Moon is between e*arth* and the Sun.

A lunar eclipse occurs at night time, when the e*arth* passes between the Sun and the Moon.

281. When does the eclipses take place?

Solar eclipse always takes place on *amavasya*. Lunar eclipse always takes place on *puranmashi*.

282. How do you calculate your events from the horoscopes of your blood relations?

The table explains the event calculation from horoscope of your blood relations.

Note your relationship with the relative. Make horoscope of that relative.

For example, you want to know about yourself from your younger brother's horoscope.

Make horoscope of younger brother.

Note 11th house and 11th Lord in your younger brother's horoscope.

Note the position of *Karaka* Jupiter in younger brother's horoscope.

The strength and P.A.C. of above factors can tell you a lot about you.

These can be very useful in case you do not have your own birth data.

In the same way, other relative's horoscopes can be used.

S. No	Relative	House	House Lord	Karaka
1.	From horoscope of Father	5th	5th Lord	Jupiter
2.	From horoscope of Mother	5th	5th Lord	Jupiter
3.	From horoscope of Elder brother	3rd	3rd Lord	Mars
4.	From horoscope of Elder sister	3rd	3rd Lord	Mars
5.	From horoscope of Younger brother	11th	11th Lord	Jupiter
6.	From horoscope of Younger sister	11th	11th Lord	Jupiter
7.	From horoscope of Wife/husband	7th	7th Lord	Jupiter/ Venus
8.	From horoscope of Son	9th	9th Lord	Sun
9.	From horoscope of Daughter	9th	9th Lord	Sun

283. How do you see relation between person and father?

Note the Lords of 1st and 9th house. Note their relative position from each other. If it is 6:8, or 2:12, the relations will not be good.

If relative position is

5:9

4:10

3:11

7:7

1:1

Then the relations will be cordial.

P.A.C. between Sun and Saturn creates misunderstanding between father and son.

The other factors should always be considered before giving final prediction.

284. How do you see relation between person and mother?

Note the Lords of 1st and 4th house. Note their relative position from each other. If it is 6:8, or 2:12, the relations will not be good.

If relative position is

5:9

4:10

3:11

7:7

1:1

Then the relations will be cordial.

P.A.C. between Moon and Saturn creates misunderstanding between mother and son.

The other factors should always be considered before giving final prediction.

285. How do you see relation between person and elder sister/ brother?

Note the Lords of 1st and 11th house.

Note their relative position from each other.

If it is not 6:8 or 2:12, the relations will be fine.

If relative position is

5:9

4:10

3:11

7:7

1:1

Then the relations will be cordial.

The other factors should always be considered before giving final prediction.

286. How do you see relation between person and younger sister /brother?

Note the Lords of 1st and 3rd house.

Note their relative position from each other.

If it is not 6:8, or 2:12, the relations will be fine.

If relative position is

5:9

4:10

3:11

7:7

1:1

Then the relations will be cordial.

The other factors should always be considered before giving final prediction.

287. How do you see relation between person and wife?

Note the Lords of 1st and 7th house.

Note their relative position from each other.

If it is not 6:8, or 2:12, the relations will be fine.

If relative position is

5:9

4:10

3:11

7:7

1:1

Then the relations will be cordial.

The other factors should always be considered before giving final prediction.

288. How do you see relation between person and mother-in-law?

Note the Lords of 1st and 10th house.

Note their relative position from each other.

If it is not 6:8, or 2:12, the relations will be fine.

If relative position is

5:9

4:10

3:11

7:7

1:1

Then the relations will be cordial.

Partner is 7th house and 4th house from 7th is tenth house of mother-in-law.

The other factors should always be considered before giving final prediction.

THE FACTORS AN ASTROLOGER NEED TO CONSIDER BEFORE GIVING PREDICTIONS

289. What are the factors an astrologer need to consider before giving predictions?

One must avoid astrology consultations on *Amavasya*, *Pooranmashi*, *Chander Grahan*, *Surya Grahan* etc.

One should be extra careful, when transit Moon is in 4th house, 8th house or 12th house from astrologer's own moon at the time of consultations.

290. How to go ahead in astrology?

Before you do that, you must know the importance of all the factors as explained below :

Age of person: Tells us about the likely possibilities of event

Sex of person: Further differentiates the different events

Females of 18 years education plus marriage

Males of 18 years education plus profession

Venus at 2-5 years makes you a doll

Venus at 20 year onwards makes you glamorous

Time of birth: Month of birth decides the Sun sign and the time decides the *Lagan*.

Your status, dominance brain level is decided

The signs get their allotted houses as per *Lagan*

Place of birth: Decides the *desh*, *kaal*, *paatr*

Cities: 18 years higher education

Villages: 18 years professional settlement/marriage etc.

There are number of factors which help us in arriving at a decision:

Note the age of person

Note *desh kaal paatr*

Note the *dhan* yogas

Note the status/*rajyogas*

Note the *dashas* between 20 to 60 years of *Parashri*

Note the *dashas* between 20 to 60 years of *Lal Kitab*

Note the double transit

Note the nature of sign falling in the ascendant

Note the nature of sign falling in the tenth house

Note the second house, ruling the family and bank balance

Note the third house which rules communications (interview, salesmanship)

Note the eleventh house signifying gains

Note the ascendant of *dashamsa*

Note the nature of planets becoming significators for profession and the planets exerting close influence on the houses ruling professional matters.

All these are important factors for assessing your professional or functional matters.

291. What will decide the results of planets and horoscope as a whole?

The interpretation will depend upon the following:—

If only a house is activated

If house and house Lord are activated

If house, house Lord and *Karaka*, are activated

If only a sign is activated

If sign and sign Lord both are activated

The net results are dependent as per separative and protective forces

Maarnay wale sai

Bachanay wala bada hota hai

Saviour is more powerful than destroyer.

The protective forces can control separative forces

If *Karaka*, *Karaka* house and *karaka* house Lord all are affected, the live *karaka* will (person) be affected.

If sign, sign Lord and *Karaka* all are affected, the significances will be affected.

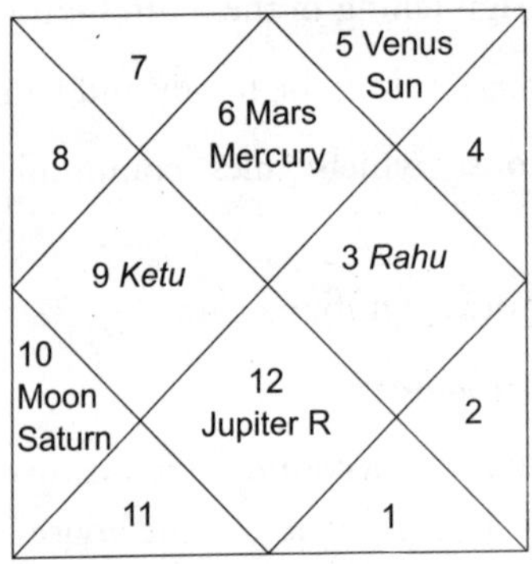

In *dasha* of Saturn, 4th house, 4th Lord Jupiter and 4th house *karaka* Moon, all are affected by separative Saturn (6th Lord), thereby will trouble mother.

Simultaneously Saturn aspects 11th house of gains, conjunct with 11th Lord Moon and aspects *Karaka* of gains Jupiter. This will affect gains and income of person.

292. How will you differentiate, whether the live personality will suffer or significances will suffer?

If *Karaka* and *Karaka* house and *Karaka* Lord all are affected, the live *karaka* (person) will be affected.

If sign, sign Lord and *karaka* all are affected, the significances will be affected.

293. How to do all this practically?

Now note double transit of Saturn and Jupiter

Note double transit of Saturn and *Rahu*

Note double transit of Saturn and *Ketu*

Note double transit of *Rahu* and *Ketu*

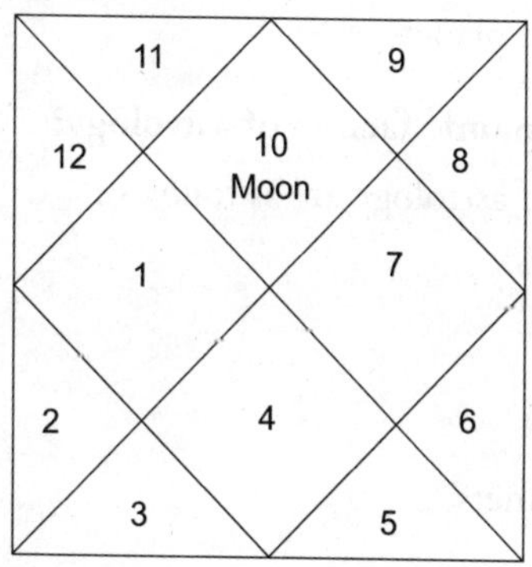

294. How will you decide the results?

Double transit of *Rahu* and *Ketu* will always be troubling

Double transit of Saturn and *Ketu* takes you towards loneliness / spiritualism etc.

Double transit of Saturn and *Rahu* is always unfavourable

Double transit of Saturn and Jupiter may be favourable or unfavourable

The above transit should be applied to affected houses from Moon as well as *Lagan*

The final decision should always be taken after combining

Static

and

Dynamic factors of astrology

295. What are static factors of astrology?

Static factors are as follows :

Sthaan of planets

Status of planets

Strength of planets in D-1 (Birth Chart)

Strength of planets in D-9 (*Navamsha*)

Strength of planets in divisional charts

Sambandh between planets

296. What are dynamic factors of astrology?

Dynamic factors of astrology are as follows :

Dasha of planets

Duration of *dasha*

Dashas to follow

Daily *gochar* of planets

Desh kaal paatr of *jatak*

Day-to-day *aacharan* of *jatak*

297. How to decide the results of a planet as per particular *lagan*?

L.L. : *Lagan* Lord

M.D. : *Maha Dasha*

A.D. : *Antar Dasha*

The following flow chart should be observed

Note the *Lagan* Lord

Note M.D. Lord

Note *mahadasha* Lord relationship with L.L.

Note A.D. Lord's relationship with M.D. Lord

Note A.D. Lords relationship with L.L.

Note A.D. relationship with different houses

Note A.D. relationship with different planets

Note A.D. relationship with transit Saturn

Note A.D. relationship with transit Jupiter

In general M.D. friendship with L.L. gives tendency for favourable results

In general M.D. enmity with L.L. gives tendency for unfavourable results

In general M.D. friendship with L.L. gives tendency for favourable results but inimical *antardashas* may be troublesome

In general M.D. enmity with L.L. gives tendency for unfavourable results but friendly *antardashas* may give tendency towards favourable results

The favourable/friendly *dashas* give favourable results only when they are strong and not weak

The unfavourable/inimical *dashas* give unfavourable results only when they are strong and not weak

Friends should always be strong, while enemies should always be weak

298. What are the best positions of the benefics in the horoscope?

Benefics should be placed in *Kendra*s and *Trikones* for best results. As the *Kendra*s are the stability houses and Trines are *karmas* of past and present. The presence of benefics in these houses blesses the significances of these houses.

299. What are the best positions of the malefic in the horoscope?

Malefic should be placed in malefic houses, 3, 11, 6, 8, 12. Malefic in third increases self-efforts and longevity. In eleventh they give gains, may be by illegal means. Malefic in 6, 8, 12 spoil the negativity of these negative houses thereby giving positive results.

300. What are the results of exchange of planets?

Exchange of planets can be either positive or negative.

The exchange of planets can give effects in following ways :

Exchange of two natural benefics

Exchange of two functional benefics

Exchange of favourable house Lords

Exchange of favourable and unfavourable house Lords

Exchange of two natural malefic planets

Exchange of two functional malefic planets

Exchange of two natural benefics gives highly favourable results.

Exchange of two functional benefics gives highly favourable results.

Exchange of favourable Lords gives favourable results

Exchange of favourable and unfavourable house Lords is good for unfavourable but bad for favourable.

Exchange of two natural malefics gives positive results

Exchange of two functional malefics gives bad results.

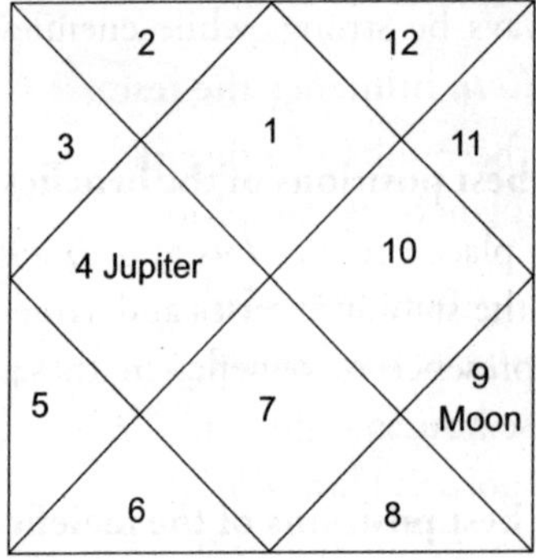

Favourable exchange between friends Moon and Jupiter.

It is exchange of two natural benefics.

It is exchange of two functional benefics.

It is exchange between *Kendra* Lord and *trikone* Lord.

In the same way you can make different combinations and analyze as per above principles.

301. What are the results of exchange of house Lords?

This should also be interpreted as shown above.

302. Which are the houses and planets to be studied for gains of money?

Gains are studied from 11th house, 5th house, 8th house etc.

11th: self-gains. 5th: gains of life partner. 8th: ancestral gains.

8th house gains are normally associated with insurance money, ancestral assets, gains after death as legal representative etc.

303. What are the results of exalted planet when they get debilitated in *navmansha*?

Exalted planet of birth chart getting debilitated in *navamsha* loses its strength and favourable results as per expectation.

304. What are the results of debilitated planet when they get exalted in *navmansha*?

Debilitated planet of birth chart getting exalted in *navamsha* gains in strength and favourable results are seen.

305. Does *Rahu* and *Ketu* influence the results of planet?

Rahu and *Ketu* affect the results of other planets in negative way, especially for Group A planets *e.g.* Sun, Moon, Jupiter and Mars.

306. How malefic and benefics planet in particular houses influence the results of the house?

Malefic try to spread malefic results while benefics try to spread benefic results in that house .They also affect the houses aspected and the planets they aspect. The results of planets are felt in houses represented by them as Lord and as *Karaka* also.

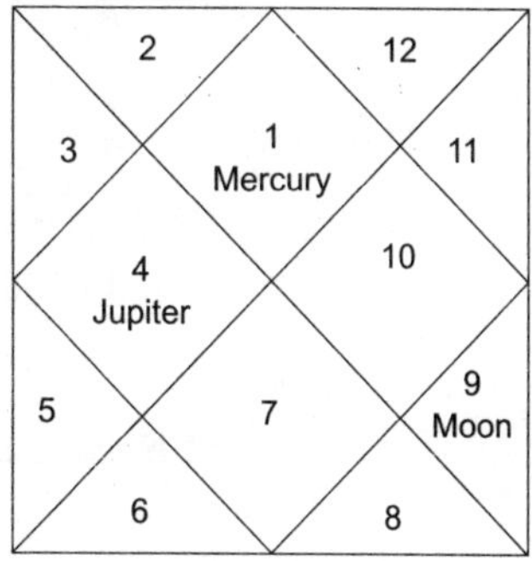

Moon as natural benefic and *Kendra* Lord will give positive results of 4th house significances like property, vehicles etc. as it is placed in trine house (9th). It is highly positive because of its placement in friendly house of Jupiter. Results of Moon gets further potentiated because its dispositer Jupiter is exalted and placed in *Kendra.*

Mercury as a functional malefic going to *Lagan* will give health problems. Mercury as sixth Lord going to *Lagan* will give good fighting and competitive spirit. Mercury as permanent Lord of 6th house of debts gives debts.

307. How does exaltation/debilitation or strength/weakness of a planet in transit affects the significance?

A benefic planet exalted in transit helps in getting its significances fulfilled favourably during that transit.

A benefic planet debilitated in transit is unable to help in getting its significances fulfilled favourably during that transit.

A malefic planet exalted in transit helps in getting its positive sides of significances fulfilled favourably during that transit.

A malefic planet debilitated in transit aggravates the problems in getting its significances fulfilled favourably during that transit.

HOW TO CATCH DISEASES BY ASTROLOGY

308. How do you catch diseases of different parts of body?

Disease happens when separative planets affect: ---

House

House Lord

Sign

Sign Lord.

The above factors should be seen from Moon *Lagan*.

Whenever the following factors are afflicted by separative planets and not protected by benefic planets, problems/diseases regarding that house are precipitated.

Whenever 1st house /1st Lord/Aries sign/Mars/1st house from Moon and 1st Lord from Moon are affected by separative planets, then there will be problems regarding head, brain, and personality of person should be expected.

Whenever 2nd house/2nd Lord/Taurus sign/Venus/2nd house from Moon/2nd Lord form Moon are affected by separative planets, then problems regarding face, right eye, speech of person should be expected.

Whenever 3rd house/3rd Lord/Gemini sign/Mercury/3rd house from Moon/3rd Lord from Moon are affected by separative planets, then problems regarding neck, ears, shoulder of person should be expected.

Whenever 4th house/4th Lord/Cancer sign/Moon/4th house from Moon/4th Lord from Moon are affected by separative planets, then problems regarding chest, heart, stomach of person should be expected.

Whenever 5th house/5th Lord/Leo sign/Sun/5th house from Moon/5th Lord from Moon are affected by separative planets, then problems regarding heart, abdomen, child birth of person should be expected.

Whenever 6th house/6th Lord/Virgo sign/Mercury/6th house from Moon/6th Lord from Moon are affected by separative planets, then problems regarding lower abdomen, kidneys, urinary system, backache should be expected.

Whenever 7th house/7th Lord/Libra sign/Venus/7th house from Moon/7th Lord from Moon are affected by separative planets, then problems regarding secret parts, sexual problems, should be expected.

Whenever 8th house/8th Lord/Scorpio sign/Mars/8th house from Moon/8th Lord from Moon are affected by separative planets, then problems regarding anus, should be expected.

Whenever 9th house/9th Lord/Sagittarius sign/Jupiter/ 9th house from Moon/9th Lord from Moon are affected by separative planets, then problems regarding hips, thighs should be expected.

Whenever 10th house/10th Lord/Capricorn/Saturn/10th from Moon/10th Lord from Moon are affected by separative planets, then problems regarding knee, gait of person should be expected.

Whenever 11th house/11th Lord/Aquarius/Saturn/11th from Moon/11th Lord from Moon are affected by separative planets, then problems regarding lower legs, left ear should be expected.

Whenever 12th house/12th Lord/Pisces/Jupiter /12th house from Moon /12th Lord from Moon are affected by separative planets, then problems regarding feet should be expected.

309. How can you be sure about the disease and its severity?

All the above diseases are strongly possible only if more than two separative planets (Mars, Saturn, *Rahu*, *Ketu*, 12th Lord) affect the above factors. The disease will be a certainty if affliction is on all the three *Lagan*s e.g., birth chart, moon *kundli*, sun *kundli*.

— the disease will be certainty if *Karaka* of the house is also afflicted by the separative planets.

310. How does a planet get afflicted as far as disease is concerned?

— A planet gets afflicted when its signs have separative planets in it

— debilitated planets give more health problems *e.g.*

Sun and Mars (fiery planets) diseases like boils, cuts, high blood pressure, acidity etc.

Moon and Venus (watery planets) watery disease

Saturn (airy planet) joint pains, nerve problems.

Mercury (airy planet) skin problems.

Jupiter (*earth*y planet) obesity, abdomen problems

— even benefic planets get afflicted, if their signs have

seperative planets in them.

311. What is the significance of Sun and parts of body affected if it is afflicted by seperative planets?

Sun represents general strength, heart, bones, right eye, lethargy, heart trouble, Arthritis, headache, stomach, brain, fractures, fever, epilepsy, acidity, skin troubles, leprosy, right eye troubles, burns etc.

312. What are the significances of Moon and parts of body being affected if afflicted by separative planets?

Moon represents mind, blood, left eye, fluids in body, breast, mental disturbances, diarrhoea, plural effusion, menstrual cycle, tuberculosis, menstrual disorder, feeding problems, anemia, and nervousness etc.

313. What are the significance of Mars and parts of body being affected if afflicted by separative planets?

Mars represents head, bone marrow, blood (haemoglobin), uterus, muscles, blood pressure etc.

314. What are the significances of Mercury and parts of body being affected if it is afflicted by separative planets?

Mercury represents skin, speech, throat, intelligence, nose, leucoderma, ear, nose, throat problems tongue, lungs, mental instability, speech problems, impotency, nerve disorders etc.

315. What are the significances of Jupiter and parts of body being affected if it is afflicted by separative planets?

Jupiter represents ears, liver, gall bladder and fat in body, spleen, chronic disease like jaundice, diabetes, digestive disorders, obesity, ear problems, and gall bladder problems, vertigo etc.

316. What are the significance of Venus and parts of body being affected if it is afflicted by separative planets?

Venus represents face, eye sight, semen, urinary system, sexual problems, reproductive system, tears, intestines, urinary infection, leucoderma, stone in glands of body, hormonal system and disorder, kidney, diabetes, lower abdomen problems, problems of face etc.

317. What are the significances of Saturn and parts of body being affected if it is afflicted by separative planets?

Saturn represents any disease, nerves, feet, knee, legs, colon, lethargy, pain in legs, depression, rectum, incurable long disease like paralysis, *Arth*ritis, tumours, cancers, intestinal troubles etc.

318. What are the significance of Rahu and parts of body affected if it is afflicted by separative planets?

Rahu represents poisons, incurable diseases, fears, phobias, depression negative thoughts, piles, leprosy, insanity etc.

319. What are the significance of *Ketu* and parts of body affected if it is afflicted by separative planets?

Ketu represents mysterious incurable diseases of any kind like irritable bowel syndrome, viral diseases, worms, amputation of a part, speech disorders, fever, boils, urticaria/skin rash, pain in feet etc.

320. What are the significances of 1st house and parts of body getting affected if it is afflicted by separative planets?

Significances of 1st house and parts of body affected when afflicted by separative planets are head, brain, whole body, headache, brain hemorrhage, head injuries, mental retardation etc.

321. What are the significances of 2nd house and parts of body being affected if it is afflicted by seperative planets?

Significances of 2nd house and parts of body affected when afflicted by separative planets are right eye, face, teeth, tongue, nose, nails, right eye vision problem, problems of gum, stammering, speech disorder etc.

322. What are the significances of 3rd house and parts of body being affected if it is afflicted by separative planets?

Significances of 3rd house and parts of body affected when afflicted by separative planets are neck, throat, right ear,shoulders, cervical spondylitis, ear infections, deafness, deaf and dumbs, upper part of food pipe (esophagus),acidity, dysphagia (difficulty in swallowing), thyroid problem etc.

323. What are the significances of 4th house and parts of body being affected if it is afflicted by separative planets?

- Significances of 4th house and parts of body being affected when afflicted by separative planets are chest, lungs, food pipe, bronchitis, pneumonia, acidity, fullness of abdomen, breast problem in females etc.

324. What are the significance of 5th house and parts of body being affected if it is afflicted by separative planets?

Significances of 5th house and parts of body being affected when afflicted by separative planets are heart, upper abdomen, stomach, liver, indigestion, heart troubles, stomach problem, spleen, duodenum, intestine, gall bladder, jaundice, gall bladder stones etc.

325. What are the significance of 6th house and parts of body being affected if it is afflicted by separative planets?

Significances of 6th house and parts of body being affected when afflicted by separative planets are kidney, large intestines, renal failure, stones in kidneys, appendicitis etc. It is house of diseases. It can cause any disease as it is permanent house of diseases and its activation during *dasha* can give health problems of any kind. In comparison to 8th house, this house gives problems of acute (recent nature) while 8th house gives long lasting problems.

326. What are the significances of 7th house and parts of body being affected if it is afflicted by separative planets?

Significance of 7th house and parts of body affected when afflicted by separative planets are sexual parts, backache, infertility, menstrual disorder in females, urinary problems, anus, impotency, urinary infections, ureteric stone, sexually transmitted infections etc.

327. What are the significances of 8th house and parts of body being affected if it is afflicted by separative planets?

Significances of 8th house and parts of body affected when afflicted by separative planets are long lasting diseases (chronic), external hemorrhoids, fissure, fistula, sex parts, longevity etc.

328. What are the significances of 9th house and parts of body being affected if it is afflicted by separative planets?

Significance of 9th house and parts of body affected if it is afflicted by separative planets are hips, thighs, upper legs, lumber spondylitis, lower backache, sciatica etc.

329. What are the significance of 10th house and parts of body being affected if it is afflicted by separative planets?

Significance of 10th house and parts of body affected when afflicted by separative planets are knee joint, knee cap, Arthritis of knee etc.

330. What are the significance of 11th house and parts of body being affected if it is afflicted by separative planets?

Significance of 11th house and parts of body affected when afflicted by separative planets are lower legs, left ear and pain in legs, varicose veins, left ear, and alternate house of diseases (6th from 6th).

331. What are the significance of 12th house and parts of body being affected if it is afflicted by separative planets?

Significances of 12th house and parts of body affected when afflicted by separative planets are feet, left eye, serious disease requiring hospitalization, calcaneal spur, pain ankles, left eye vision problems, hospitalization, sleep disorders, paralysis etc.

332. Does slow moving planets play a role in diseases?

— P.A.C. of slow moving planets, like malefic Saturn, *Rahu* give long, chronic diseases *e.g.*, tuberculosis, cancer, tumours etc.

333. What are the main factors regarding progeny, which should be avoided while doing *kundli milan*?

Afflictions to 5th house and its Lord can adversely affect the progeny. Nadi *dosha* can lead to still birth (dead baby), miscarriages etc.

Nadi *dosha* should never be ignored especially if 5th house, 5th Lord and *Karaka* Jupiter, Venus are also afflicted.

334. What are the factors which help us in arriving at a decision in astrology? Explain with example.

There are number of factors which help us in arriving at a decision. The analysis flow is explained keeping profession in mind.

Note the age of person

Note *desh kaal paatr*

Note the *dhan* yogas

Note the status/rajyogas

Note the *dashas* between 20 to 60 years

Note the functional benefics and functional malefics

Note the double transit

The nature of sign falling in the ascendant

The nature of sign falling in the tenth house

Second house ruling the family and cash

The impact of the third house which rules self-efforts

The eleventh house signifying income and gains

The ascendant of *dashamsha* sign in tenth house

Planets in tenth house

Strength of tenth house and tenth Lord

Note the most powerful planet in horoscope

The nature of planets becoming significators for profession

And the planets exerting close influence on the houses ruling professional matters is important.

Now, we will apply the above factors to the example horoscope.

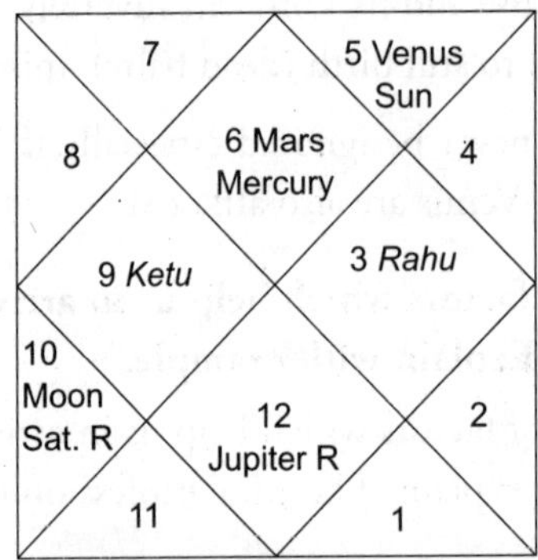

1. STRENGTH OF HOROSCOPE AS A WHOLE

— there are seven planets in *Kendra*s and *Trikones* giving strength to horoscope (this will give status and wealth to person)

— all the *Kendra*s have planets in them (this will give status and stability)

— *Kendras* have dominance of melefics like *Rahu*, *Ketu* and Mars (the status and stability will be associated with troubles and hurdles)

— exalted *Lagan* Lord in *Lagan* (person will be capable of achieving a lot)

— presence of three *panch mahapurush* yogas (these give status, wealth, honour, stability etc.)

Bhadar yoga (exalted Mercury in *Lagan*). This gives extra ordinary intelligence with sharp application of brain)

Hansa yoga (own sign Jupiter in Pisces in *Kendra* from *Lagan*). This gives status, money, educated partner etc.

Shash yoga (own sign Saturn in Capricorn *Lagan* from Moon). The yoga gives stability, maturity, excellent education, business etc.)

—PRESENCE OF FOUR PLANETS IN OWN SIGN

1st Lord mercury in 1st in own sign Virgo. (Mercury :— it is exalted and placed in *Lagan* making *Bhadra* yoga (*panch mahapurush* yoga). *Bhadar* yoga gives intelligence, longevity, good calculations, business sense etc.

5th Lord Saturn in 5th in own sign Capricorn (Saturn : — It is 5th and 6th Lord in own sign Capricorn in own sign and placed in *trikone*. It is forming *Shash* yoga being conjunct with moon. It gives good technical education, good intelligence etc.

7th Lord Jupiter in 7th in own sign Pisces. (Jupiter : — It is placed in *Kendra* in own sign Pisces making *Hansa* yoga. It gives wealth, wisdom, applied knowledge, consultancy, convincing powers etc. Jupiter being 4th Lord and 7th Lord will give property, vehicles and good, educated, intelligent, wise partner.

12th Lord Sun in 12th in own sign Leo. (Sun : — Sun in own sign in Leo but placed in 12th house. Its degrees are 15 degrees 37 minutes placed in *Yuva avastha*. Sun is *vargottam* as it is placed in same Leo sign in *navamsa*. These factors promise good private life, foreign visits but hospitalisation also.

— PRESENCE OF TWO PLANETS ASPECTING THEIR OWN SIGN

8th Lord Mars aspects its own sign Scorpio. (Mars :— Mars is placed in *Lagan* with exalted *Lagan* Lord Mercury. It is *vargottam*. It is in *Bala avastha*. It is greatest enemy for *Lagan*. It is aspected by its friend Jupiter from 7th house.

These factors promise longevity as 8th Lord Mars aspects its own house of longevity. But 8th Lord's placement in *Lagan* gives accidents, health problems, obstructions in life.

11th Lord Moon aspects its own sign cancer.

Moon : — Moon is 11th Lord placed in 5th house (*trikone*) which is good. It is *pakshbali* being six houses away from Sun. It is placed in inimical sign Capricorn with enemy Saturn making it weak and afflicted. Its degrees are 24 degrees 2 minutes in Capricorn in *Bala avastha*.

These factors promise habit of speculation, but gains on long run will be restricted and delayed because of conjunction of Saturn (6th Lord of debts and diseases etc.)

335. Which horoscope to study, *lagan* or Moon?

Before answering this question, certain basic points should be noted.

Planets belong to two groups :—

Group A :— Sun, Moon, Jupiter, and Mars

Group B : —Mercury, Venus and Saturn

Note *Lagan* sign and group

Note Moon sign and group

Note Sun sign and group

Decide the group with majority and give prediction with that.

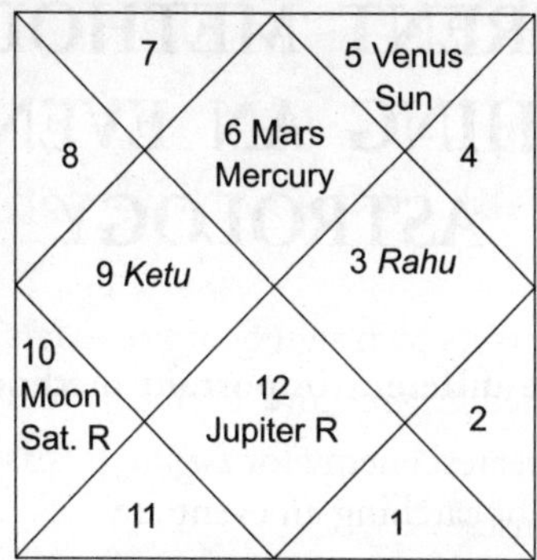

The above horoscope has Virgo *Lagan* (Group B planet).

Moon sign is Capricorn (Group B planet).

Sun sign is Leo (Group A planet).

Two out of three belong to B Group so the prediction priority should be given to Moon *Lagan*.

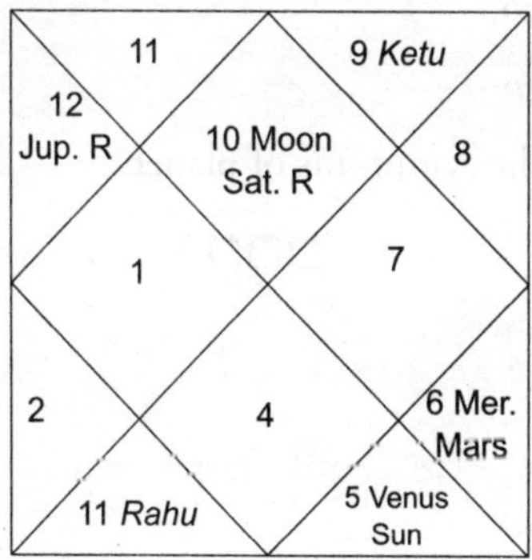

In my personal opinion, one should always study birth chart as well as Moon chart.

Apply transit also on birth chart as well as Moon chart.

DIFFERENT METHODS OF CATCHING AN EVENT BY ASTROLOGY

336. What are the different important methods of catching an event?

Different methods of catching an event are

1. By *dasha* of a planet
2. By nature of a planet as malefic or benefic
3. By significance of a planet
4. By Moon *kundli*
5. By transit of planets
6. By *prashna kundli*
7. By *desh kaal paatr*
8. By recognising the symptoms of planets.

GIVING INTERPRETATION WITHOUT AN ACCURATE HOROSCOPE

337. Can one give interpretation without an accurate Horoscope?

Every planet has either good or bad effects on the person. Even if you don't have the horoscope, you still, can do some improvement in your life by recognizing the troubling planet at a particular time. This can be done by observing certain happenings/events in your life. A particular planet affects

Your nature,

Your health,

Your relationships,

Your profession,

Your attitude,

Your body parts,

Your mental thinking.

Different aspects of life etc.

When one does not have an accurate horoscope, try recognizing a planet by symptoms and take preventive/promotional measures.

A particular planet affects your nature, your health, your relationships, your profession, your attitude, your body parts, your mental thinking, different aspects of life etc. By recognising these changes, planet can be recognised and remedy can be done to suppress the unfavourable results and simultaneously promoting positive results.

Broadly speaking, the results of planets can be divided into 12 categories : —

1. Personal level
2. Medical level

3. Professional level
4. Family/relative
5. *Karaka* effects
6. Weakness as per degrees
7. Weakness as per position
8. Weakness as per aspect
9. Weakness as per conjunction
10. Weakness as per *Lal Kitab*
11. Miscellaneous observations
12. Remedies in brief

338. How to catch an event in horoscope as per *prashna kundli*?

Note the time of question

Try to catch as per Moon

Try to catch as per Moon's *Nakshatra*

Try to catch as per *Lagan*'s *Nakshatra* Lord

Try to catch as per *Lagan* Lord

Try to catch as per *Lagan* Lord *Nakshatra*

Try to catch as per planets aspecting *Lagan*

Try to catch as per planets aspecting *Lagan* Lord

339. How to catch an event in horoscope as per *lagan kundli*?

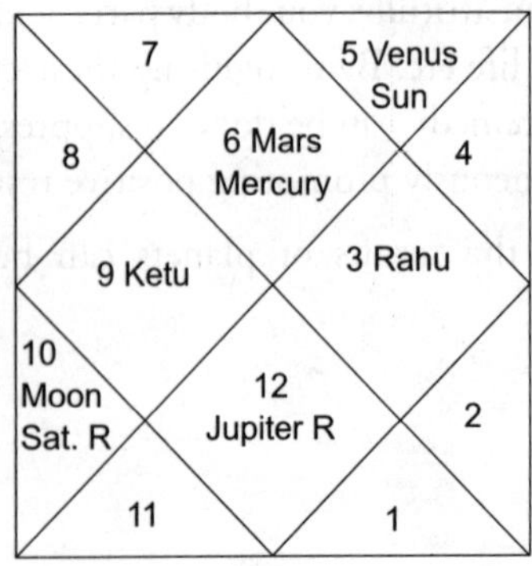

As per *dasha* Lord's placement

As per *dasha* Lord's aspects

As per *dasha* Lord's conjunction

As per *dasha* Lord's ownership

As per *dasha* Lord as *Karaka*

Jupiter, *dasha* Lord is placed in 7'h house in own sign gives activities related to 7th house (partnership).

Jupiter aspects 11th, 1st, 3rd house activating gains by self-effort and partnership.

There is no conjunction with Jupiter.

Jupiter is Lord of 4th house of vehicles and seventh house of partnership.

Jupiter is *Karaka* for money, spouse and children etc.

The above analysis indicates the activation of vehicles, partnership, children and money etc. in the *dasha* of Jupiter between the ages of 25 years to 41 years starting 18th April 1998 to 2014.

340. How to catch an event in horoscope as per Moon *kundli*?

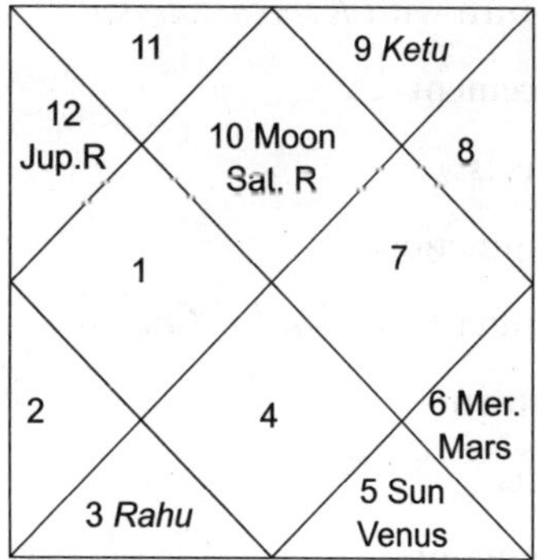

As per *dasha* Lord's placement

As per *dasha* Lord's aspects

As per *dasha* Lord's conjunction

As per *dasha* Lord's ownership

As per *dasha* Lord as *Karaka*

Jupiter is placed in 3rd house of self-efforts.

Jupiter is aspecting 7th house, 9th house and 11th house indicating gains with self-efforts and partnership.

Jupiter has no conjunction with any planet.

It is Lord of 3rd house of self-efforts and 12th house of expenses, foreign visits, hospitalisation and losses etc.

Jupiter is *Karaka* for money, spouse and children etc.

The above analysis indicates the activation of self-efforts, partnership, gains as well as losses or unwarranted expenses etc. in the *dasha* of Jupiter between the ages of 25 years to 41 years starting 18th April 1998 to 2014.

341. How to catch an event as per transit from Moon?

As per Saturn's placement

As per Saturn's aspects

As per Saturn's conjunction

As per P.A.C. of Saturn with *Karaka*/*Karakas*

As per Jupiter's placement

As per Jupiter's aspects

As per Jupiter's conjunction

As per P.A.C. of Jupiter with *Karaka*/*Karakas*

As per *Rahu*'s placement

As per *Rahu*'s aspects

As per *Rahu*'s conjunction

As per P.A.C. of *Rahu* with *Karaka*/*Karakas*

As per *Ketu*'s placement

As per *Ketu*'s aspects

As per *Ketu*'s conjunction

As per P.A.C. of *Ketu* with *karaka*/*karakas*

One should apply transit of outer planets for activation of any activity.

342. How to catch an event as per transit from lagan?

Apply transit of slower moving planets.

As per Saturn's placement

As per Saturn's aspects

As per Saturn's conjunction

As per P.A.C. of Saturn with *Karaka*/*Karakas*

As per Jupiter's placement

As per Jupiter's aspects

As per Jupiter's conjunction

As per P.A.C. of Jupiter with *Karaka*/*Karakas*

As per *Rahu*'s placement

As per *Rahu*'s aspects

As per *Rahu*'s conjunction

As per P.A.C. of *Rahu* with *Karaka*/*Karakas*

As per *Ketu*'s placement

As per *Ketu*'s aspects

As per *Ketu*'s conjunction

As per P.A.C. of *Ketu* with *Karaka*/*Karakas*

343. How to catch the event as per running *dasha*?

In majority of the horoscopes, the *dasha* will indicate the event as per P.A.C. of *dasha* Lords.

344. How to do all this practically?

Make 12 blank horoscopes

Note the transit of Saturn

Note the transit of Jupiter

Note the transit of *Rahu*

Note the transit of *Ketu*

Now note double transit of Saturn and Jupiter

Now note double transit of Saturn and *Rahu*

Now note double transit of Saturn and *Ketu*

Now note double transit of *Rahu* and *Ketu*

Double transit of *Rahu* and *Ketu* will always be troubling

Double transit of Saturn and *Ketu* takes you towards loneliness / spiritualism etc.

Double transit of Saturn and *Rahu* is always unfavourable

Double transit of Saturn and Jupiter may be favourable or unfavourable depending upon the activation of group of houses/ house Lords/*Karaka*s etc.

The above transit should be applied to affected houses from Moon as well as *Lagan*

345. How to catch a query after getting the above factors?

Note the position of Saturn in transit

Note the position of Jupiter in transit

Note the signs of double transit of Saturn and Jupiter

Note the houses where these signs are placed in the horoscope

The event will be related to those houses of horoscope

Combine with *vimshotri dasha*

Combine with *Lal Kitab*

Synthesize all the above factors

For example : —

Saturn in Virgo (6)

Saturn will have effects on 6, 8, 12, 3 signs

Jupiter is in Pisces (12)

Jupiter will have effects on 12, 4, 6, 8 signs

Common signs among the above transit are 6, 8, and 12 signs

Note the house numbers where these signs are placed in horoscope.

The event favourable or unfavourable will be related to that house/ houses.

Correlate with *dasha* for favourable or unfavourable results.

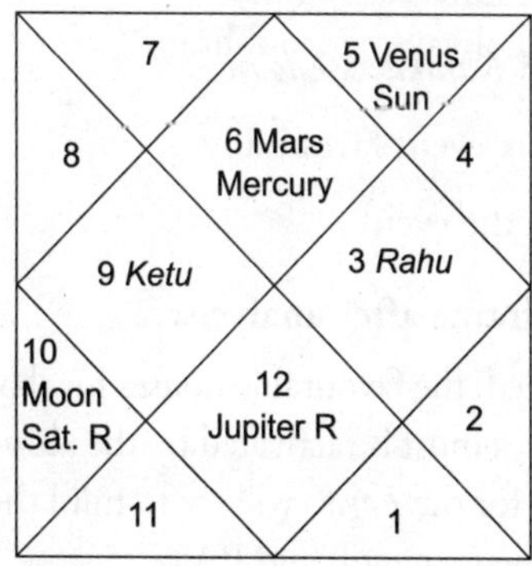

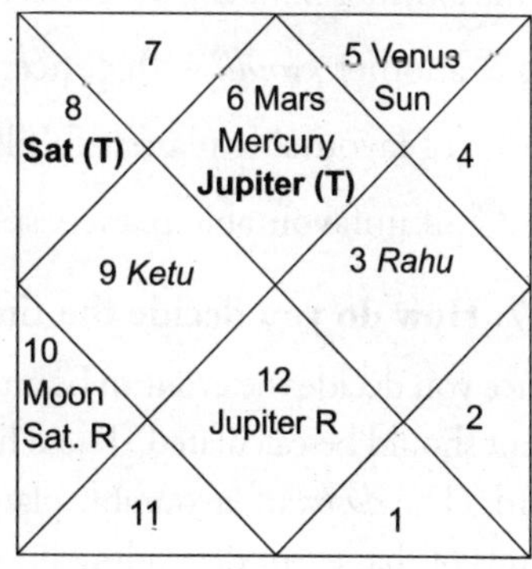

Double transit in September 2017.

Saturn in transit in Scorpio and Jupiter in transit in Virgo.

Saturn activates sign number 8, 10, 2, 5

Saturn activates Moon, Saturn, Venus, and Sun

Jupiter activates sign number 6, 10,12,2

Jupiter activates Moon, Saturn, and Jupiter

Double transit is taking on sign number 10 (5th house) and sign number 2 (9th house)

Double transit is taking on planet Moon and Saturn.

Activation of Moon as a *Karaka* and activation of 2nd and 6th houses from 4th house of mother can give health problems to mother.

ANALYZING PRASHNA KUNDLI

346. How do you analyze *prashna kundli*?

Make *prashna kundli* whenever you are doing astrological analysis

Catch the question

Decide the concerned house

Decide the *Karaka* for question

Make another *kundli* with concerned house as *Lagan*

Make another *kundli* with concerned *Karaka* as *Lagan*

P.A.C. of favourable planets fulfills the event favourably

P.A.C. of unfavourable planets spoils the event

347. How do you decide the time frame after analysis?

Once you decide the event to be analyzed, the favourable houses for that event should be calculated. These houses must be activated by the *dasha* Lords. The *dasha* of favourable planets for the *Lagan* will try to fulfil the results of that event depending upon their strength and P.A.C.

348. What are the guidelines while analyzing an event or query?

Decide house as per event or decide event as per house activated

Never shift your focus from concerned house

Never shift your focus from concerned house Lord

Never shift your focus from concerned house *Karaka*

Never shift your focus from concerned event *Karaka*

Analyze the above factors in full details

Treat concerned house as *Lagan* and analyze

Decide the end results as per strength of house

Decide the end results as per strength of house Lord

Decide the end results as per strength of house *Karaka*

Decide the end results as per strength of *dasha* Lord

Decide the end results as per strength of *antardasha* Lord

Decide the end results as per strength of *dasha* Lord in transit

Decide the end results as per strength of *antardasha* Lord in transit

Decide the end results as per strength of *Karaka* in transit

349. Give some simple hints on analysis?

Make your horoscope

Break your horoscope in 12

Make 12 different horoscopes with 1st house, 2nd house, 3rd house and so on as *Lagan*

Study these 12 horoscopes as independent horoscopes in context with significances

Placement of benefics in 1, 5, and 9 from *Lagan* of that horoscope promotes the significances

Placement of benefics in 4,7,10 from *Lagan* of that horoscope promotes the significances

Placement of benefics in 3, 6, 10, and 11 from *Lagan* of that horoscope promotes the significance after lot of struggle and hard work

Placement of malefic in 1, 5, and 9 from *Lagan* of that horoscope reduces the significance

Placement of malefic in 4,7,10 from *Lagan* of that horoscope reduces the significance

Placement of malefic in 2, 12 from *Lagan* of that horoscope reduces the significance

Placement of malefic in 3, 6, 10, and 11 from *Lagan* of that horoscope fulfills after lot of struggle

350. When the planet will be favourable?

Planet will be favourable in following circumstances

— no inimical planet should be in its house or houses,

— no inimical planet in its *Karaka* houses,

— no inimical planet in its exalted house and

— no inimical planet in its debilitated house.

351. Does age and position of planets in horoscope helps in analysis?

As per *Lal Kitab*, a particular planet gets activated at a particular age irrespective of your *Parashri dasha*. Certain activities of life can also activate a particular planet.

JUDGING A HOROSCOPE

352. How do you judge a horoscope?

21 point programme

1. See how many planets in *Kendras*/ *Trikons*
2. How many planets in own sign
3. How many planets aspecting own house.
4. How many planets are exalted
5. How many planets are debilitated
6. How many planets are *digbali*
7. How many planets in 6th, 8th, 12th house
8. How many planets in friend's house
9. How many planets in inimical houses
10. Any *yogkaraka* planets in horoscope
11. How many retrograde planets
12. How is *Lagan*
13. How is *Lagan* Lord?
14. *Dasha* at birth and subsequent *dashas* (*Kendra* or *trikone*/6/8/12 etc.)
15. How is Moon placed?
16. Any exchange of planets
17. Position of *Rahu* and *Ketu* in horoscope
18. Presence/absence of *mahapurush* yogas
19. Most powerful planets in the horoscope
20. Presence of combust planets
21. Correlation of *dasha* pattern with age and *desh*, *kaal*, *paatr*

353. What are fertile signs?

Watery signs (Cancer, Scorpio, and Pisces) are fertile signs.

354. Are there any specific period during a year when women are most fertile?

Watery signs are called as fertile signs.

Every year when the new Moon is in a watery sign (Cancer, Scorpio or Pisces) these are three time periods, when women are most fertile.

355. How can one use this principle?

The above fertility periods can be used for i.v.f. (in vitro fertilization) and natural conception dates.

356. Is *prashna kundli* useful in analyzing child birth?

Yes, it is very useful. *Lagan* Lord or Moon posited in 5th house in *prasna kundli* with P.A.C. of benefics indicates promise of child. 5th Lord in *Lagan* with P.A.C. of benefics indicates promise of child.

357. How to analyze an event as per different *varshphals* and *dasha* pattern?

Make *varshphals* of three consecutive years and note the position of planet as per event.

If you want to analyze education, note the placement of Moon in different *varshphals* and predict. Placement of Moon in 6, 8, 12th houses is not good for education.

(DETAILS IN *LAL KITAB* AND REMEDIES BOOK BY THE AUTHOR.)

358. How to make a performa to analyze the position of different factors as per performa?

After studying and analyzing all the points as mentioned above, one should compile all the datas in a performa for immediate recollection of the important datas.

This performa will be able to show you the basics of all the planets in birth chart.

This performa will be able to show you the basics of all the houses in birth chart.

This performa will be able to show you the basics of all the house Lords in birth chart.

This performa will be able to show you the basics of all the *dasha* Lords in birth chart.

This performa will be able to show you the basics of all the planets in Moon chart.

This performa will be able to show you the basics of all the houses in Moon chart.

This performa will be able to show you the basics of all the house Lords in Moon chart.

This performa will be able to show you the basics of all the *dasha* Lords in Moon chart.

This performa will be able to show you the yogas in birth chart.

This performa will be useful as a ready reckoner in case of requirement of any information regarding the horoscope.

Nowadays lots of softwares are there for getting the datas and calculations, but working on a performa in few cases will help you in utilization of the datas which are available with you. This definitely helps in analysis and flow of learning and predicting different events.

Name:________________________Tel.no:________________________

D.O.B : ________________________ T.O.B. : ________________________

P.O.B. : ________________________

Planets	Degree	*Avastha*	*Nakshatra*	Nak.Lord
SUN				
MOON				
MARS				
MERCURY				
JUPITER				
VENUS				
SATURN				
RAHU				
KETU				
LAGNA				

Lagan Kundli

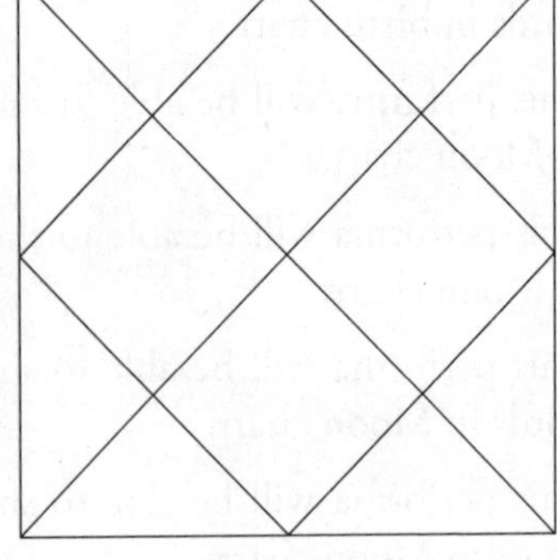

Moon *Kundli*

LAGAN KUNDLI (D-1)

Placement	Benefics	Malefics	Neutral
Planets in Trines			
Planets in *Kendras*			
Planets In 6,8,12			
Planets in 3,11			

MOON KUNDLI (D-1)

Placement	Benefics	Malefics	Neutral
Planets in Trines			
Planets in *Kendras*			
Planets In 6,8,12			
Planets in 3,11			

YOGAS (General)

MAHABHAGYA YOGA

BHADRA YOGA

RUCHAK YOGA

HANS YOGA

MALAVYA YOGA

SHASHA YOGA

GAJ KESARI YOGA (where)

BUDH ADITYA YOGA (where)

YOGAS OF MOON

KEMDRUM YOGA

DHURDHARA YOGA

ANAPHA YOGA

SUNPHA YOGA

RAJ YOGA

COMBINATION of *KENDRAS* & *TRIKONAS*

DHAN YOGA

COMBINATIONS of 2, 5,9,11& *LAGAN*

VIPREET RAJ YOGA

PLACEMENT of 6,8,12 LORDS IN 6,8,12

BALANCE OF *DASHA* AT BIRTH

- TRINES/*KENDRA*/6, 8, 12/2, 11, 3

DASHA PATTERN & CORRELATION WITH AGE AS PER *DESH, KAAL, PAATR*

Note the number of planets in:-

(A) • Fixed signs Moveable signs Dual signs

• Fiery signs Earthy signs Airy signs Watery signs

(B) • *Lagan* sign Moon sign Lagan Lord sign Moon sign Lord

NAVMANSH (D-9) ANALYSIS

CHECK *LAGAN* SIGN/LORD of D-1 BECOMING *VARGOTTAM*

LORD of *KENDRA*/TRINE

LORD of 6, 8, 12

CHECK POSITION of D-9 *LAGAN* LORD

CHECK POSITION of PLANETS IN D-9

ANALYSIS OF HOUSES & THEIR LORDS (LAGAN KUNDLI)

Houses & Lords	Planets Posited	Aspected by	Conjunct with
1st House			
1st Lord			
2nd House			
2nd Lord			
3rd House			
3rd Lord			
4th House			
4th Lord			
5th House			
5th Lord			
6th House			
6th Lord			
7th House			
7th Lord			
8th House			
8th Lord			
9th House			
9th Lord			
10th House			
10th Lord			
11th House			
11th Lord			
12th House			
12th Lord			

ANALYSIS OF HOUSES & THEIR LORDS (Moon *Kundli*)

Houses & Lords	Planets Posited	Aspected by	Conjunct with
1st House			
1st Lord			
2nd House			
2nd Lord			
3rd House			
3rd Lord			
4th House			
4th Lord			
5th House			
5th Lord			
6th House			
6th Lord			
7th House			
7th Lord			
8th House			
8th Lord			
9th House			
9th Lord			
10th House			
10th Lord			
11th House			
11th Lord			
12th House			
12th Lord			

HOUSES ACTIVATED BY *DASHA* & *GOCHAR*
(Double Transit)

Houses Activated	I	II	III	IV	V	VI	VII	VIII	IX	X	XI	XII
In D-1 by *Dasha*												
In D-1 by *Gochar*												
In Ch.K by *Dasha*												
In Ch.K by *Gochar*												

359. What are the effects of Moon in *Rahu/Ketu* axis?

If Moon is in *Rahu Ketu* axis in the horoscopes of both boy and girl, the married life and progeny will be affected. This is because besides one seven axis affliction by *Rahu Ketu*, fifth house also would be under the influence of either *Rahu* or *Ketu*.

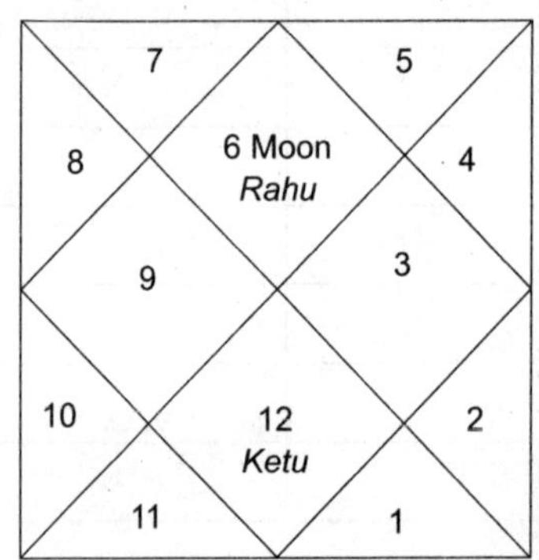

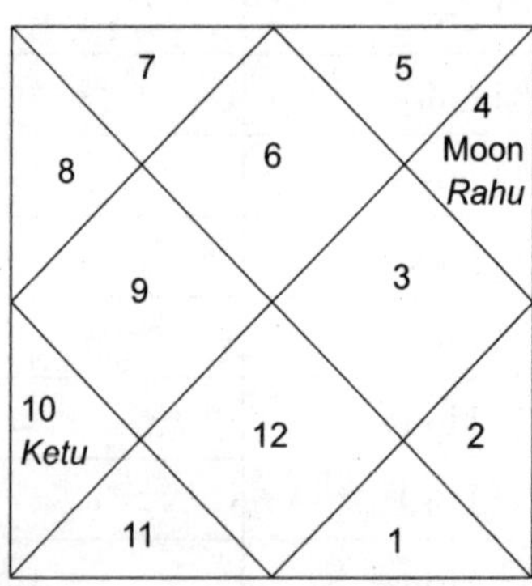

Both the horoscopes have afflicted Moon as it is in *Rahu Ketu* axis. In both the horoscopes 1st, 5th and 7th houses from Moon *Lagan* are afflicted by *Rahu*.

360. What are the main ways by which a planet can give results?

Make flow chart

Dasha of a planet gives results in four ways

1. As Lord of different houses.
2. As a benefic or malefic
3. As a natural *karaka*
4. As Lord of permanent houses of *kaal purush kundli*

— AS LORD OF DIFFERENT HOUSES :— Mars will give results of 4th house and 9th house for Leo *Lagan.*

The Lordship varies as per rising *Lagan.*

— PLANET CAN BEHAVE EITHER AS A BENEFIC OR MALEFIC : —

This is further divided into

Natural benefic or natural malefic

Functional benefic or functional malefic

— AS A NATURAL *Karaka* (the results of planet give its results as a *karaka* also which are very important.)

— AS LORD OF PERMANENT HOUSES of *Kaal Purush Kundli*

No planet will shed its basic nature in spite of getting modified by sign, Lordship, *Lagan*, its strength etc.

One cannot change either the basic horoscope or the *dasha* pattern of life but still variations occur depending upon the

— *desh kaal paatr*

(The role of planet gets modified by *desh, kaal, paatr. Manglik dosh* is not considered in childhood but is fully considered in adulthood at the time of marriage.

The results will depend upon the strength of planet and strength of houses).

— event at a particular time and age (transit of different planets at that time)

— *raja* yoga and other favourable yogas also will be of no use, if they are without strength and their *dasha* does not operates in your lifetime at the right moment.

RIGHT *DASHA* OF RIGHT PLANET AT RIGHT AGE MAKES EVERYTHING RIGHT.

❏❏❏

CHARITY BEGINS AT HOME

361. How can you modify the results of a planet by remedies?

The remedies can help you in diluting the negative effects of planets. As per *Karma* theory, every planet who is unfavourable for a particular horoscope would trouble you either physically, financially, professionally, mentally, spiritually etc.

If you repay the dues by 'cash or kind' before a planet's *dasha* comes, the *Bal*ance of your negative *karmas* gets diluted. You are then either given grace, punished with less penalty etc. It is like either you pay the penalty in cash or bear the consequences. Before advising remedies to anyone, you must do the remedies for yourself by mantras, worshipping, donations etc. The charity should begin at home.

362. What do you mean by charity begins at home and what can be achieved by doing charity for different relations?

Principle of "charity begins at home" should be fully followed by everyone. Giving respect to elders, all family members and doing the needful for your dear ones improves your planets. The blessings and good wishes of your elders and dear ones can give you an extra advantage of rectifying the problems of life.

In fact, no one can do charity for parents but still taking care of your old father, sick father, financially weak father, *jatak* is able to rectify the negativities of your horoscope. This helps in diluting any dispute with higher authority, boss, seniors, heart problems, eye problems, brain problems etc. All these things can happen on their own because Sun is the live *Karaka* of above significances.

By taking care of your old mother, sick mother, financially weak mother, *jatak* is able to rectify the negativities of Moon. This helps in diluting any mental stress, educational hurdles etc. This helps in peace at home, satisfaction, relaxation at mental level, improved educational grades, etc. All these things can happen on their own because Moon is the live *Karaka* of above significances.

By taking care of your elder brother, sick brother, financially weak brother, one is able to rectify the negativities of Jupiter. This helps in diluting financial problems; you become wiser; achieve wisdom, expressive power; applied knowledge improves; husband, son gets benefic results. All these things can happen on their own because Jupiter is the live *Karaka* of above significances.

By taking care of your elder sister, sick sister, financially weak sister, one is able to rectify the negativities of Jupiter. This helps in diluting financial problems, you become wiser, achieve wisdom, expressive power and applied knowledge improves and husband, son get benefic results. All these things can happen on their own because Jupiter is the live *Karaka* of above significances.

By taking care of your younger brother, sick brother, financially weaker brother, one is able to rectify the negativities of Mars. This improves your health, energy level, dominance, command, improving fertility etc. All these things can happen on their own because Mars is the live *karaka* of above significances.

By taking care of your younger sister, sick sister, financially weak sister, one is able to rectify the negativities of Mercury. This helps in improving your intelligence, speaking power, analytical power, calculations, business sense etc. All these things can happen on their own because Mercury is the live *Karaka* of above significances.

By taking care of your husband, sick husband, financially weak husband, one is able to rectify the negativities of Jupiter by taking care of your husband. This helps in diluting financial problems, you become wiser, achieve wisdom, your expressive power, applied knowledge and convincing power improves. Husband and son get benefic results. All these things can happen on their own because Jupiter is the live *Karaka* of above significances.

By taking care of your husband teacher/*preacher*/*gurus* etc., financially weak teacher/*preacher*/*gurus* etc., one is able to rectify the negativities of Jupiter. This helps in diluting financial problems. You become wiser and achieve wisdom. Expressive power, applied knowledge and convincing power improves. Husband, son get benefic results.

All these things can happen on their own because Jupiter is the live *Karaka* of above significances.

By taking care of your wife, sick wife, financially weak wife, one is able to rectify the negativities of Venus. This helps in improving your knowledge, beauty, glamour, comforts , sperms, etc. All these things can happen on their own because Venus is the live *Karaka* of above significances.

By taking care of your old grandparents, sick grand parents, financially weak grand parents, *jatak* is able to rectify the negativities of *Rahu* and *Ketu*. This helps in diluting any mental stress, hurdles in life, sudden unexpected troubles etc. This helps in peace at home, satisfaction and relaxation at mental level, professional level etc. All these things can happen on their own because *Rahu* and *Ketu* are the live *Karaka* of obstructions, hurdles, unexpected troubles.

By taking care of your servants and helpers, *jatak* is able to rectify the negativities of Saturn. This helps in diluting any mental stress, delays in different projects, health issues etc. This helps in satisfaction and relaxation at mental level, improvement in health etc. All these things can happen on their own because Saturn is the live *Karaka* of illness, delays, slowness, negativities etc.

REMEDIAL MEASURES IN ASTROLOGY

363. What is the importance of universal remedies in astrology?

Before you jump into the remedial astrology, certain things should be kept in mind. The attitude of the astrologer should be very co-operative, patient, pious, charitable and accommodative. Astrologer must have faith in his remedies and the logics of the remedies should be crystal clear to him. Only when you have faith in your remedies, then only you can make others believe in your remedies.

Now the question which arises is: Can destiny be denied? No,but it can definitely be delayed, diluted, directed in the right direction.

51 Universal Remedies for Happiness At Home Are :—

1. Try to maintain a good moral character (general improvement of all planets).
2. Feed street dogs (dilutes the bad effects of *Ketu*).
3. Eat In kitchen (dilutes the bad effects of *Rahu*).
4. Keep water in bedroom at night and pour it in plants in morning(sucks negativity of any kind).
5. Feed more than 100 *chapattis* to pet animals once a month (dilutes the bad effects of *Ketu*, *Rahu* etc.)
6. Do regular purification of the property at least once a month preferably on *Amavasya* (sucks all negativities and promotes positivity).
7. Donate during the *shraadhs* to get blessings of ancestors.

   The general remedies for different planets are as follows:

8. **Sun :—** respect father and elderly males, obey government, do remedies of *surya grahan*, don't argue with boss.

   Sun :— Do not eat salt on Sunday. Do not eat or drink in the *hora* of Sun.

9. **Moon :—** respect and serve mother, elderly ladies; take silver

coin and rice from mother, do remedies of *chander grahan*, pour water on *"Shivling"*.

Moon :— chant *mantra* of Moon *"Om Namah Shivaey"*, put white flowers in running water on Monday, drink water in silver utensils, don't serve and drink milk after sunset, pour milk on *babool* tree.

10. **Mars :—** respect youngers and try to help them, read *"Hanuman Chalisa"* daily, distribute and eat sweets, do blood donation.

    Mars :— eat *gur* and red *masoor* on Tuesday, put red flowers in running water, don't eat and drink in the *hora* of Mars.

11. **Mercury :—** help and give sweets to *behan, bua, beti,* help eunuch, give water to *tulsi* plant daily, give sweets and study material to young girls less the 12 years of age.

    Mercury :— eat small *elaichi* and *tulsi* leaves on Wednesday, put *elaichi* in running water, donate green *moong dal* to beggars, don't eat and drink in the *hora* of Mercury.

12. **Jupiter :—** have good moral character, don't indulge in religious arguments, respect gurus, apply kesar on forehead.

    Jupiter :— put 12 flowers of chameli in running water, leave yellow flowers in front of Vishnuji, drink water in gold utensil, don't eat and drink in the *hora* of Jupiter.

13. **Venus :—** respect wife, respect maid and young female colleagues in the office, feed *"peda"* to the cow, don't wear torn clothes, one should use perfumes.

    Venus :— put white flowers in running water, chant mantra of *Om Namah Shukraey*, feed *jwaar* to cow and pure *ghee*, don't eat and drink in the *hora* of Venus.

14. **Saturn :—** do not lie, have good moral character, feed minimum 10 blinds in a year.

    Saturn :— put coconut oil mixed with camphor on the head, put black *urad* in running water, donate one fist of black *urad* to beggars, do not eat and drink in the *hora* of Saturn.

15. **Rahu :—** eat in kitchen, clean your toilet seat on every Wednesday and Saturday. On Saturday evening after Sunset

and before stars appear on the sky, feed some over fried things and tea to the lepers.

Rahu :— do not eat and drink in the *hora* of Saturn, put flowers of black *dhatura* on *"Shivling"*,

16. **Ketu :—** apply *kesar* on the forehead, feed biscuits to stray dogs daily, donate one double colour blanket to the priest or to the religious person on Monday or Thursday aged 40-50 years of age.

    Ketu :— don't use iron utensils, do not eat and drink in the *hora* of Jupiter and Saturn.

    Planet's positive results can be further improved by your daily *aacharan* as follows :—

17. Wake up before sunrise and purify yourself and recite *navgrah mantras.*
18. Do *surya namaskar* daily with 12 steps to improve Sun.
19. Give water to Sun within 8 minutes of sunrise for improving significance of Sun.
20. Water *tulsi* and other plants for Mercury.
21. Keep water for birds in northeast for Jupiter and Moon.

    Bajra in southwest for pigeons for *Rahu.*

22. Read *"Hanuman Chalisa"* daily for Mars, Saturn, *Rahu* and *Ketu.*
23. Make 3 pieces of *chapatti* one for dog for *Ketu*, one for cow for Moon and Venus, one for crow for *Rahu* and Saturn.
24. Food to home female servant for Saturn, *Rahu.*
25. Feed small insects for *Rahu*, Saturn.
26. Satnaza for birds and animals for all planets.
27. Help blinds for Sun, Moon, Venus and Saturn.
28. Help orphans for Venus, Jupiter.
29. Help needy students for Mercury, Jupiter.
30. Help in schools for Mercury, Jupiter.
31. Donating for water charity for Moon, Jupiter.

    Do not do if Moon in 6th house.

32. Donating for religious places for Jupiter.
33. Doing services in shoe counter of religious place, for *Rahu*, Saturn.
34. Donate items of *Rahu*, *Ketu* and Saturn (soft coke, barley, coconut, *til*, tea etc.) regularly to handicaps, blinds and lepers to dilute the bad effects of *Rahu*, Saturn and *Ketu*) for overall improvement.
35. Donating for the marriage of poor girl for Mars, Venus and Mercury.
36. Water *peepal* tree daily for Jupiter in day and Saturn at night.
37. Apply *kesar* on forehead for Jupiter.
38. Food to lady priest and feed sweeper.
39. Cut coconut from top and fill it with *desi ghee*, sugar and place it under earth with top open for ants to eat, at least once a month. This keeps bad effects of Saturn, *Rahu*, *Ketu*, and Mars along with Venus under control.
40. Feeding minimum ten blinds once a year for professional progress. This keeps bad effects of Saturn under control.
41. Feeding street dogs with sweet biscuits or sweet *rotis* for harmony at home as well as professional place. This keeps bad effects of *Ketu* under control.
42. Leave four coconuts in a temple on first day followed by one coconut everyday for next three days for recovery from health problems. For chronic or long diseases, keep on donating one coconut every Saturday.
43. Take a silver coin and rice from mother or mother-in-law and keep it with you lifelong for success in all ventures of life (blessings of Moon with wealth and prosperity).
44. Donate a double colour blanket at religious place for promoting professional beginning.
45. Feed street dogs for diluting the Ill effects and misunderstanding at office.
46. Wash 1.25 kg. Jon (barley) in 0.5 kg. milk and pour the milk in

tulsi plant and immerse *jonin* flowing water for recovery of money.

Whenever going for recovery take silver coin and rice with you.

47. Sprinkle *Ganga jal* on both sides of the door of business premises in morning before entry to prevent losses in business.
48. Leave some money whenever you go to cremation ground or cross cremation ground for prevention of health problems and for speedy recovery.
49. Keep 10 *"chhuaaray"* in red cloth or rapped in red *"mauli"* in all your vehicles to prevent accidents.
50. In cases of precious babies or for that matter, all expecting mothers should tie 6 feet *mauli* around their right arm till the delivery. After the delivery she should tie the new *mauli* around her arm and the old *mauli* should be tied around the baby's arm till the age of 2 years.
51. If unknown problems are there, then rotate peacock feather from head to toe for 12 times and sprinkle it outside the house.

Pray and serve for the betterment of others also.

364. What is the use of regular purification and how to do purification?

Regular purification of the property is one of the best remedy more so in cases of persons not having horoscopes or accurate time. Purification is very useful for all the family members irrespective of whether you believe in astrology or not.

Purification is done in two steps :—

1. Sucking the negativity
2. Promoting the positivity

Sucking The Negativity

Sucking of negativity is done on *amavasya* or Saturday after Sunset.

— clean the property with a piece of cloth.

— sprinkle water along the walls.

— burn *"guggal"*.

— sprinkle rock salt/keep rock salt in earthen pots (*diyaas*) in all corners in a clockwise direction

— leave it all night.

Promoting The Positivity

Next day of *Amavasya* or Sunday morning

— clean the property in the morning.

— sprinkle rice or *"phullian"*.

— after half an hour collect the *"phullian"* and feed the birds.

— sprinkle *Ganga jal* or holy water

— burn incense (sandalwood) or *dhoop* or *havan samagri*.

— take three rounds of property with peacock feather.

— all along the purification process, keep worshiping.

365. What are the logics behind different steps of purification?

By cleaning, you wash off the negativity. Sprinkling water all along settles the negativity.

"Guggal" removes the negativity from atmosphere.

Rock salt sucks the negativity throughout night.

The left over negativity is removed by cleaning.

Distribution of *"phullian"* (made of rice) is a kind of donation, if any dues are still left over. By feeding *"phullian"* to birds, the donations are offered to creatures of God. Birds are represented by Mercury, permanent sixth Lord of *kaal purush kundli*. Mercury is the permanent Lord of loans, credits, diseases, disputes etc. Offering *"phullian"* to them dilutes or removes the above problems.

Sprinkling *Ganga jal* or holy water settles the negativity and promotes positivity.

Lighting of *hawan samagri* etc. finally promotes the positivity and aura of property.

Peacock feather further removes any hidden negativities.

❑❑❑

EXAMPLE HOROSCOPE WITH PRACTICAL ANALYSIS

Before we go to the practical analysis of a horoscope, there are certain parameters to be remembered for smooth flow of analysis. As explained earlier.

Horoscope is a picture of your life which is based on the past *karmas* and can be modified to a certain extent with present *karmas*.

The analysis of the horoscope should be done at two levels: —

1. STATIC ANALYSIS
2. DYNAMIC ANALYSIS

Static analysis includes the potential of Stability/Strength/ Smoothness etc. in life.

Dynamic includes delivery of results as per *Dasha*, Double transit and *Desh kaal paatr*a etc.

After analyzing the above two parameters, the role of remedial astrology comes to play. The results of past *karmas* cannot be denied but can definitely be diluted by certain measures done with full faith and devotion.

Before remedial measures are taken, one must be very sure of the results of a planet as per *dasha* and *desh kaal paatr*. After static analysis, one should be crystal clear whether to prevent the negativity or to promote positivity. (Details available in the Remedial book by the author.)

Practical flow for static analysis.

1. Strength of horoscope as a whole
2. Strength of all the planets
3. Strength of all the houses
4. Strength of all the *lagnas*
5. Strength of different *Karaka*s
6. Special yogas present
7. Strength of planets in divisional charts

Practical flow for Dynamic analysis.

Dasha of planets

Duration of *dasha*

Dashas to follow

Daily *gochar* of planets

Desh kaal paatr of *jatak*

Day to day aacharan of *jatak*

MALE

DATE OF BIRTH

TIME OF BIRTH

PLACE OF BIRTH

Everyone has endless queries regarding different events of life at different times. It is very important to study the potential of a horoscope before predicting any event. Before going to analytical part of astrology, one must have the following data and charts with you.

Birth chart

Moon chart

Sun chart

Minimum 16 divisional charts

Dasha pattern from date of birth to 120 years.

Gochar of different planets at different stages of life

Different charts of close blood relatives if possible

First of all one should assess

1. Strength of horoscope as a whole
2. Strength of all the planets
3. Strength of all the houses
4. Strength of all the *lagnas*
5. Strength of different *Karaka*s

6. Special yogas present
7. Strength of planets in different divisional charts

After assessment of the above static features present in the horoscope since birth, the assessment of fulfilment or failures of events should be dealt with in a dynamic way by applying *dasha*, transit and *desh kaal paatr*.

Dasha is the most important factor as it either delivers or denies the event. *Dasha* at birth followed by different *dashas* sets the trend of life and quality of events at different stages of life.

Dasha along with transit gives the real time of happening of different events.

Now we will apply the above factors to the example horoscope.

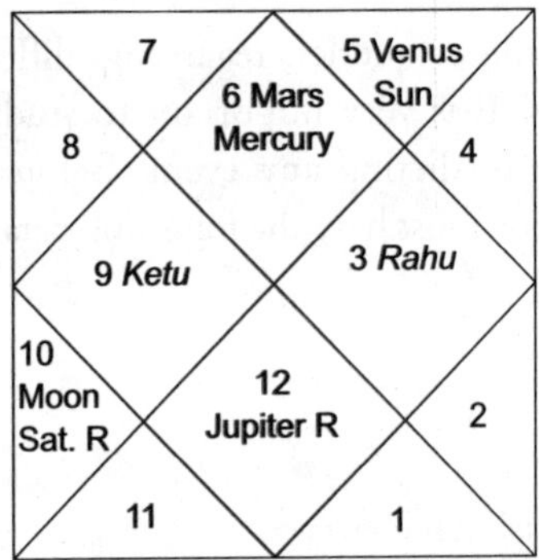

2. STRENGTH OF HOROSCOPE AS A WHOLE

— there are seven planets in *Kendras* and *Trikones* giving strength to horoscope (this will give status and wealth to person)

— all the *Kendras* have planets in them (this will give status and stability)

— *Kendras* have dominance of melefics like *Rahu*, *Ketu* and Mars (the status and stability will be associated with troubles and hurdles)

— exalted *Lagan* Lord in *Lagan* (person will be capable or achieving a lot)

— presence of three *panch mahapurush* yogas (these give status, wealth, honour, stability etc.)

Bhadar yoga (exalted Mercury in *Lagan*). This gives extra ordinary intelligence with sharp application of brain)

Hansa yoga (own sign Jupiter in Pisces in *Kendra* from *Lagan*). This gives status, money, educated partner etc.

Shash yoga (own sign Saturn in Capricorn *Lagan* from Moon). The yoga gives stability, maturity, excellent education, business etc.)

— PRESENCE OF FOUR PLANETS IN OWN SIGN

1st Lord Mercury in 1st in own sign Virgo. (Mercury: — it is exalted and placed in *Lagan* making *Bhadra* yoga (*panch mahapurush* yoga). *Bhadra* yoga gives intelligence, longevity, good calculations, business sense etc.

5th Lord Saturn in 5th in own sign Capricorn (Saturn : — It is 5th and 6th Lord in own sign Capricorn in own sign and placed in *trikone*. It is forming *Shash* yoga being conjunct with Moon. It gives good technical education, good intelligence etc.

7th Lord Jupiter in 7th in own sign Pisces. (Jupiter :— It is placed in *Kendra* in own sign Pisces making *Hansa* yoga. It gives wealth, wisdom, applied knowledge, consultancy, convincing powers etc. Jupiter being 4th Lord and 7th Lord will give property, vehicles and good, educated, intelligent, wise partner.

12th Lord Sun in 12th in own sign Leo. (Sun :— Sun in own sign in Leo but placed in 12th house. Its degrees are 15 degrees 37 minutes placed in *Yuva avastha* Sun is *vargottam* as it is placed in same Leo sign in navamsa. These factors promise good private life, foreign visits but hospitalisations also.

— PRESENCE OF TWO PLANETS ASPECTING THEIR OWN SIGN

8th Lord Mars aspects its own sign Scorpio. (Mars :—Mars is placed in *Lagan* with exalted *Lagan* Lord Mercury. It is *vargottam*. It is in

Bala avastha. It is greatest enemy for *Lagan*. It is aspected by its friend Jupiter from 7th house.

These factors promise longevity as 8th Lord Mars aspects its own house of longevity. But 8th Lord's placement in *Lagan* gives accidents, health problems, obstructions in life.

11th Lord Moon aspects its own sign cancer.

Moon :— Moon is 11th Lord placed in 5th house (*trikone*) is good, it is *pakshbali* being six houses away from Sun. It is placed in inimical sign Capricorn with enemy Saturn making it weak and afflicted. Its degrees are 24 degrees 2 minutes in Capricorn in *Bala avastha*.

These factors promise habit of speculation but gains on long run will be restricted and delayed because of conjunction of Saturn.

2. STRENGTH OF ALL THE PLANETS

SUN : — Sun in own sign in Leo but placed in 12th house.

Its degrees are 15 degrees 37 minutes placed in *Yuva avastha*.

Sun is *vargottam* as it is placed in same Leo sign in *navamsa*.

It is aspected by *Ketu* from 4th house.

These factors promise good private life, foreign visits but hospitalisations also.

MOON : — Moon is 11th Lord placed in 5th house (*trikone*) is good, it is *pakshbali* being six houses away from Sun. It is placed in inimical sign Capricorn with enemy Saturn making it weak and afflicted. Its degrees are 24 degrees 2 minutes in Capricorn in *Bala avastha*.

These factors promise habit of speculation but gains on long run will be restricted and delayed because of conjunction of Saturn.

MARS :— Mars is placed in *Lagan* with exalted *Lagan* Lord Mercury. It is *vargottam*. It is in *Bala avastha*. It is greatest enemy for *Lagan*. It is aspected by its friend Jupiter from 7th house.

These factors promise longevity as 8th Lord Mars aspects its own house of longevity. But 8th Lord's placement in *Lagan* gives accidents, health problems, obstructions in life, sudden health problems.

MERCURY :— It is exalted and placed in *Lagan* making *Bhadra* yoga (*panch mahapurush* yoga). It is afflicted being conjunct with inimical planet Mars. Conjunction of Mars as 8th Lord in *Lagan* with *Lagan* Lord gives accidents, health problems, obstructions in life.

Bhadra yoga gives intelligence, longevity, good calculations, business sense etc.

JUPITER :— It is placed in *Kendra* in own sign Pisces making *Hansa* yoga. It gives wealth, wisdom, applied knowledge, consultancy, convincing powers etc. Jupiter being 4th Lord and 7th Lord will give property, vehicles and good, educated, intelligent, wise partner.

Jupiter being afflicted by aspect of 6th Lord Saturn and 8th Lord Mars will create problems in house and property because 4th house is already under the influence of *Rahu–Ketu* axis.

VENUS : — It is placed in 12th house in inimical sign Leo with 12th Lord Sun. It is *vargottam* being placed in Leo in *navamsha*. Venus in 12th or 6th house gives lots of money and prosperity. It is being aspected by *Ketu* from 4th house which gives troubles with vehicles and property.

SATURN :— It is 5th and 6th Lord in own sign Capricorn and placed in *trikone*. It is forming *Shash* yoga being conjunct with Moon.

It gives good technical education, good intelligence etc.

RAHU :— *Rahu* in Gemini sign placed in *Kendra*. Its dispositer Mercury is exalted and placed in *Lagan*. This will potentiate the results of *Rahu* giving cleverness, diplomacy, cunningness etc. in profession.

KETU :— *Ketu* is placed in 4th house in Sagittarius sign. Its dispositer Jupiter is placed in *Kendra* in Pisces forming *Hansa* yoga. It will give good education, good applied knowledge, property, vehicles etc.

3. STRENGTH OF ALL THE HOUSES

After studying the strength of planets, one should analyse the strength of all the twelve houses. The planet alone cannot give the results of its both houses in the same way. P.A.C. of houses will be different although Lord can be same. So all the individual houses should be studied for specific results of that house.

1ST HOUSE :— First house is Virgo with its Lord Mercury placed in exalted position forming *Bhadra* yoga. *Lagan* or 1st house is strong so the person will be able to achieve lots of things in life like good health, wealth, status, honour etc. As the first house has 8th Lord Mars placed in it and aspected by retrograde Saturn and retrograde Jupiter makes one prone to diseases. Aspect of retrograde planets with *Lagan* and *Lagan* Lord makes one prone to health problems.

2ND HOUSE :— Second house is Libra with its Lord Venus in 12th house with 12th Lord Sun who is inimical to Venus. This will lead to losses and extra expenses on diseases, hospitalisation etc. As we have already seen the proneness of the person to diseases because of P.A.C. of retrograde planets Saturn and Jupiter with *Lagan* and *Lagan* Lord. Saturn is a natural *Karaka* of diseases also.

3RD HOUSE :— Third house is Scorpio, whose Lord Mars is placed in *Lagan* with exalted *Lagan* Lord Mercury. This makes the person self-made with own efforts. Aspect of 7th Lord Jupiter on 1st house, 3rd house as well as 1st Lord, 3rd Lord can lead to partnership or association of life partner in business.

4TH HOUSE :— Fourth Lord Jupiter is placed in *Kendra* in 7th house in own sign Pisces. The position of Jupiter forming *Hansa* yoga gives property, vehicles and good education with intelligence. P.A.C. of 5th Lord Saturn of own sign further improves the higher education.

5TH HOUSE :— Fifth Lord Saturn in own sign Capricorn. It is forming *Shash* yoga being conjunct with Moon It gives good technical education, good intelligence, promise of children etc.

6TH HOUSE :— Sixth Lord Saturn in own sign Capricorn in 5th house. It is forming *Shash* yoga being conjunct with Moon. Saturn as 6th Lord of house of competition gives success in higher education, success in competition, technical education, good intelligence etc. 6th Lord Saturn's association with Moon (eleventh Lord of gains) gives gains in competition and education.

7TH HOUSE :— Seventh Lord Jupiter is placed in *Kendra* in 7th house in own sign Pisces. The position of Jupiter forming *Hansa* yoga in 7th house gives good life partner, who will be educated, intelligent , good adviser and supportive.

8TH HOUSE :— Eighth house is Aries with its Lord Mars placed in 1st house conjunct with Mercury, who is placed in exalted position forming *Bhadra* yoga. 8th house is aspected by its Lord Mars promising long, *pooran aayu* to *jatak*.

9TH HOUSE :— Ninth house is Taurus with its Lord Venus in 12th house with 12th Lord Sun, who is inimical to Venus. This will lead to losses and extra expenses on foreign visits or higher studies, hospitalisation.

10TH HOUSE :— Tenth house is Gemini with its Lord Mercury placed in exalted position forming *Bhadra* yoga in *Lagan* so the person will be able to achieve lots of things in professional life. As the tenth Lord is conjunct with 8th Lord Mars placed in *Lagan* and aspected by retrograde 6th Lord Saturn associating loans with business. (7th Lord Jupiter also aspecting 10th house and tenth Lord Mercury by retrogradation).

11TH HOUSE :— Eleventh Lord Moon is placed in 5th house (*trikone*) is good. It is strong in *pakshbal* being six houses away from Sun. It is placed in inimical sign Capricorn with enemy Saturn making it weak and afflicted thereby restricting the amount of gains. These factors promise habit of speculation, but gains on long run will be restricted and delayed because of conjunction of Saturn.

12TH HOUSE :— 12th Lord Sun in own sign in Leo. Sun is *vargottam* as it is placed in same Leo sign in *navamsa*. It is aspected by *Ketu* from 4th house. These factors promise good private life, foreign visits, and hospitalisations.

STRENGTH OF ALL THE LAGNAS

Birth chart lagan :— First house is Virgo with its Lord Mercury placed in exalted position forming *Bhadra* yoga. *Lagan* or 1st house is strong so the person will be able to achieve lots of things in life like good health. As the first house has 8th Lord Mars placed in it makes him prone for sudden health problems, obstructions in life etc. *Lagan* is aspected by retrograde Saturn and retrograde Jupiter. Aspect of retrograde planets with *Lagan* and *Lagan* Lord makes one prone to diseases.

Moon lagan :— Moon sign Lord is Capricorn with its Lord Saturn in it providing strength to it. Moon's conjunction with inimical Saturn delays the activities, which person is planning mentally. Saturn being Lord of sixth house of diseases and as disease *karaka* also makes one disease prone and mentally tense etc.

Sun lagan :— Sun *Lagan* is Leo with its own Lord Sun in it thereby making Sun *Lagan* strong.

What is important here is that all the three lagnas have their *Lagan* Lords in *Lagan* thereby providing strength and protection to *Lagan*.

4. STRENGTH OF DIFFERENT *KARAKAS*

We have already discussed the role of all the planets above as house Lords. But the role of planets as different *Karaka*s is different. Different planets as *Karaka*s will behave as below.

Sun :— Sun is *Karaka* for father, boss, government, bones, heart etc. In this horoscope, Sun is placed in 12th house with enemy Venus. It is aspected by *Ketu* and retrograde Jupiter making it weaker from health angle.

Moon :— Moon is *Karaka* for mother, mind, blood, fluids in body etc. In this case Moon is conjunct with inimical Saturn. Saturn is Lord of 6th house (house of diseases). Saturn itself is the natural *Karaka* for diseases. The health of mother will thus be affected. But before giving such prediction, 4th house, and 4th Lord must also be analyzed.

Mars :— Mars is *Karaka* for younger brother, muscles, bone marrow etc. In this case Mars is well placed in *Lagan* with exalted *Lagan* Lord mercury.

Mercury :— Mercury is *Karaka* for education, knowledge, mathematics, business, speech, communication etc. Mercury's exalted and *digbali* position forming *Bhadra* yoga will make person very intelligent, educated, and business minded with good command on speech.

Jupiter :— Jupiter is *Karaka* for money, applied knowledge, consultancy, adviser, health and healing etc. Jupiter is placed in *Kendra* in own sign Pisces making *Hansa* yoga. It gives wealth, wisdom, applied knowledge, consultancy, convincing powers etc. Jupiter being 4th Lord and 7th Lord will give property, vehicles and good educated, intelligent, wise partner.

Venus :— Venus is *Karaka* for wife, semen, sex, glamour, vehicles, luxuries etc. Venus is placed in 12th house in inimical sign Leo with 12th Lord Sun. It is *vargottam* being placed in Leo in *navamsha.* Venus in 12th or 6th house gives lots of money and prosperity. It is being aspected by *Ketu* from 4th house, which gives troubles with vehicles and property. Mars as 8th Lord is also afflicting 4th house and 4th Lord Jupiter. Venus as well 4th house are afflicted by *Ketu,* this makes one prone for accidents.

Saturn :— Saturn is *Kuraka* for diseases, nerves, patience, slowness, lethargy etc. Saturn is forming *panchmahapurush shash* yoga. It is 5th and 6th Lord in own sign Capricorn and placed in *trikone.* It is forming *Shash* yoga being conjunct with Moon. It gives good technical education, good intelligence, patience etc.

Rahu :— *Rahu* is *Karaka* for suddenness, cunningness, cleverness, diplomacy.

Rahu in Gemini sign placed in *Kendra.* Its dispositer Mercury is exalted and placed in *Lagan.* This will potentiate the results of *Rahu* giving cleverness, diplomacy, cunningness etc. in profession.

Ketu :— *Ketu* is *Karaka* for mystery, feet, spiritualism, *Moksha* etc. *Ketu* is placed in 4th house in Sagittarius sign. Its dispositer Jupiter is placed in *Kendra* in Pisces forming *Hansa* yoga. It will give good education, good applied knowledge, property, vehicles etc.

5. SPECIAL YOGAS PRESENT

This horoscope has many special powerful yogas like:

— *Bhadra* yoga

— *Hansa* yoga

— *Shash* yoga etc.

All these yogas make the horoscope powerful.

6. STRENGTH OF PLANETS IN DIFFERENT DIVISIONAL CHARTS

Before giving final prediction regarding any event, the role of divisional charts must be analyzed. As we see in real life, the person passes through many events simultaneously. On the one hand one gets promotion and gains, simultaneously mother of the person can be in trouble. This can happen during the *dasha* of eleventh Lord as it indicates gains and promotion but simultaneously 11th is 8th from 4th house of mother. This does not happen with everyone, because the role of divisional charts come into play. *Chaturamsha* D 4 must be analyzed before giving final prediction about mother.

ANALYZING AN EVENT/SIGNIFICANCE

For analyzing any significance,

— one should try to note the house representing that significance.

— the house Lord of the significant house.

— the *karaka* of the significant item.

— All these three factors should be seen from Moon horoscope also.

— for superfine tuning, analyze concerned divisional chart

Brief table below gives the important significant items and the factors to be considered.

S.NO.	Significance	Factors to be seen
1	Body	*Lagan*, *Lagan* Lord, Sun, dispositer of Sun
2	Wealth	2nd house, 2nd Lord, Jupiter
3	Self-efforts	3rd house, 3rd Lord, Mars, *Lagan*, *Lagan* Lord
4	Younger brother	3rd house, 3rd Lord, Mars
5	Property	4th house, 4th Lord,
6	Plot	4th house, 4th Lord, Mars
7	Apartment	4th house, 4th Lord, Venus
8	House (old)	4th house, 4th Lord, Saturn
9	Mother	4th house , 4th Lord, Moon
10	Vehicles	4th house, 4th Lord, Venus
11	Education	2nd house, 2nd Lord, 4th house, 4th Lord, Mercury, Jupiter.
12	Basic (primary)	2nd house, 2nd Lord, 4th house, 4th Lord, Mercury, Jupiter
13	Higher education	2nd house, 2nd Lord, 4th house, 4th Lord, 5th house, 5th Lord, Mercury, Jupiter, 5th house, 5th Lord from Moon
14	Graduation	2nd house, 2nd Lord, 4th house, 4th Lord, 5th house, 5th Lord, Mercury, Jupiter, 5th house, 5th Lord from Moon
15	Post-graduation	2nd house, 2nd Lord, 4th house, 4th Lord, 5th house, 5th Lord, 9th house, 9th Lord Mercury, Jupiter, 9th house, 9th Lord from Moon
16	Research	2nd house, 2nd Lord, 4th house, 4th Lord, 5th house, 5th Lord, 8th house, 8th Lord, 9th house, 9th Lord Mercury, Jupiter, 8th house, 8th Lord from Moon

17	Spiritual education	2nd house, 2nd Lord, 4th house,4th Lord, 5th house, 5th Lord, 8th house,8th Lord, 9th house,9th Lord, 12th house, 12th Lord, Mercury, Jupiter, 12th house, 12th Lord from Moon
18	Children	5th house, 5th Lord, Jupiter, along with Venus in males
19	Speculation	5th house, 5th Lord, Mercury, Jupiter
20	Legal matters	6th house, 6th Lord, Jupiter, Saturn, Mars
21	Competition	6th house, 6th Lord, Jupiter, *Rahu*
22	Loans	6th house, 6th Lord, Jupiter, Mercury
23	Partner	7th house, 7th Lord, Jupiter
24	Life partner	7th house, 7th Lord, Jupiter along with Venus in males
25	Business partner	7th house, 7th Lord, Jupiter along with *dhan* yogas
26	Longevity	8th house, 8th Lord, Saturn, 3rd house, 3rd Lord
27	Obstructions in life	8th house, 8th Lord, *Rahu*, *Ketu*
28	Father	9th house, 9th Lord, Sun
29	Fortune	9th house, 9th Lord, Jupiter
30	Profession	10th house, 10th Lord, Saturn, Sun, Mercury, Jupiter
31	Government job	10th house,10th Lord, Sun
32	Consultancy	10th house, 10th Lord, Jupiter
33	Business	10th house,10th Lord, Mercury
34	Politician	10th house, 10th Lord, Sun, Saturn
35	Laborious Jobs	10th house, 10th Lord, Saturn

36	Gains	11th house,11th Lord, Jupiter, no P.A.C. of 6th, 8th, 12th houses or Lord
37	Elder brother	11th house, 11th Lord, Jupiter
38	Expenses	12th house, 12th Lord, Jupiter
39	Hospitalisation	12th house, 12th Lord, Saturn
40	Jail	12th house, 12th Lord, Mars
41	*Moksha*	12th house, 12th Lord, *Ketu*
42	Foreign	12th house, 12th Lord, 9th house, 9th Lord, 7th house, 7th Lord, *Rahu*
43	Donations	12th house,12th Lord, Jupiter
44	Enjoyment and pleasure	12th house, 12th Lord, Venus and *Rahu*
45	Short travels	3rd house, 3rd Lord
46	Long travels	7th house, 7th Lord, 9th house, 9th Lord, 12th house, 12th Lord

The above table should be used very carefully. One must

Recognize the event first.

Will I have wealth in life?

Will I have gains in life?

For analyzing wealth, your stress should be more on 2nd house, 2nd Lord and *Karaka* Jupiter.

For analyzing gains, your stress should be more on 11th house, 11th Lord and *Karaka* Jupiter.

All the analysis which have been done so far is static. Now we will shift to dynamic analysis.

The predictions should be made after synthesizing Static and Dynamic factors:

The static factors are:

The strength of planets,

Strength of house

Strength of *Karaka* and

Running *dasha* at that time etc.

Transit of Saturn and Jupiter

Transit of *dasha* Lords

Transit of *Karaka* for the event

Desh kaal paatr

Dynamic factors of astrology are as follows :—

Dasha of planets

Duration of *dasha*

Dashas to follow

Daily *gochar* of planets

Desh kaal paatr of *jatak*

Day to day aacharan of *jatak*

Now we will do practical analysis of the horoscope. In brief, note the *dasha* at birth, *dasha* to follow at different age, transit of planets, *desh, kaal, paatr*.

Dasha at birth was Mars. *Dasha* to follow are as given below.

Dasha	**Starting of *dasha***	**Ending of *dasha***	**Age of person**
MARS	2-9-1963	17-4-1970	1-7 years
RAHU	18-4-1970	17-4-1988	7-25 years
JUPITER	18-4-1988	17-4-2004	25-41 years
SATURN	18-4-2004	17-4-2023	41-60 years
MERCURY	18-4-2023	17-4-2040	60-77 years
KETU	18-4-2040	17-4-2047	77-84 years
VENUS	18-4-2047	17-4-2067	84-104 years
SUN	18-4-2067	17-4-2073	104-110 years
MOON	18-4-2073	17-4-2083	110-120 years

❑❑❑

PRACTICAL APPLICATION RELATING TO DASHA AND TRANSITS

Use of the *Dasha* Pattern

On broader analysis, Mars *dasha* is age of play school.

Rahu dasha from 7-25 years will be main period of higher school followed by higher education and may be getting job.

Jupiter *dasha* from 25-41 years will be main *dasha* for earning, profession, business, partnership, marriage, progeny etc.

Saturn *dasha* from 41-60 years will be main *dasha* for earning, profession, business, partnership, marriage of children etc.

Mercury *dasha* from 60-77 years will be main *dasha* for earning, profession, business, partnership, deep studies, worshipping etc. and so on. These above possibilities are general for everyone as per *desh, kaal, paatr*.

Now we have to see the activation of different houses as per *dasha*. This should be done as per P.A.C. (Position, Aspect, Conjunction.)

Now from practical angle you should make a table as given below and then analyze the different *dashas* as per different age.

Dasha of planet at birth	Posited and Lordship	Aspected Houses	Aspected by Planets	Aspected planets	Conjunct With Planet	Total number of activated houses
MARS	1,3,8	4,7,8	SAT.(R) (5,6) JUP(R) 4,7	JUPITER 4,7 *KETU* 4	MERCURY 1,10	1,3,4,5,6, 7,8,10
RAHU	10	2,4,6	SAT.(R) (5,6) JUP(R) 4,7	*KETU* 4	—	2,4,5,6, 7,10

JUPITER (R)	7, 4,7	1,2,3,12, 10, 11	SAT.(R) (5,6) MER. 1,10	MER.1,10 MARS 3,8 SUN 12 VENUS 2,9 *RAHU* 10	—	1,2,3,4,5, 6,7,8,910, 11,12
SATURN (R)	5, 5,6	1,2,6,7, 10,11	—	MER. 1,10 MARS 3,8 JUP. 4,7 *KETU* 4 *RAHU* 10	MOON 11	1,2,3,4,5, 6,7,8,10, 11
MERCURY	1 1,10	7	SAT. R (5,6) JUP.R 4,7,	JUP. 4,7	MARS 3,8	1,3,4,5,6, 7,8,10
KETU	4	8,10,12	MARS 3,8 *RAHU* 10	*RAHU* 10 SUN 12 VENUS 2,9	—	2,3,4,8, 9, 10,12
VENUS	12 2,9	6	KETU 4, JUP. R 4,7	—	SUN 12	2,4,6,7,9, 12
SUN	12 12	6	*KETU* 4, JUP. R 4,7	—	VENUS 2,9	2,4,6,7,9, 12
MOON	5 11	11	—		SATURN 5,6	5,6,11

The table above shows the activation of different houses during different *dashas*. These are the results of *dasha* Lord activation. Next step is to see activation by *antardasha* Lords. After this, combine *mahadasha* and *antardasha* results and find out the common houses.

Example :—

TABLE A

M. D. Houses	**A.D. Houses**	**HOUSE ACTIVATED BY A.D.**	**COMMON HOUSES**
MARS	MARS	1,3,4,5,6,7,8,10	1,3,4,5,6,7,8,10
1,3,4,5,6,7,8,10	*RAHU*	2,4,5,6,7,10	4,5,6,7,10
	JUP. R	1,2,3,4,5,6,7,8,9, 10,11,12	1,3,4,5,6,7,8,10
	SAT. R	1,2,3,4,5,6,7,8, 10,11,	1,3,4,5,6,7,8,10

	MER	1,3,4,5,6,7,8,10	1,3,4,5,6,7,8,10
	KETU	2,3,4,8,9,10,12	3,4,8,10
	VENUS	2,4,6,7,9,12	4,6,7,
	SUN	2,4,6,7,9,12	4,6,7,
	MOON	5,6,11	5,6,
RAHU	*RAHU*	2,4,5,6,7,10	2,4,5,6,7,10
2,4,5,6,7,10	JUP. R	1,2,3,4,5,6,7,8,9, 10,11,12	2,4,5,6,7,10
	SAT. R	1,2,3,4,5,6,7,8 10,11	2,4,5,6,7,10
	MER	1,3,4,5,6,7,8,10	4,5,6,7,10
	KETU	2,3,4,8,9,10,12	2,4,10
	VENUS	2,4,6,7,9,12	2,4,6,7
	SUN	2,4,6,7,9,12	2,4,6,7
	MOON	5,6,11	5,6
	MARS	1,3,4,5,6,7,8,10	4,5,6,7,10

NOTE :— WHILE DECIDING COMMON HOUSES IN CASE OF *Rahu/Ketu*, WE SHOULD CONSIDER THE HOUSES ACTIVATED BY THEIR DISPOSITER ALSO.

In the same way, you can do it for all the *mahadashas* and *antardashas*. Now we see, so many houses getting activated. True, everyone at every stage is passing through lots of activities at same time. Now the main activities are decided by the common houses activated by both *mahadasha* Lord and *antardasha* Lord. Still many common houses can be there. Here comes the role of double transit of Saturn and Jupiter. Now the final outcome will be indicated by the common houses activated by M.D. AND A.D. ALONG WITH DOUBLE TRANSIT.

In the same way the whole exercise should be done with Moon as *Lagan*.

To make the job much easier, one can make table of double transit.

Catch the double transit in a particular year, note the signs having double transit and see which houses of your horoscope get activated by those signs.

Double transit is same for everyone as it activates particular signs. The house will be different for everyone as per the *Lagan* and Moon sign *Lagan*.

The *dasha* pattern of the example horoscope is given below.

Maha dasha	***Antardasha***	**Begininining**	**Ending**
MARS	MARS.	2-9-63	17-9-63
	RAHU	17-9-63	5-10-64
	JUPITER	5-10-64	10-9-65
	SATURN	10-9-65	20-10-66
	MERCURY	20-10-66	17-10-67
	KETU	17-10-67	15-03-68
	VENUS	15-03-68	15-5-69
	SUN	15-5-69	20-9-69
	MOON	20-9-69	21-4-70
RAHU	*RAHU*	21-4-70	02-01-73
	JUPITER	02-01-73	28-5-75
	SATURN	28-05-75	03-04-78
	MERCURY	03-04-78	21-10-80
	KETU	21-10-80	08-11-81
	VENUS	08-11-81	08-11-84
	SUN	08-11-84	03-10-85
	MOON	03-10-85	03-04-87
	MARS	03-04-87	21-04-88
JUPITER	JUPITER	21-04-88	09-06-90
	SATURN	09-06-90	20-12-92
	MERCURY	20-12-92	28-03-95
	KETU	28-03-95	03-03-96

	VENUS	03-03-96	02-11-98
	SUN	02-11-98	21-08-99
	MOON	21-08-99	20-12-2000
	MARS	20-12-2000	26-11-2001
	RAHU	26-11-2001	21-04-2004
SATURN	SATURN	21-04-2004	25-04-2007
	MERCURY	25-04-2007	03-01-2010
	KETU	03-01-2010	11-02-2011
	VENUS	11-02-2011	12-04-2014
	SUN	12-04-2014	25 03-2015
	MOON	25-03-2015	24-10-2016
	MARS	24-10-2016	01-12-2017
	RAHU	01-12-2017	08-10-2020

Once you have the *dasha* pattern, you can now use the TABLE NUMBER A for getting different houses being activated and prepare your own table as given below in TABLE NUMBER B.

TABLE B

EVENT	M.D.	A.D.	COMMON HOUSE	DOUBLE TRANSIT	FINAL HOUSE
JOINED SCHOOL	MARS	SATURN	1,3,4,5, 6,7,8,10	2,4	4
FOREIGN VISIT	*RAHU*	JUPITER	2,4,5,6, 7,10	7	7
FOREIGN VISIT FROM SCHOOL	*RAHU*	SATURN	2,4,5,6, 7,10	4,5,12,9,	4,5
PASSED HIGH SCHOOL	*RAHU*	MERCURY	4,5,6,7, 10	4,6,9, 10,11	4,6,10
ADMISSON IN ENGINEERING	*RAHU*	*KETU*	2,4,10	10,	10
LOVE AFFAIR	RAJI	VENUS	2,4,6,7	2,4,7	2,7
SISTER GOT MARRIED	*RAHU*	VENUS	2,4,6,7	2,4,7	2,7

PASSED ENGINEERING	*RAHU*	MOON	5,6	5,6	5,6
FIRST JOB	*RAHU*	MOON	5,6	5,6	5,6
FATHER EXPIRED	*RAHU*	MOON	5,6	6	6
MARRIAGE	*RAHU*	MARS	4,5,6,7,10	5,7	7
BOUGHT CAR	JUPITER	JUPITER	1,2,3,4,5, 6,7, 8,910, 11,12	2,4,5,7, 10, 11	4,11
STARTED OWN BUSINESS	JUPITER	JUPITER	1,2,3,4,5, 6,7, 8,910, 11,12	2,4,5,7, 10, 11	7,11
BLESSED WITH DAUGHTER	JUPITER	JUPITER	1,2,3,4,5, 6,7, 8,910, 11,12	2,4,5, 7,9, 10	5,9
BLESSED WITH SON	JUPITER	MERCURY	1,3,4,5, 6,7, 8,10	5,7,11	5,7
BOUGHT CAR	JUPITER	MERCURY	1,3,4,5, 6,7, 8,10	4,11,12	4
ROBBERY WITH INJURY	JUPITER	SUN	2,4,6,7, 9,12	2,3,4,6, 8,9,10,12	2,4,6, 9,12
SURGERY IN AMERICA	JUPITER	MARS	1,3,4,5, 6,7, 8,10	5,6,7,8, 9,12	5,6,7, 8
DOWNFALL	JUPITER	*RAHU*	2,4,5,6, 7,10	3,4,6,7, 10,11,12	6,7,12

Now, we will try to study whether the above principles will hold good. Normally, the following events can take place in the life of a person living in an average middle class family of metropolitan city. The events will differ as per *desh*, *kaal*, *paatr*.

Dasha at birth : event

3 years old : joins school

5 years old : primary school

11 years old : secondary school

18 years old : joins college

23 years old : leaves college and joins job

30 years old and so on.

Many events take place simultaneously along with the above events like travelling, love affair, health problems, marriage, birth of child, marriage in the family, vehicle purchase, schooling of children, property, sickness or death of close blood relations, disputes and differences etc.

Different events can get activated by activation of a house/house Lord/*Karaka* by *dasha* Lords. Event can get activated by *dasha* either in birth chart or in Moon chart. Always try to analyze the events in birth as well as Moon chart.

Now we will note the event, *dasha*, *gochar* and see the co-relation of event.

EVENTS :—

1. JOINED SCHOOL IN MARCH, 1966.
2. FOREIGN VISIT IN MAY, 1973.
3. FOREIGN VISIT FROM SCHOOL SIDE IN MAY, 1977.
4. PASSED HIGH SCHOOL WITH 80% IN APRIL, 1981.
5. ADMISSION IN ENGINEERING IN JULY, 1981.
6. LOVE AFFAIR IN 83-84.
7. SISTER GOT MARRIED IN MAY, 83.
8. PASSED ENGINEERING IN APRIL, 86.
9. JOB IN JULY 86
10. FATHER EXPIRED ON 9TH AUGUST, 86.
11. MARRIAGE WITH THE SAME GIRL IN OCT., 87.
12. BOUGHT OLD CAR IN MAY, 88.
13. STARTED OWN BUSINESS FEB., 1989
14. BLESSED WITH DAUGHTER ON 26TH JULY, 89.
15. SON WAS BORN IN 1994.
16. BOUGHT A NEW CAR MARCH, 1995

17. ROBBERY ON 24TH MARCH, 99 WITH INJURY.
18. SURGERY IN AMERICA IN JUNE, 2001.
19. DOWNFALL AROUND 2002

- The events take place only when *dasha* activates the events and double transit of Saturn and Jupiter blesses those houses or house Lords or *Karaka.*
- Note the event.
- Note the *dasha.*
- Note the houses activated by *dasha* Lords.
- Note the house Lords activated by *dasha* Lords.
- Note the *karakas* activated by *dasha* Lords.
- Apply the above factors in birth chart and Moon *kundli.*
- Apply double transit of Saturn and Jupiter on above factors.

JOINED SCHOOL IN APRIL, 1966 :—

For joining school at nursery and play school levels, the activation of 2nd, 3rd and 4th houses is required. 2nd house is the house of speech, 3rd house is house of sports and play, 4th house is the basic house of education.

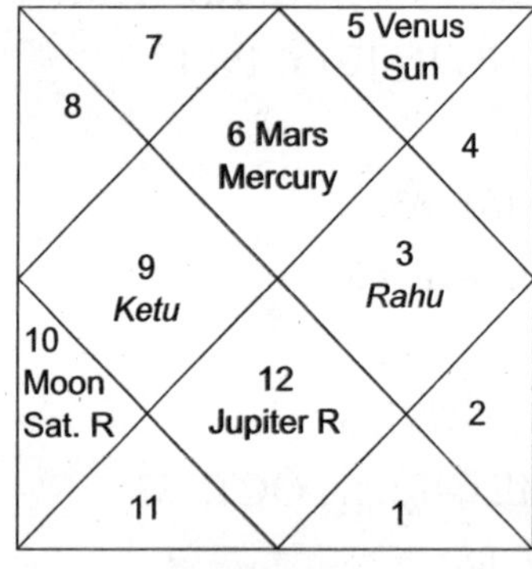

Birth Chart

11
9
Ketu
12
Jup. R
10 Moon
Sat.R
8
1
7
2
4
6
Mer.
Mars
3 Rahu
5 Ven
Sun

Moon Chart

March 1966 in *dasha* of Mars/Saturn/Venus

Mars in *Lagan* with Mercury, *Karaka* of intelligence and education. It is aspecting 4th house of basic education. Mars is aspecting Jupiter, *Karaka* for education.

Saturn from 5th aspects 2nd house of speech and learning.

Venus is 2nd Lord of speech and learning.

TRANSIT OF SATURN AND JUPITER

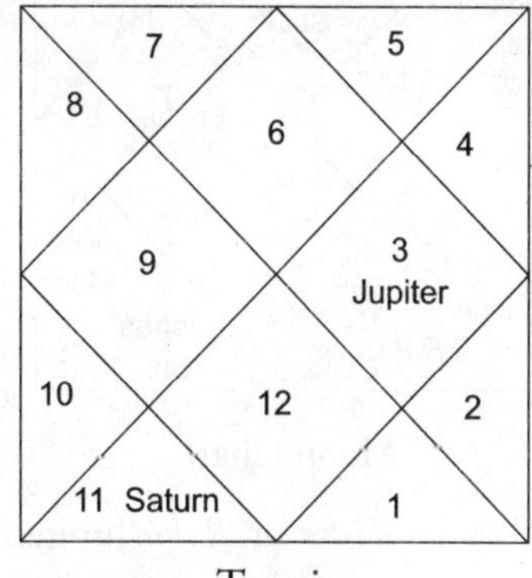

Transit

7
5 Venus
Sun
8
6 Mars
Mercury
4
9
Ketu
3
Rahu
10
Moon
Sat. R
12
Jupiter R
2
11
1

Birth Chart

Transit Over Birth Chart

Saturn in transit in Aquarius aspects 3rd house and 2nd Lord Venus. Jupiter in transit in Gemini aspects 2nd house and 4th house of education.

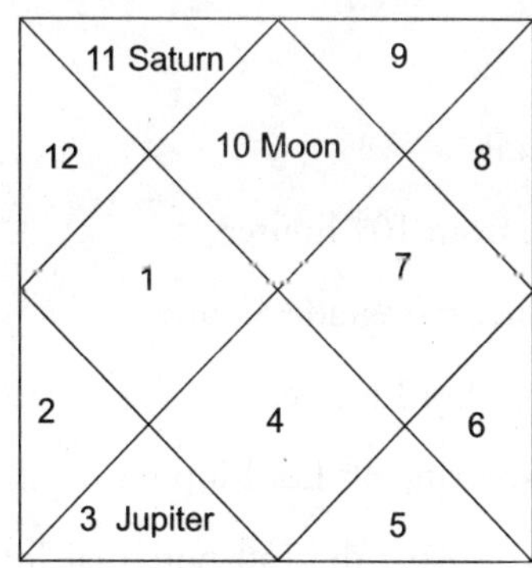

Transit

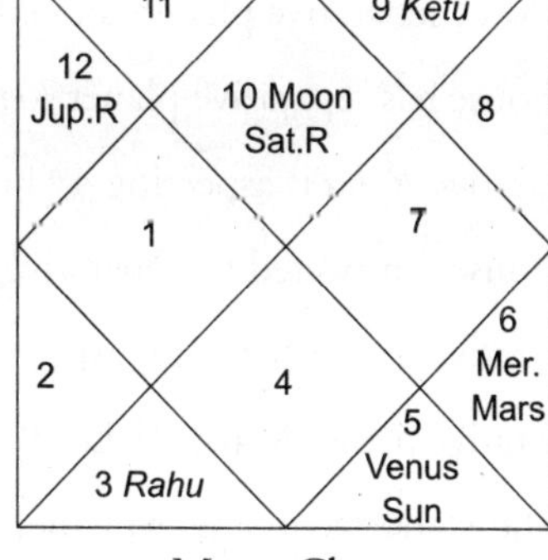

Moon Chart

Transit Over Moon Chart

Saturn is transiting over 2nd house of speech and aspecting 4th house of education.

Jupiter is aspecting 2nd house from Gemini.

FOREIGN VISIT IN MAY 1973 :—

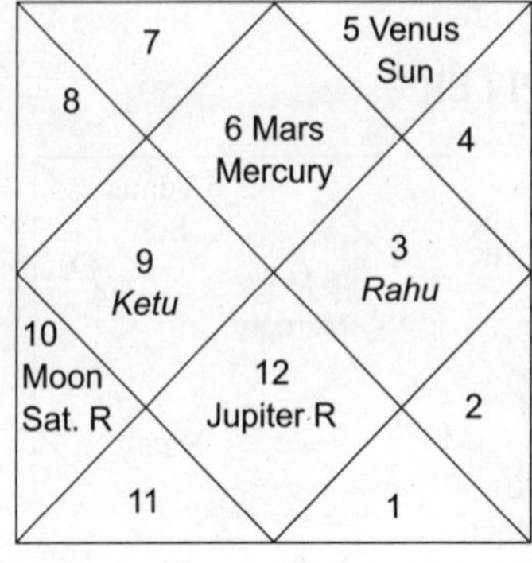

Birth Chart

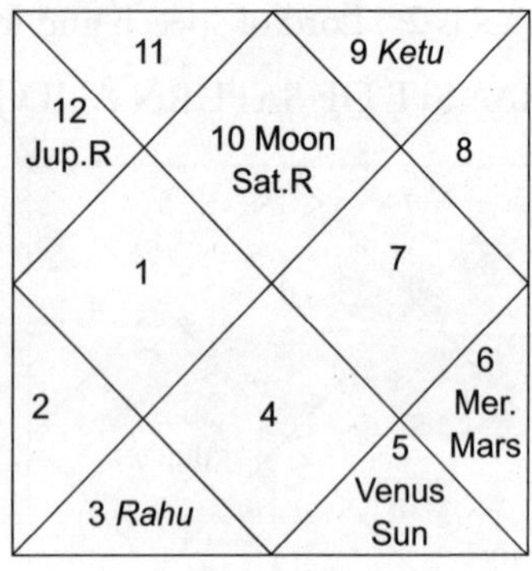

Moon Chart

Went to foreign country in May 1973 in *dasha* of *Rahu*/Jupiter/Saturn

For going to foreign country, one must have afflicted fourth house of residence.

This should be followed by the activation of 7th house/9th house/12th house of foreign travelling by the *dasha* Lords.

Dasha of separative planets should be there.

4th house has separative planet *Ketu* in it.

Separative *Rahu* is aspecting 4th house from 10th house.

4th house is aspected by separative planet retrograde Saturn.

Separative planet Saturn is aspecting 4th Lord Jupiter.

Separative planet Mars (8th Lord) is aspecting 4th Lord Jupiter.

So the static factors as explained above have the full potential for going abroad.

Now we will apply *dasha* and *gochar*.

Rahu :—

- Separative *Rahu* is aspecting 4th house from 10th house.

- *Rahu* is natural *Karaka* for travelling abroad.

Jupiter :—

Jupiter is Lord of 7th house and is aspecting 12th house by retrograde aspect.

Jupiter is also aspecting 12th Lord Sun by retrograde aspect.

Jupiter is also aspecting 9th Lord Venus by retrograde aspect.

- Saturn :—
- Saturn is aspecting 7th house and 7th Lord Jupiter.

With the static affliction of 4th house and 4th Lord Jupiter as explained above, the dynamic factors of *dasha* precipitated the event of foreign travel.

The *dashas* have activated all the houses (7th, 9th, and 12th) of foreign travelling.

TRANSIT OF SATURN AND JUPITER

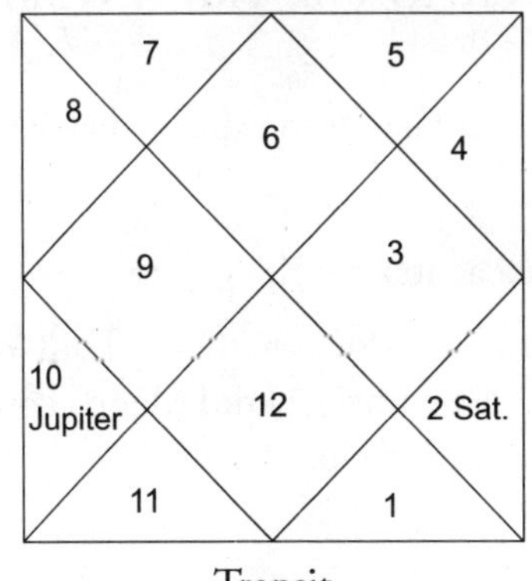

Transit

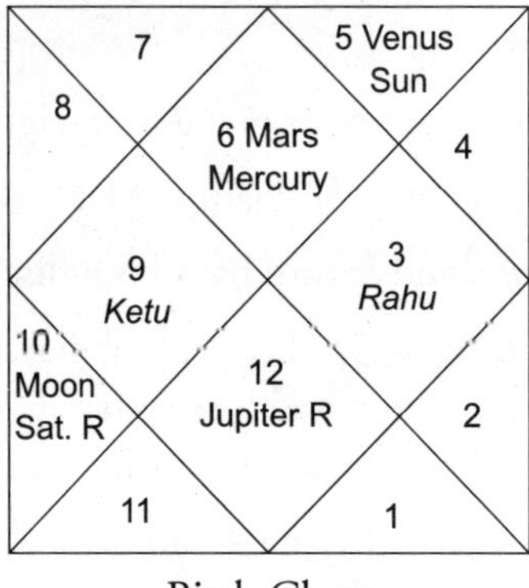

Birth Chart

Transit Over Birth Chart

Transit Saturn was in Taurus (9th house of foreign travels)

Transit Jupiter was in Capricorn and aspected 9th house of foreign travels. It aspected *Lagan* and *Lagan* Lord also.

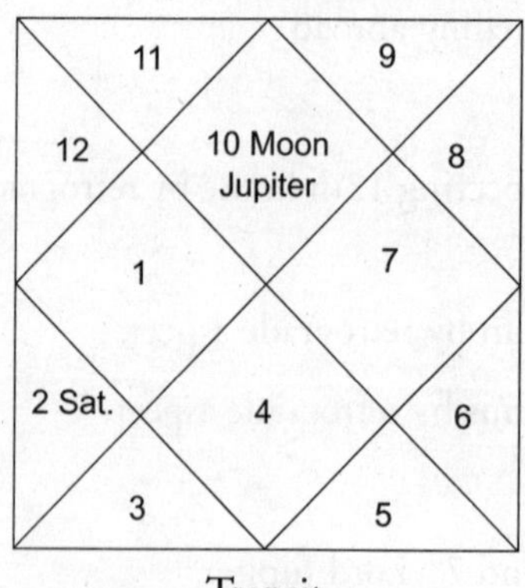

Transit

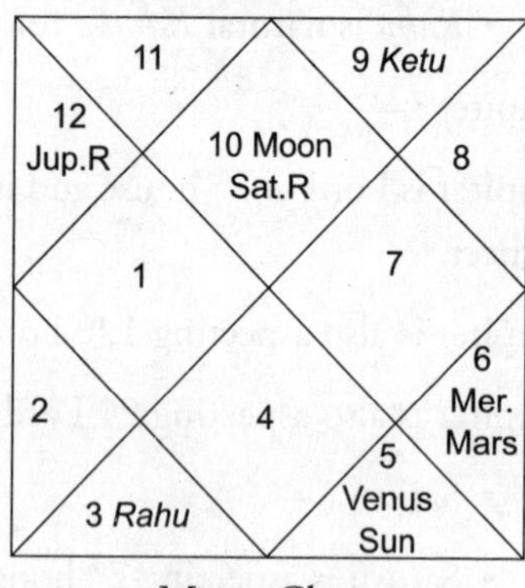

Moon Chart

Transit Over Moon Chart:

Transit Saturn was in Taurus the 5th house and aspected 7th house of foreign travels. Transit Jupiter was in Capricorn and aspected 9th house of foreign travels. Transit Jupiter was in Capricorn and aspected 7th house of foreign travels. It was transiting over Saturn (*Lagan* and *Lagan* Lord) of Moon chart also.

FOREIGN VISIT WITH EDUCATIONAL TRIP IN MAY 1977:—

Explanation for going to foreign country has been explained above.

Dasha of *Rahu* /Saturn/Mars

Rahu and Saturn have been discussed as above.

Saturn is 5th Lord of higher education along with 6th Lord of competition and is conjunct in 5th house with 11th Lord Moon (Lord of gains) thereby promising gains from education.

Mars is aspecting 4th house/4th Lord Jupiter.

MOON HOROSCOPE :—

Mars is placed in 9th house of foreign with 9th Lord Mercury.

Mars is 4th and 11th Lord of Moon *kundli* and placed in 9th house of foreign visits.

Mars is aspecting 12th house of foreign and also aspecting 12th Lord Jupiter.

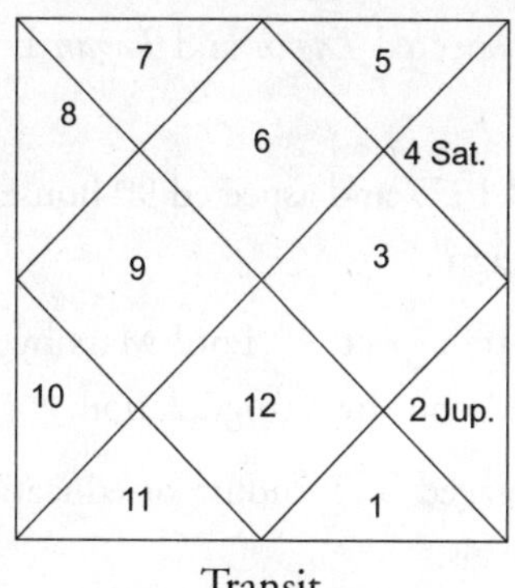

Transit

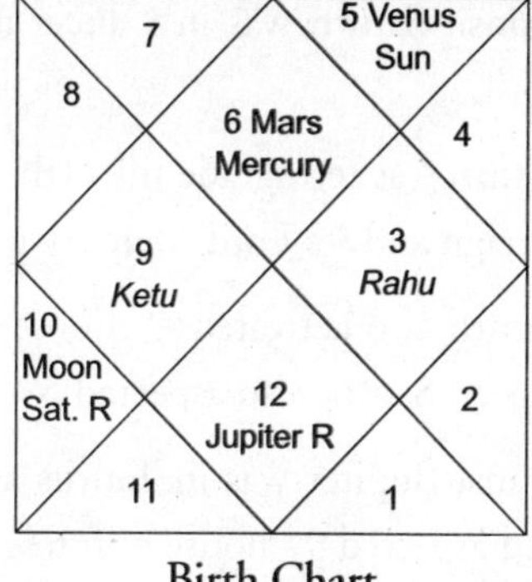

Birth Chart

Transit Over Birth Chart

Transit Saturn was In Cancer and aspected *Lagan* and *Lagan* Lord both.

Saturn was retrograde till 11th April 1977 and aspected 12th house of foreign and 12th Lord Sun of foreign.

Saturn also activated 4th house, 4th Lord Jupiter, 5th house, 5th Lord Saturn (houses and house Lords of education).

Transit Jupiter was in Taurus and placed in 9th house of foreign travels.

It aspected *Lagan* and *Lagan* Lord also. It aspects Mercury (*karaka* for education).

It aspects 5th house of education. It aspects 5th Lord Saturn (Lord of education house).

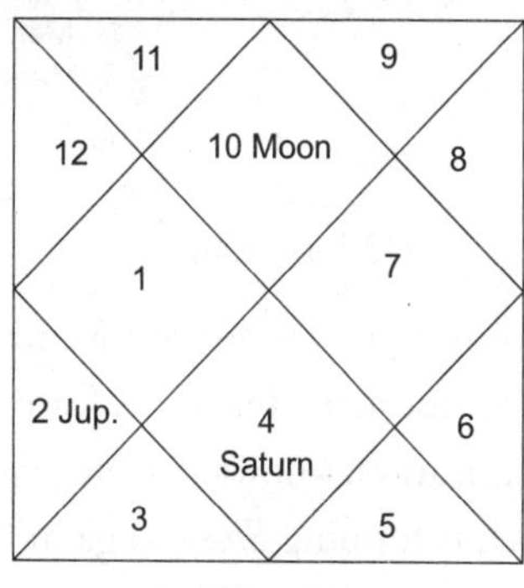

Transit

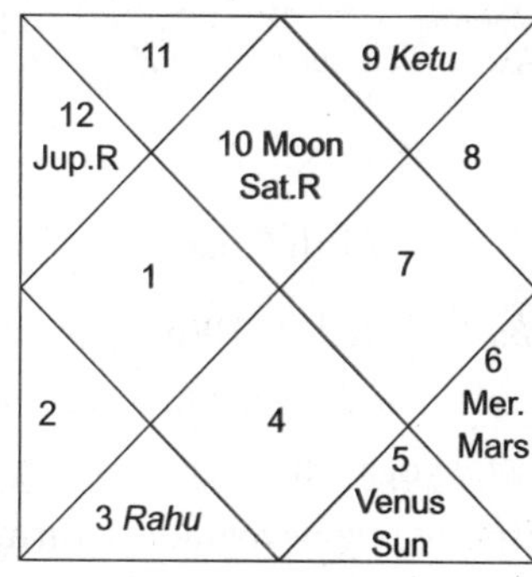

Moon Chart

Transit Over Moon Chart

Transit Saturn was in Cancer and aspected *Lagan* and *Lagan* Lord both.

Saturn was retrograde till 11th April 1977 and aspected 9th house of foreign and 9th Lord Mercury of foreign.

Saturn also activated 4th house by 10th aspect, 4th Lord Mars by 3rd aspect, Saturn also aspected 5th Lord Venus by retrogradation.

Transit Jupiter was in Taurus and placed in 5th house of education and aspected 9th house of foreign travels.

It also aspects 9th Lord Mercury. It aspected *Lagan* and *Lagan* Lord Saturn. It aspects Mercury (*Karaka* for education).

PASSED HIGH SCHOOL WITH DISTINCTION IN APRIL, 1981:—

Dasha of *Rahu* /Mercury /Jupiter followed by *Rahu*/*Ketu*/*Rahu* in April 1981.

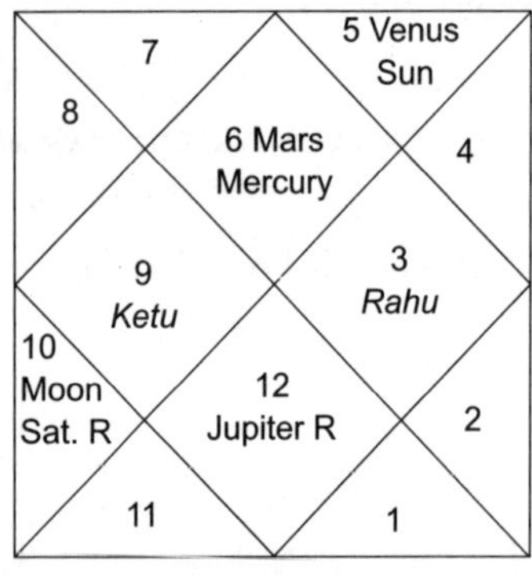

Birth Chart

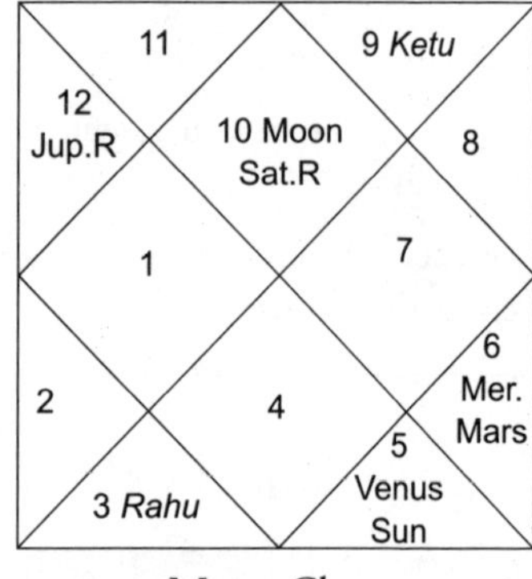

Moon Chart

Rahu is placed in 10th house in Gemini sign whose Lord Mercury is exalted and placed in *Lagan*. *Rahu*'s dispositer Mercury is forming *Bhadra* yoga which gives very good education, knowledge etc. *Rahu* is aspected by retrograde Saturn, which is forming *Shash* yoga in 5th house. *Rahu* is aspected by retrograde Jupiter forming *Hansa* yoga.

The association of *Rahu* with three *panch mahapurush* yogas gives extraordinary powers to *Rahu.*

Mercury is *Lagan* Lord and placed in *Lagan* in an exalted state giving *Bhadra* yoga giving extra ordinary intelligence and educational progress. The association of Mercury with two *panch mahapurush* yogas (*Shash* and *Hansa*) gives extra ordinary powers to Mercury.

Ketu is placed in Sagittarius in *Kendra.* Its dispositer Jupiter is forming *Hansa* yoga and is aspected by exalted Mercury, which is forming *Bhadra* yoga. Jupiter is also aspected by 5th Lord Saturn of own sign and forming *Shash* yoga. So, the indirect association of *Ketu*'s dispositer Jupiter with three *panch maha purush* yogas gives extra ordinary education and intelligence to the *jatak.*

TRANSIT OF SATURN AND JUPITER

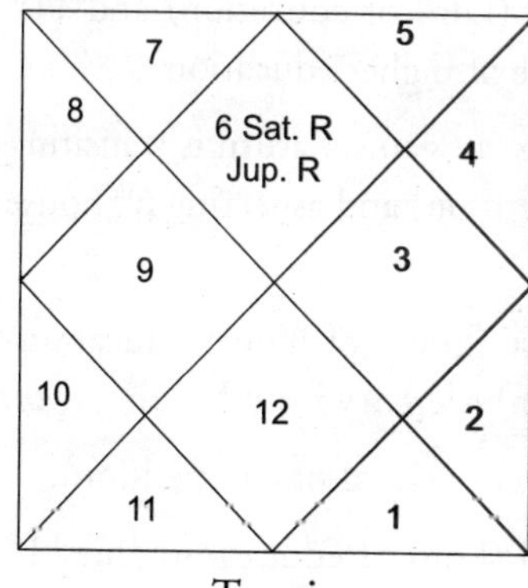

Transit

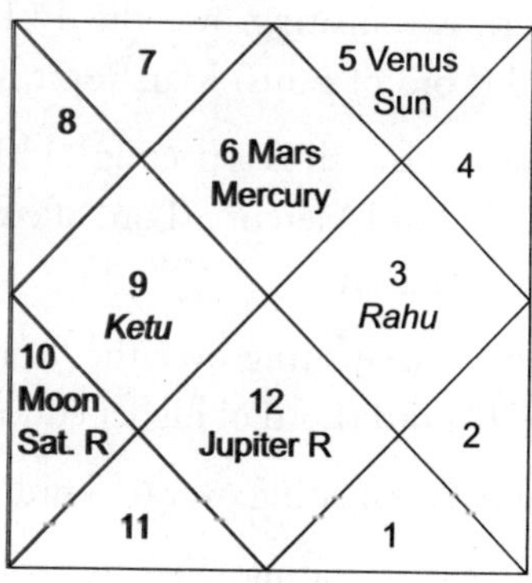

Birth Chart

Transit Over Birth Chart

Saturn in transit is placed in Virgo and is transiting over 10th Lord Mercury (Lord of profession and *Lagan* Lord also.) Mercury is *Karaka* for education also.

Jupiter in transit is placed in Virgo and is transiting over 10th Lord Mercury (Lord of profession and *Lagan* Lord also.) Mercury is *Karaka* for education also.

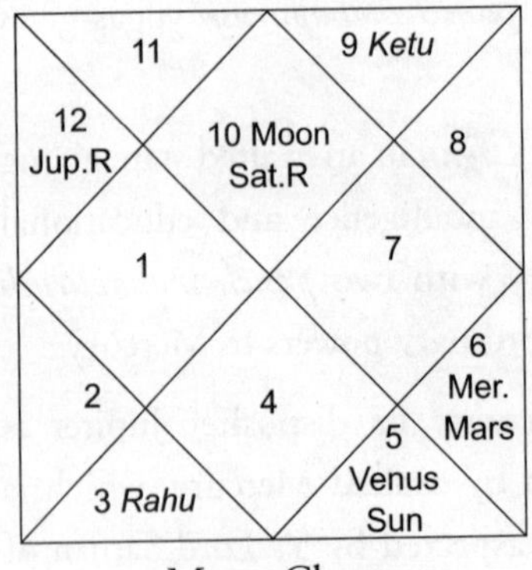

Moon Chart

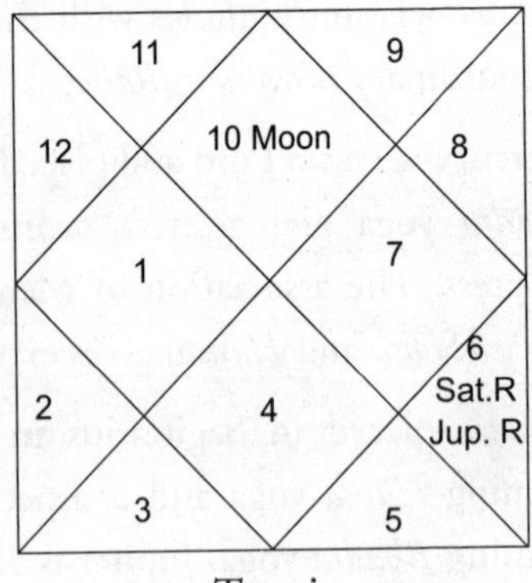

Transit

Transit Over Moon Chart:

Saturn is transiting over the 9th house (house of higher education) and 9th Lord (Lord of higher education) Mercury.

Saturn is transiting over the 4th Lord (Lord of education) and 11th Lord (Lord of gains) Mars in 9th house of higher education.

Saturn in transit is aspecting 11th house of gains. Saturn is transiting over 6th Lord Mercury (Lord of competition) and aspecting 6th house of competition.

Jupiter is transiting over the 9th house (house of higher education) and 9th Lord (Lord of higher education) Mercury from Moon *Lagan*.

Jupiter is transiting over 6th Lord Mercury (Lord of competition).

Jupiter is transiting over the 4th Lord (Lord of education) and 11th Lord (Lord of gains) Mars in 9th house of higher education from Moon *Lagan*.

So we can see the simultaneous transit of Saturn activating 6th house, 6th Lord Mercury, 9th house, 9th Lord Mercury, 11th house, 11th Lord Mars thereby clearing the way for success with gains of higher education.

So we can see the simultaneous transit of Jupiter activating 6th Lord Mercury, 9th house, 9th Lord Mercury, 4th Lord Mars and 11th Lord Mars from Moon *Lagan*, thereby clearing the way for success with gains of higher education.

Jupiter is transiting over *Lagan* and *Lagan* Lord Mercury and is aspecting 5th house and 9th house (houses of higher education.)

Jupiter is aspecting Moon (11th Lord of gains). Jupiter is aspecting 5th house of higher education and 5th Lord Saturn (Lord of higher education and competition (6th Lord).

The double transit of Saturn and Jupiter have fully activated the houses and Lords of higher education with gains.

JOINED ENGINEERING IN A PRESTIGIOUS COLLEGE :—

Dasha of *Rahu*/*Ketu*/Saturn July, 1981

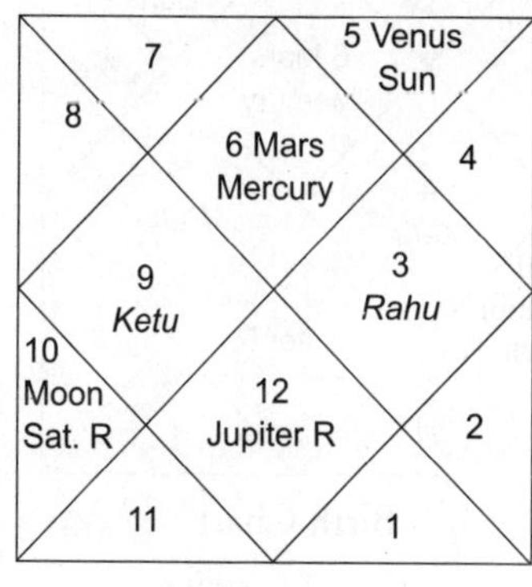

Birth Chart

Moon Chart

All the *dashas* are of separative planets thereby precipitating separation from home to another town for education. All the three *dashas* are of natural malefics giving technical education. Link between 5th house and 10th house gives professional education.

Rahu is placed in 10th house in Gemini sign, whose Lord Mercury is exalted and placed in *Lagan*. *Rahu*'s dispositer Mercury is forming *Bhadra* yoga which gives very good education, knowledge etc. *Rahu* is aspected by retrograde Saturn which is forming *Shash* yoga in 5th house. *Rahu* is aspected by retrograde Jupiter forming *Hansa* yoga. The association of *Rahu* with three *panch mahapurush* yogas gives extra ordinary powers to *Rahu*.

Ketu is placed in 4th house and is aspecting 10th house of profession. *Ketu*'s dispositer is Jupiter, which is placed in 7th house in own sign Pisces forming *Hansa* yoga. *Ketu* is aspected by retrograde Saturn, who is forming *Shash* yoga in 5th house. *Ketu* is aspecting 12th house along with 12th Lord Sun leading to shifting away from home for studies.

Saturn is Lord of 5th house (higher education) aspects 10th house, tenth Lord Mercury by retrograde aspects. Saturn is Lord of 6th house of competition also. *Jatak* joined engineering in prestigious college away from home.

TRANSIT OF SATURN AND JUPITER

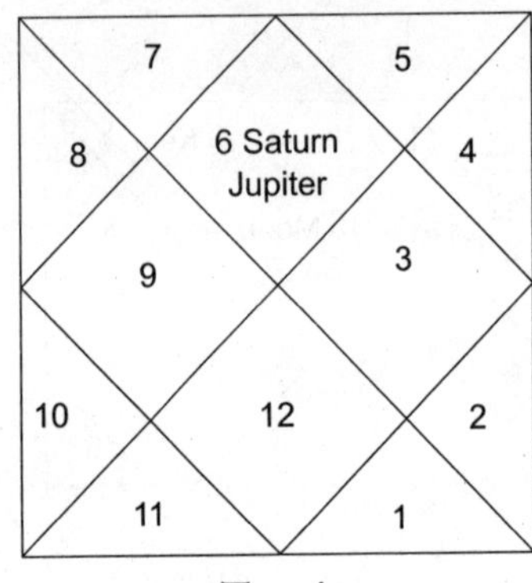

Transit

7
5 Venus
Sun
8
6 Mars
Mercury
4
9
Ketu
3
Rahu
10
Moon
Sat. R
12
Jupiter R
2
11
1

Birth Chart

Transit Over Birth Chart

Saturn in transit is placed in Virgo and is transiting over 10th Lord Mercury (Lord of profession and *Lagan* Lord also.) Mercury is *Karaka* for education also.

Jupiter in transit is placed in Virgo and is transiting over 10th Lord Mercury (Lord of profession and *Lagan* Lord also.) Mercury is *Karaka* for education also.

Jupiter is transiting over *Lagan* and *Lagan* Lord Mercury and is aspecting 5th house and 9th house (houses of higher education.)

Jupiter is transiting over 10th Lord Mercury and is aspecting 5th house and 9th house (houses of higher education.)

Jupiter is aspecting Moon (11th Lord of gains). Jupiter is aspecting 5th house of higher education and 5th Lord Saturn (Lord of higher education and competition (6th Lord) and Jupiter is transiting over 10th Lord Mercury.

The double transit of Saturn and Jupiter have fully activated the houses and Lords of higher education with gains.

Simultaneous activation of 5th and 10th houses or their Lords leads to professional courses.

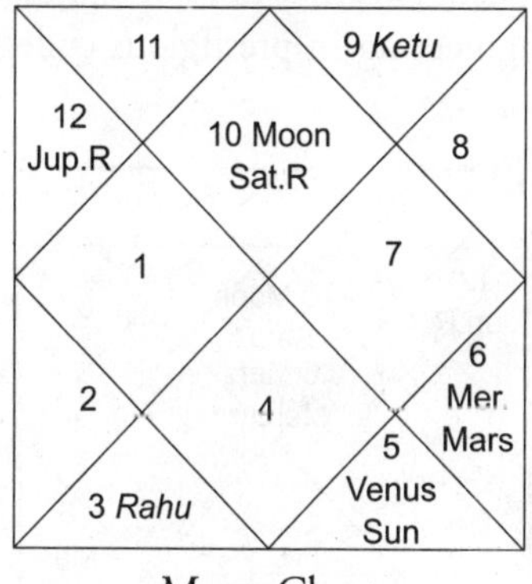

Moon Chart

Transit

Transit Over Moon Chart:

Saturn is transiting over the 9th house (house of higher education) and 9th Lord (Lord of higher education) Mercury from Moon *Lagan*.

Saturn is transiting over the 4th Lord (Lord of education) and 11th Lord (Lord of gains) Mars in 9th house of higher education from Moon *Lagan*.

Saturn in transit is aspecting 11th house of gains and 6th house of competition.

So, we can see the simultaneous transit of Saturn activating 6th house, 6th Lord Mercury, 9th house, 9th Lord Mercury (from Moon),10th Lord Mercury (from *Lagan*), 11th house, 11th Lord Mars thereby clearing the way for success with gains of higher education and professional studies.

Jupiter is transiting over the 9th house (house of higher education) and 9th Lord (Lord of higher education) Mercury from Moon *Lagan*.

Jupiter is transiting over the 4th Lord (Lord of education) and 11th Lord (Lord of gains) Mars in 9th house of higher education from Moon *Lagan*.

So we can see the simultaneous transit of Jupiter activating 6th Lord Mercury, 9th house, 9th Lord Mercury, and 4th and 11th Lord Mars from Moon *Lagan*, thereby clearing the way for success with gains of higher education.

LOVE AFFAIR IN 1983-1984 :—

Dasha of *Rahu*/Venus

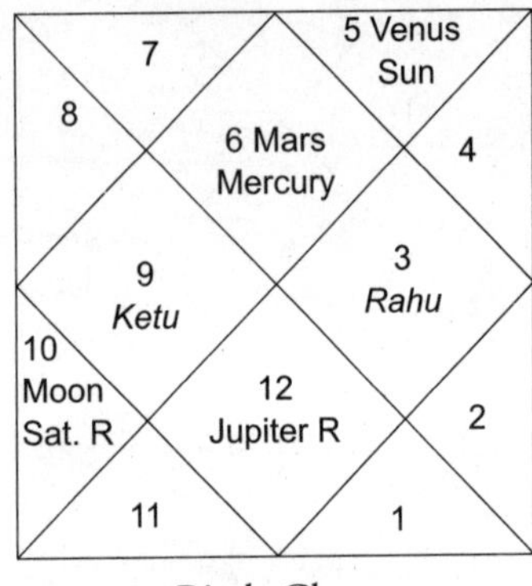

Birth Chart

11
9 *Ketu*
12
Jup.R
10 Moon
Sat.R
8
1
7
6
Mer.
Mars
2
4
5
Venus
Sun
3 *Rahu*

Moon Chart

Both *Rahu* and Venus are natural significators of love and affairs. Connection between 5th and 7th house and their Lords leads to love affair or love marriage. In this horoscope 5th Lord Saturn is aspecting 7th house and 7th Lord. As fifth is house of romance and love while 7th house is house of life partner, so there is clear connection of fifth and seventh. Saturn which is Lord of 5th house of romance and love is also aspecing *Lagan* and *Lagan* Lord thereby making relationship between first, fifth and seventh houses thereby leading to love marriage. *Rahu* is aspected by Saturn Lord of 5th house of love affairs. Saturn is aspecting 7th house (house of life partner) and 7th Lord Jupiter which finally led to marriage with the same girl. *Rahu*'s dispositer Mercury is aspecting 7th house (house of life partner) and 7th Lord Jupiter which finally led to marriage with the same girl.

Venus is natural *Karaka* for love and wife in case of males. It is placed in 12th house of private life with 12th Lord Sun. Involvement of *Rahu* gives inter-caste relationship or marriage.

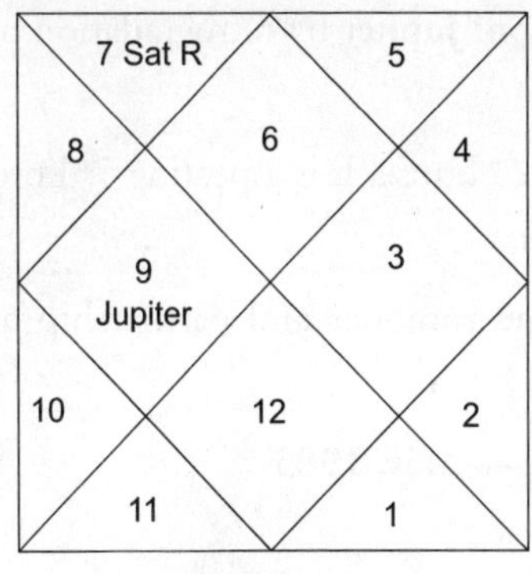

Transit

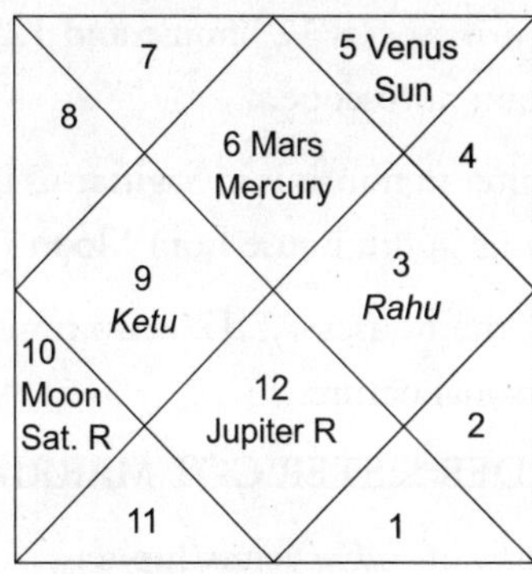

Birth Chart

TRANSIT OF SATURN AND JUPITER :—

Transit Over Birth Chart:

Saturn retrogrades in Libra from February 1983 onwards and aspects 7th house and 7th Lord Jupiter. Jupiter is *Karaka* also for life partner. Saturn aspects the 8th house of secrecy also.

Jupiter in Sagittarius in 4th house aspects the 12th house as well as 12th Lord Sun (12th house is house of private life or secret life). Jupiter in Sagittarius in 4th house aspects Venus (*Karaka* of love and romance) in birth chart.

Jupiter retrogrades in Sagittarius in April 84 thereby aspecting 7th house (house of life partner) and 7th Lord Jupiter. Jupiter is *Karaka* also for life partner.

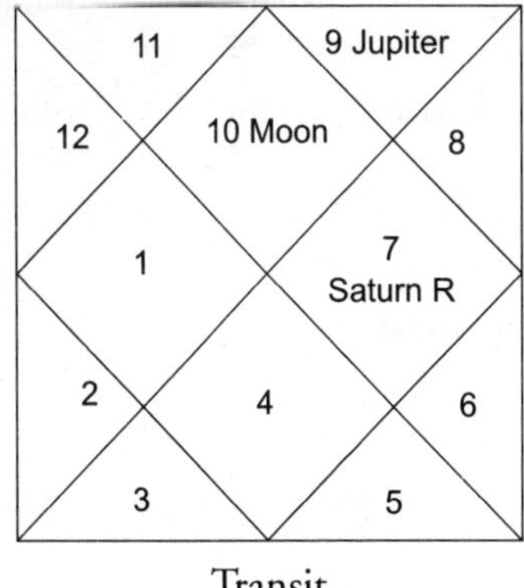

Transit

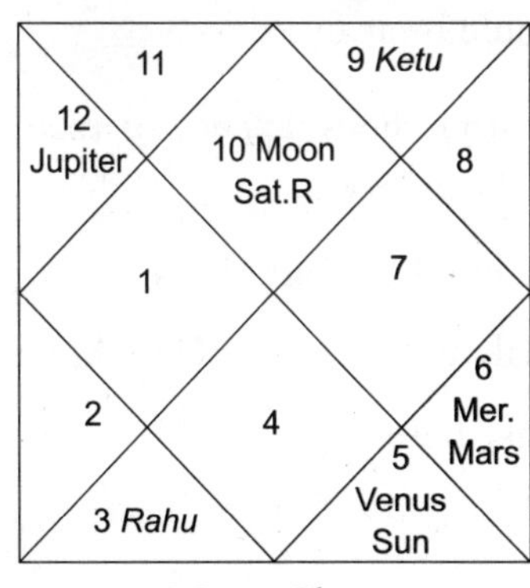

Moon Chart

Transit Over Moon Chart:—

Saturn aspects 12th house and 12th Lord Jupiter by retrogradation in Moon horoscope.

Jupiter in transit is in Sagittarius in 12th house. It is aspecting 5th Lord Venus in 8th house from Moon *Lagan.*

So, the houses 5,7,12 activation gives romance and partnership of personal nature.

ELDER SISTER GOT MARRIED:— May, 1983

Dasha of *Rahu*/Venus/Jupiter

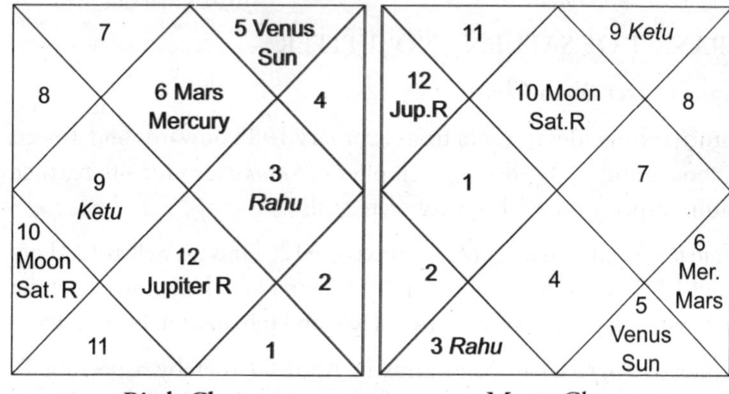

Birth Chart Moon Chart

For analyzing marriage of elder sister or brother, following factors should be analyzed :—

Treat 11th house as *Lagan* because 11th house represents elder brother or elder sister.

Analyze 11th Lord Moon

Analyze from Jupiter (*Karaka* for elder sister).

Make horoscope with 11th house as *Lagan.*

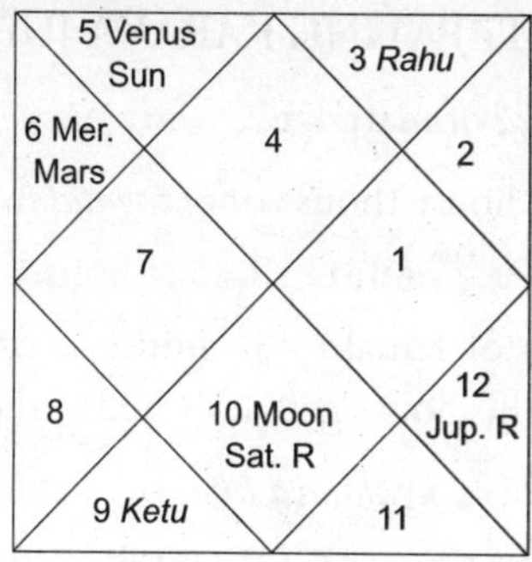

In case of females, 8th house is the *"mangalalaya" bhav* (family of life partner). In majority of females this house gets activated at the time of marriage.

Rahu is natural *Karaka* of marriage.

Rahu is in 12th house of private life and is aspecting 8th house of *mangalalaya bhava.*

Venus is natural *Karaka* of marriage.

Venus is in 2nd house of *kutumbh sthaan* with 2nd Lord Sun of *kutumbh sthaan.*

Venus is aspecting 8th house of *mangalayay bhava.*

Jupiter is the *karaka* of husband for females.

Jupiter being retrograde aspects and activates 12th house of private life.

Jupiter being retrograde aspects and activates 2nd house of family.

Jupiter being retrograde aspects and activates 8th house of *mangalalaya.*

Jupiter being direct aspect activates 12th Lord Mercury.

Jupiter by direct aspect activates 5th Lord Mars of romance and love.

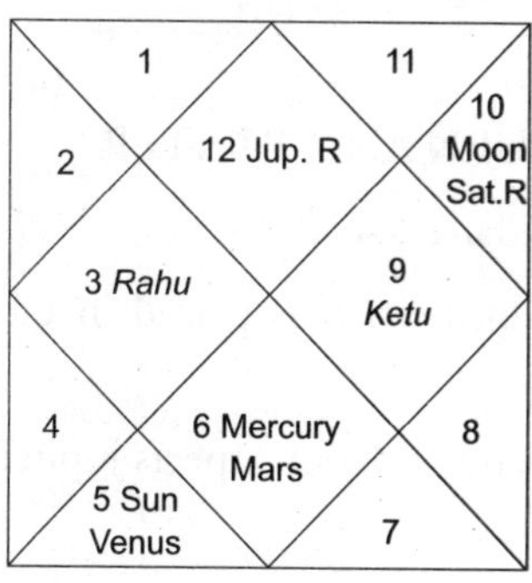

HOROSCOPE BY TREATING KARAKA JUPITER AS LAGNA

Rahu is natural *karaka* of marriage.

Rahu is activating 8th house (house of *mangalalaya*) by 5th aspect, 12th house of private life by 9th aspect.

(In case of marriage of females, 8th house is *mangalayay bhav*. In majority of females, this house gets activated at the time of marriage.)

Venus is the 8th Lord (*mangalalaya bhav*).

Venus is aspecting 12th house of private life.

Jupiter is the *Karaka* of husband for females.

Jupiter being retrograde activates 12th house of private life.

Jupiter aspect over 2nd Lord Mars activates 2nd house of family.

Jupiter being retrograde aspects and activates 8th house of *mangalalaya*.

Jupiter activates 7th house and 7th Lord Mercury (7th house is house of life partner).

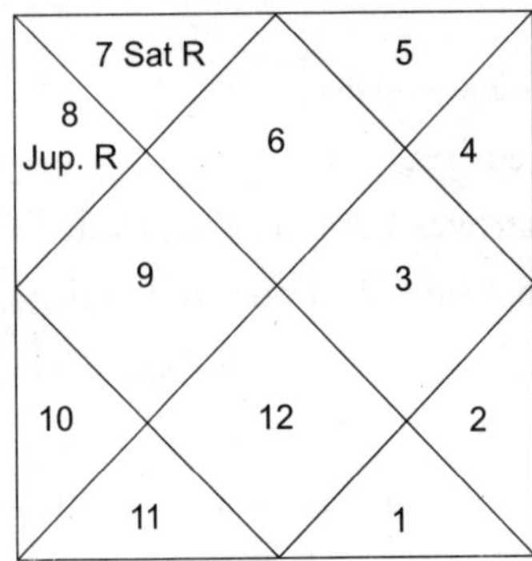

Transit

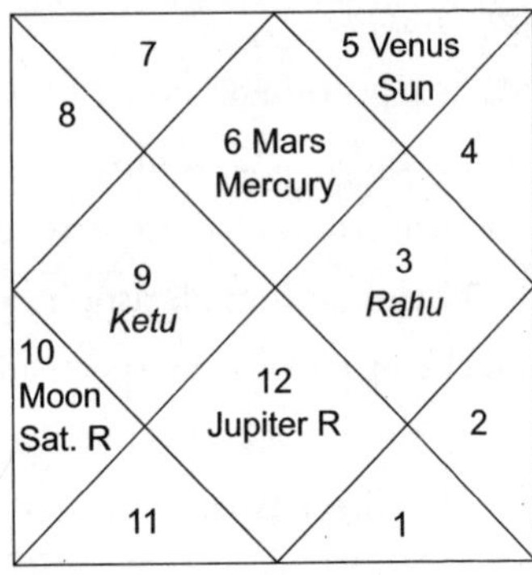

Birth Chart

TRANSIT OF SATURN AND JUPITER

Transit Over Birth Chart :—

Saturn in transit in birth chart is placed in Libra and aspects 11th house (house of elder sister).

Saturn in transit by retrogradation aspects Jupiter the *Karaka* of elder sister.

Jupiter in transit in Scorpio aspects 11th house of elder sister.

Jupiter in transit in Scorpio aspects Jupiter (*Karaka* for elder sister).

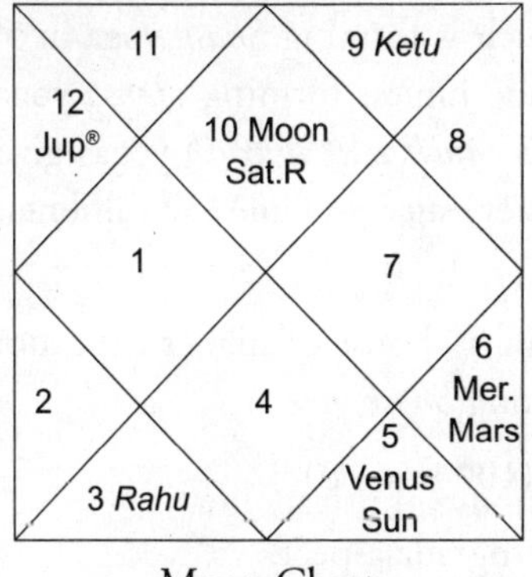

Moon Chart

11
9
8
Jup R
12
10 Moon
1
7
Sat R
2
4
6
3
5

Transit

Transit from Moon chart: —

Saturn in transit by retrogradation associates with 11th house and 11th Lord Mars (Lord of 11th house of elder sister in Moon *kundli*).

Jupiter is transiting over 11th house of Moon *kundli*.

Jupiter in transit in Scorpio aspects Jupiter (*Karaka* for elder sister) from 11th house of elder sister.

PASSED ENGINEERING IN APRIL 1986 :—

Dasha of *Rahu*/Moon/Jupiter

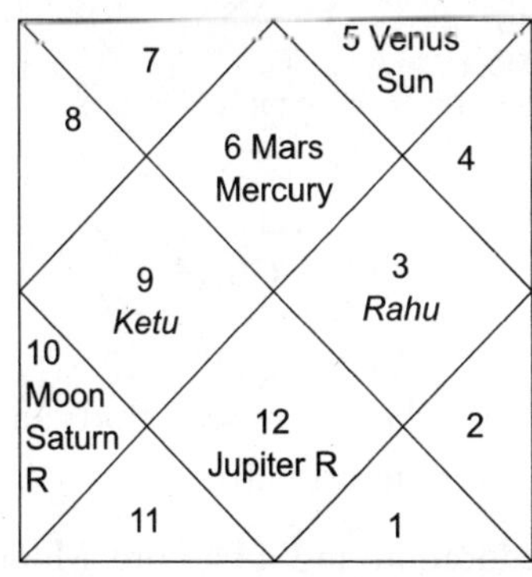

Birth Chart

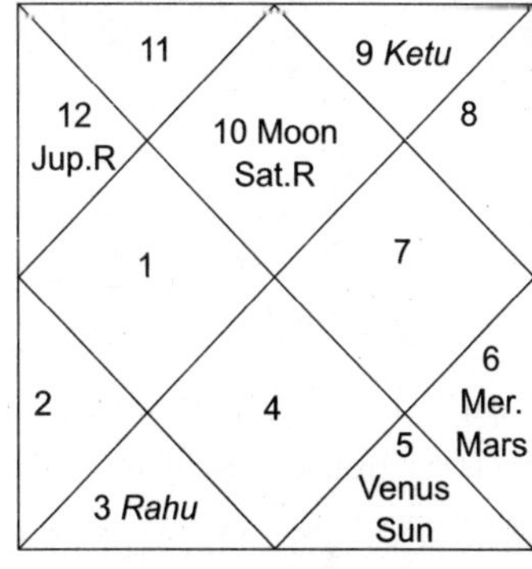

Moon Chart

Rahu is placed in 10th house in Gemini sign whose Lord Mercury is exalted and placed in *Lagan*. *Rahu*'s dispositer Mercury is forming *Bhadra* yoga which gives very good education, knowledge etc. *Rahu* is aspected by retrograde Saturn which is forming *Shash* yoga in 5th house. *Rahu* is aspected by retrograde Jupiter forming *Hansa* yoga. The association of *Rahu* with three *panch mahapurush* yogas gives extra ordinary powers to *Rahu* to achieve success, fame and fulfilment of efforts.

Moon is 11th Lord of gains placed in 5th house of higher education with 5th Lord Saturn (Saturn is forming *Shash* yoga.)

Jupiter is Lord of 7th house of fame (10th from 10th).

Jupiter is aspecting 10th house by retrograde aspect.

Jupiter is aspecting 10th Lord Mercury (*karaka* for education).

The simultaneous activation of 5th house and 10th gives professional education. Activation of 11th house gives gains from higher studies.

TRANSIT OF SATURN AND JUPITER

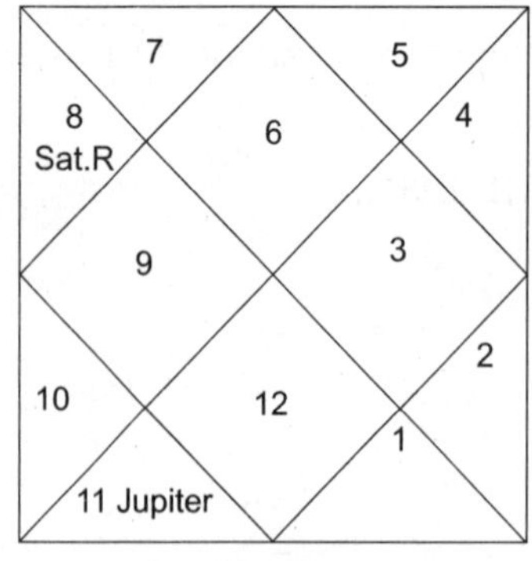

Transit

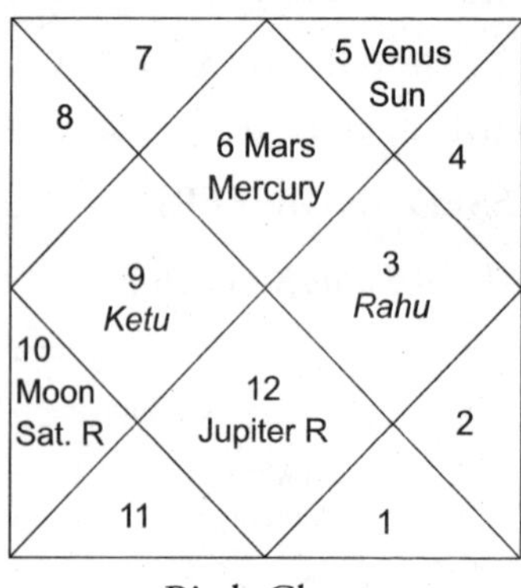

Birth Chart

Transit from birth chart : —

Saturn in transit is placed in Scorpio the 3rd house of self-efforts and aspects 5th house as well as 5th Lord Saturn in birth chart.

Saturn aspects 5th house of higher education and 11th Lord Moon (Lord of gains) by 3rd aspect from 3rd house of self-efforts in birth chart.

Jupiter in transit is placed in Aquarius in 6th house of competition and aspects 10th house of profession and Jupiter aspects Venus (Lord 9th house of higher education.)

Jupiter in transit is placed in Aquarius in retrogradation in 6th house of competition and aspects 9th house of higher education.

Jupiter in transit is placed in Aquarius in retrogradation in 6th house of competition and aspects 10th Lord Mercury (Lord of profession) and 9th Lord Venus (Lord of higher education and profession) in birth chart.

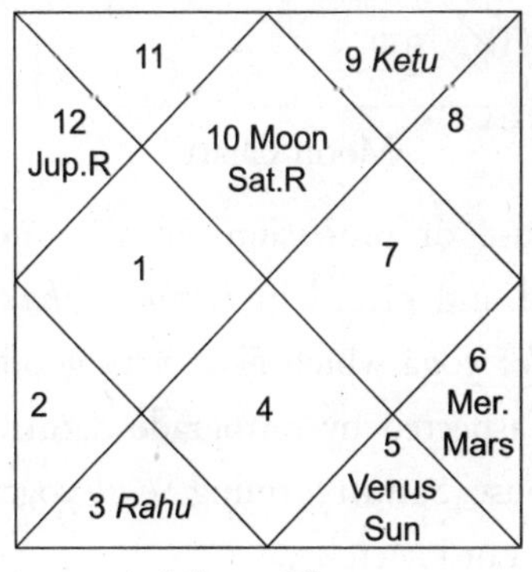

Moon Chart

11
Jupiter
9
12
10 Moon
8 Sat. R
1
7
2
4
6
3
5

Transit

Transit Over Moon Chart :—

Saturn in transit is placed in Scorpio the 11th house of gains and aspects *Lagan* as well as *Lagan* Lord Saturn in Moon *kundli.*

Saturn aspects 5th house of higher education and 5th Lord Venus also by 10th aspect from 11th house of gains.

Jupiter in transit is placed in Aquarius in 2nd house and aspects 6th house of competition and 5th Lord Venus of higher education.

Jupiter in transit is placed in Aquarius in 2nd house and aspects 10th house of profession and 10th Lord Venus (Lord of higher education and profession) in Moon *kundli.*

Simultaneous activation of fifth, sixth, tenth and eleventh houses by *dasha* and double transit of Saturn and Jupiter gives success in higher education.

JOB IN JULY, 1986 :—

Dasha of *Rahu*/Moon/Saturn

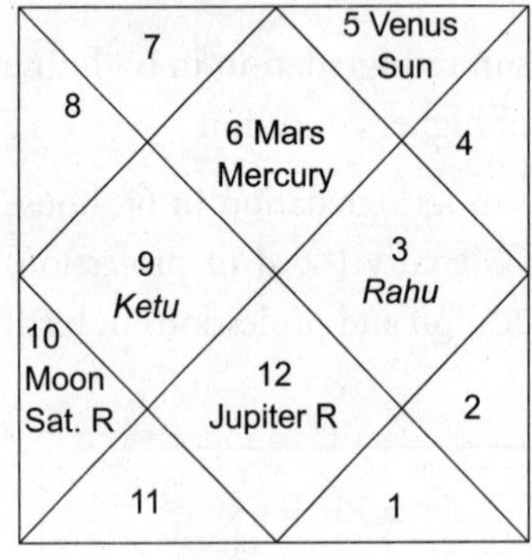

Birth Chart

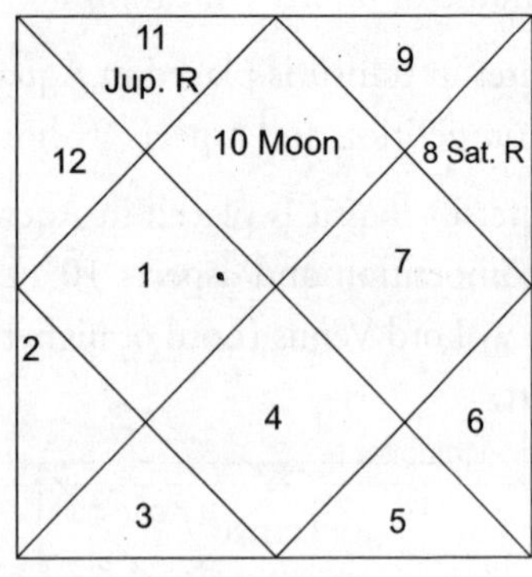

Moon Chart

Rahu is placed in 10th house (house of profession) in Gemini sign whose Lord Mercury is exalted and placed in *Lagan*. *Rahu's* dispositer Mercury is forming *Bhadra* yoga which gives very good education, knowledge etc. *Rahu* is aspected by retrograde Saturn which is forming *Shash* yoga in 5th house. Saturn forming *Shash* yoga is aspecting both 10th house and 10th Lord Mercury.

Rahu is aspected by retrograde Jupiter forming *Hansa* yoga.

The association of *Rahu* with three *panch mahapurush* yogas gives extra ordinary powers to *Rahu* to achieve success, fame and fulfilment of efforts.

Moon is 11th Lord of gains placed in 5th house of higher education with 5th Lord Saturn (Saturn is forming *Shash* yoga.) Saturn is placed in 5th house with Moon who is 11th Lord of gains.

Saturn by retrograde aspect is aspecting 10th house and 10th Lord Mercury.

Saturn is also aspecting 11th Lord Mars from Moon *Lagan*. Saturn is also aspecting 7th house of fame (being 10th from 10th house).

TRANSIT OF SATURN AND JUPITER

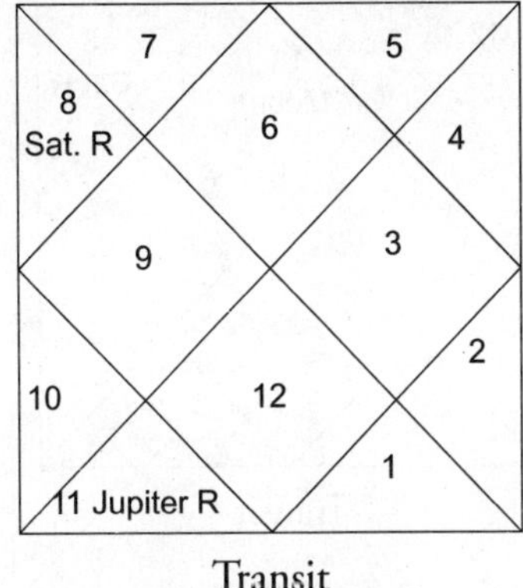

Transit

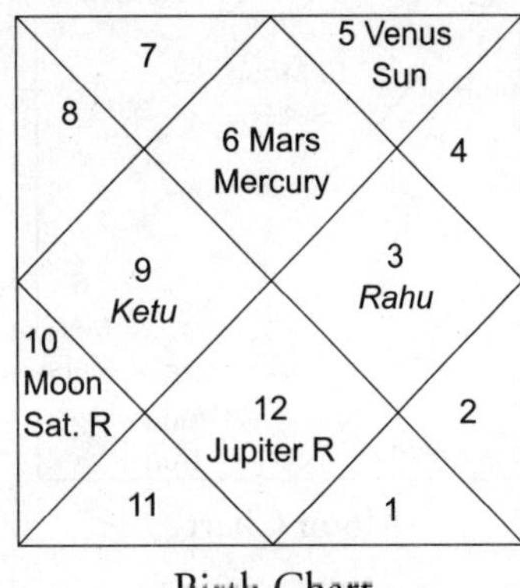

Birth Chart

Transit Over Birth Chart :—

Saturn in transit is placed in Scorpio the 3rd house of self-efforts and aspects 5th house as well as 5th Lord Saturn in birth chart.

Saturn aspects 5th house of higher education and 11th Lord Moon (Lord of gains) by 3rd aspect from 3rd house of self-efforts in birth chart.

Saturn by retrogradation aspects 11th house of gains.

Saturn by retrogradation activates 2nd house and 2nd Lord Venus (house and Lord of money).

Jupiter in transit is placed in Aquarius in 6th house of competition and aspects 10th house of profession and Venus (Lord of 2nd house of money and 9th Lord of fortune).

Jupiter in transit is placed in Aquarius in retrogradation in 6th house of competition and aspects 9th house of higher education.

Jupiter in transit is placed in Aquarius in retrogradation in 6th house of competition and aspects 10th Lord Mercury (Lord of profession) and 9th Lord Venus (Lord of higher education and profession) in birth chart.

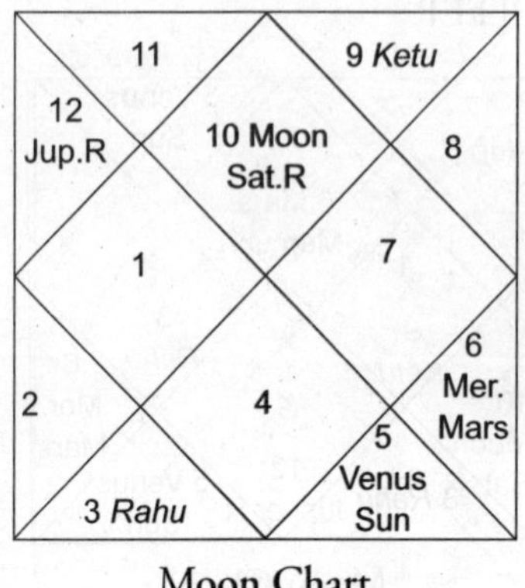

Moon Chart

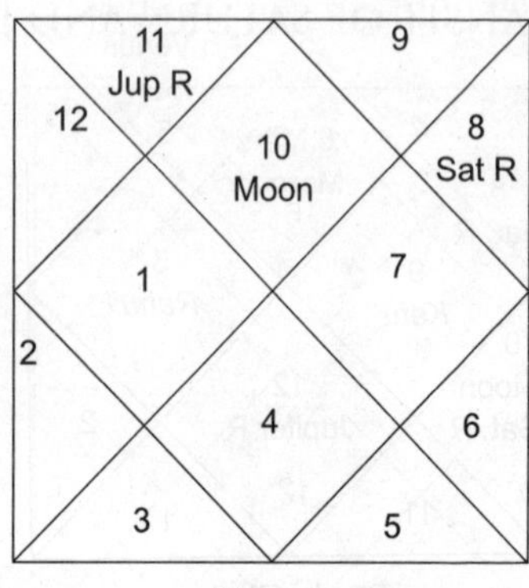

Transit

Transit Over Moon Chart :—

Saturn in transit is placed in Scorpio the 11th house of gains and aspects *Lagan* as well as *Lagan* Lord Saturn in Moon *kundli*.

Saturn aspects 5th house of higher education and 5th Lord Venus also by 10th aspect from 11th house of gains.

Jupiter in transit is placed in Aquarius in 2nd house and aspects 6th house of competition and 5th Lord Venus of higher education.

Jupiter in transit is placed in Aquarius in 2nd house and aspects 10th house of profession and 10th Lord Venus (Lord of higher education and profession) in Moon *kundli*.

Simultaneous activation of second house (money house), sixth (house of competition), tenth (house of profession) and eleventh house (house of gains gave him job).

FATHER EXPIRED IN CAR ACCIDENT IN AUGUST 1986 :—

Dasha of *Rahu*/Moon/Saturn

Here we see an incidence of getting gains of a job on one side and unfortunate incidence of death of father on the other side. For analyzing death of father from one's horoscope, following points are to be noted. Analyze from 9th house, 9th Lord and *Karaka* Sun.

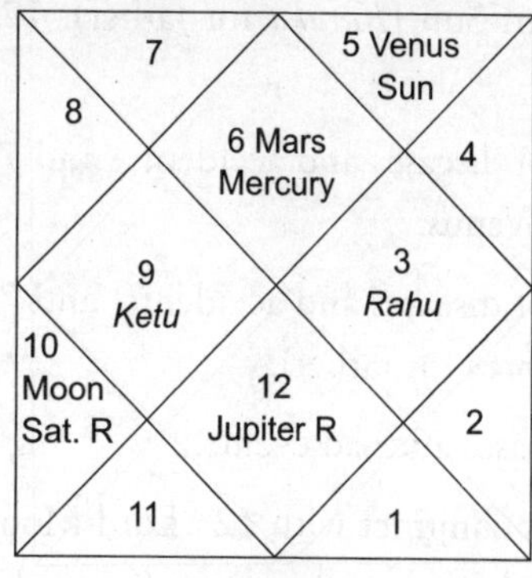

Birth Chart

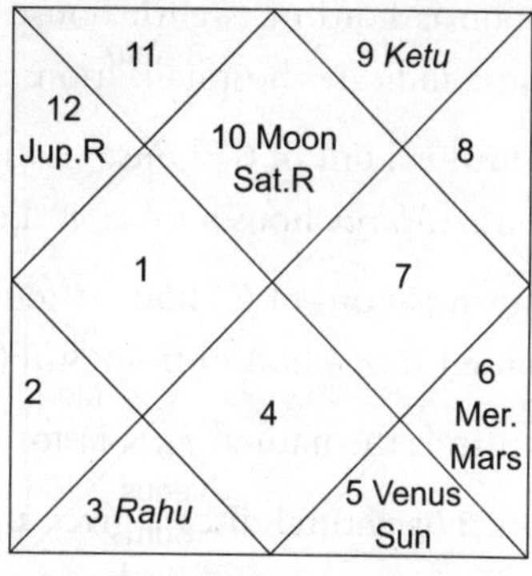

Moon Chart

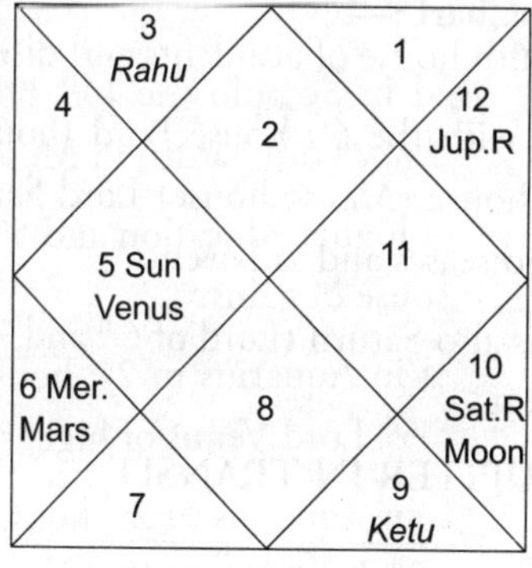

9th House As *Lagan*

Rahu is placed in 2nd house (*Marak bhav*) from 9th house and aspecting 6th house of accidents from ninth. *Rahu* is also aspecting 8th house of suddenness and death by 7th aspect.

Rahu is placed in 11th house from 9th Lord Venus. 11th house is bad for health as it is 6th from 6th house.

Rahu is placed in 11th house from Sun (*Karaka* for father). 11th house bad for health as it is 6th from 6th house.

Rahu is aspecting 7th house (*Marak bhav*) from Sun as well as Venus (9th Lord).

Moon is Lord of twelfth house from 9th Lord Venus. 12th house indicates hospitalisation.

Moon is Lord of twelfth house from Sun (*Karaka* for father). 12th house indicates hospitalization.

Saturn is Lord of 6th house (house of diseases and accidents) and 7th house (*Marak* house) from 9th Lord Venus.

Saturn is Lord of 6th house (house of diseases and accidents) and 7th house (*Marak* house) from Sun (*Karaka* for father).

Saturn is the natural *Karaka* for diseases and sad events.

Saturn is natural disease giver and is conjunct with 12th Lord Moon from Venus (Lord of 9th house of father) as well as Sun (*Karaka* for father).

Moon is placed in 6th house of accidents and diseases.

Moon is conjunct with the 6th house Lord (house of diseases and accidents) and 7th house (*Marak* house) Lord Saturn. Saturn is the natural *Karaka* for diseases and sad events.

Moon's dispositer is also Saturn (Lord of 6th and 7th houses) and it is conjunct with Moon.

SATURN AND JUPITER IN TRANSIT

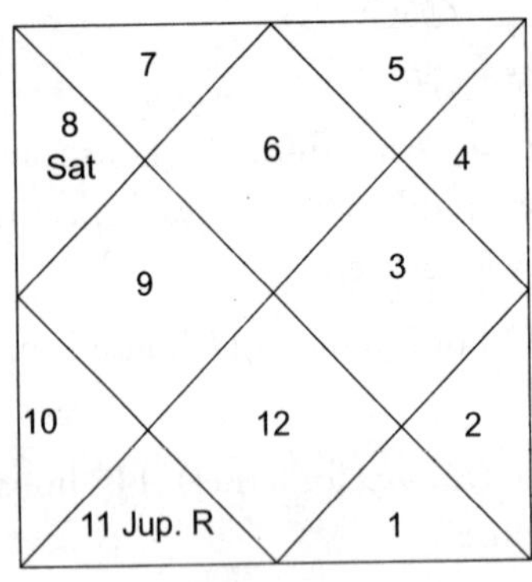

Transit

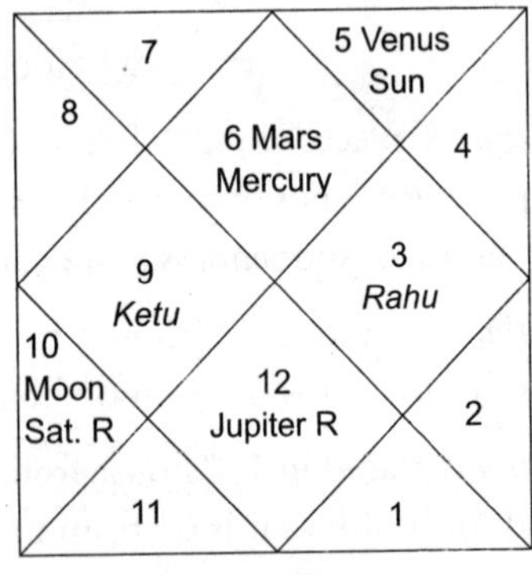

Birth Chart

Transit Over Birth Chart:—

Saturn in transit is placed in Scorpio, 7th house (*Marak*) from 9th house of father.

Saturn aspects 9th house, 9th Lord Venus and *Karaka* for father (Sun).

Saturn is *Badhakpati* for father house (Taurus) 9th Lord from fixed *Lagan* is *Badhakpati*. So Saturn as *Badhakpati* for father is transiting through the *Marak bhava* for father and is aspecting Taurus (*Lagan* for father), Venus (Lord of Taurus) and Sun (*Karaka* for father).

Jupiter in transit is placed in Aquarius and aspects 9th Lord Venus and Sun (*Karaka* for father).

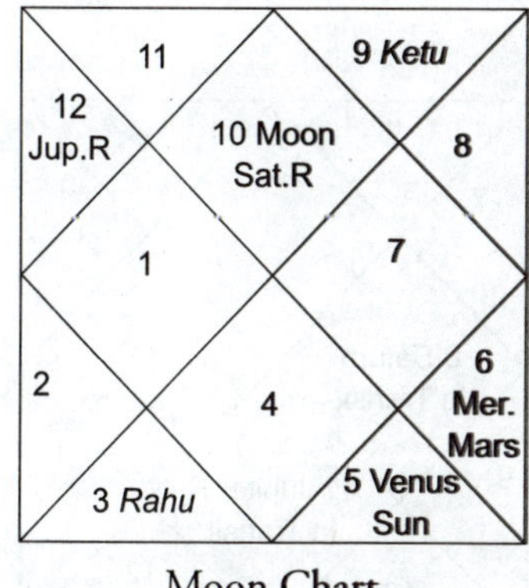

Moon Chart

Transit

Transit Over Moon Chart :—

Saturn in Scorpio aspects Sun *Karaka* for father. Jupiter in Aquarius aspects Sun, *Karaka* for father.

Saturn in Scorpio aspects 12th house and 12th Lord Sun from 9th house of father). Jupiter in Aquarius aspects Sun (12th house and 12th Lord Sun from 9th house of father).

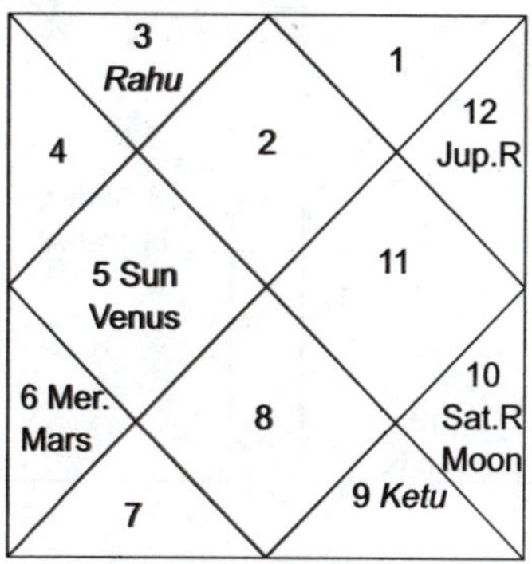

9th HOUSE AS LAGNA

Moon is 12th Lord from Sun *Lagan*. Moon is in 6th house of accidents with 6th Lord Saturn. Moon is aspecting 12th from 6th house. Moon is conjunct with *Badhakpati* Saturn in *Badhak* house. Taurus being a fixed sign, 9th Lord is *Badhakpati* for it.

Saturn is the *Badhakpati* for 9th house of father. (For moveable *lagnas* 11th Lord is *Badhakpati*. For fixed *lagnas* 9th Lord is *Badhakpati*. For dual *lagnas* 7th Lord is *Badhakpati*).

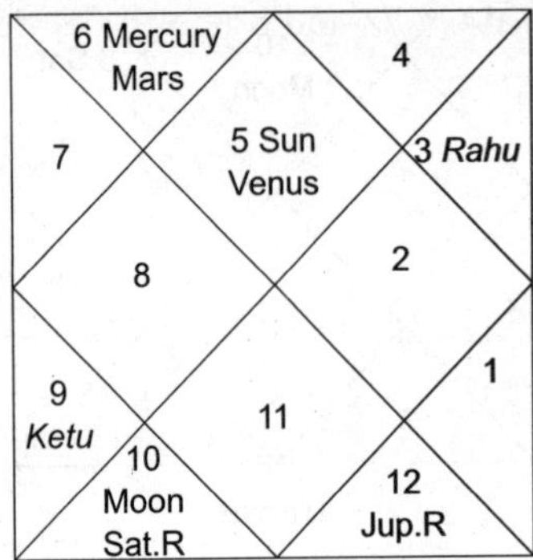

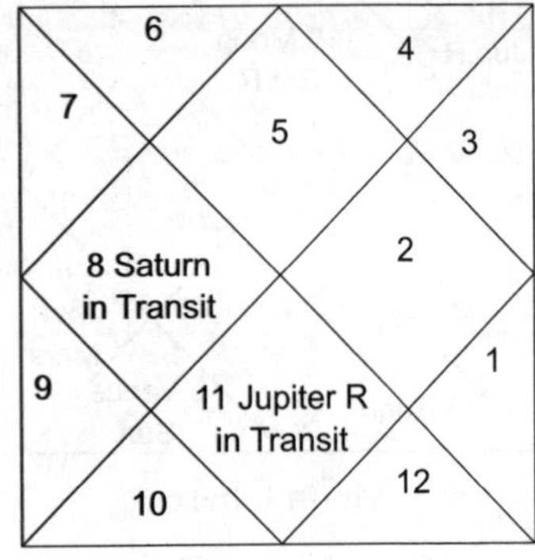

Saturn is conjunct with 12th Lord Moon from *Karaka* Sun as well as 9th Lord Venus of birth chart.

From 9th Lord Venus of birth chart and ***karaka*** Sun, Saturn is Lord of 6th house of accident as well as ***markesh*** as 7th Lord.

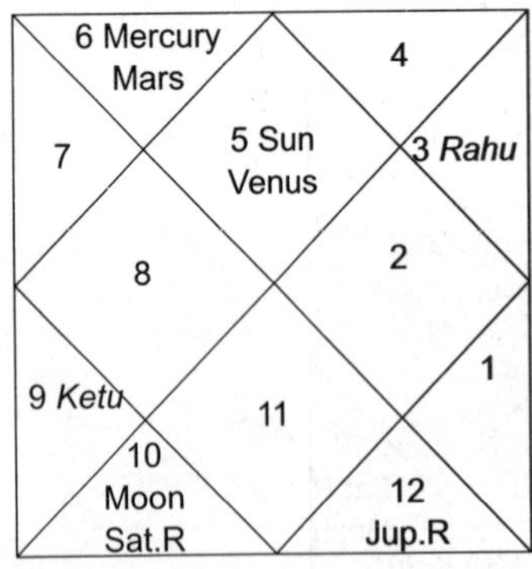

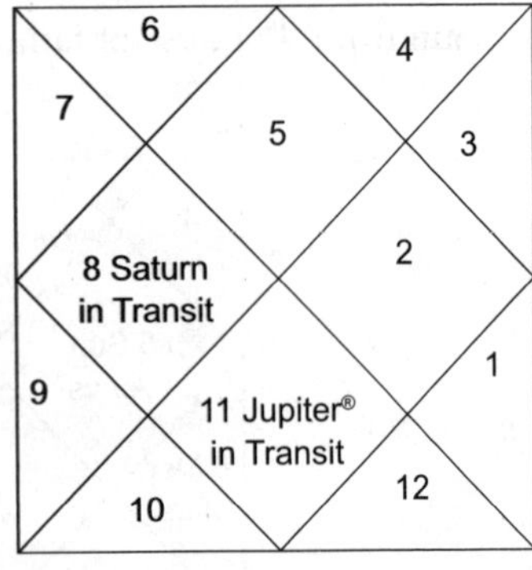

HOROSCOPE BY TREATING 9TH LORD VENUS AND *KARAKA* SUN AS *LAGNA*

TRANSIT OF SATURN AND JUPITER

Saturn in transit is placed in Scorpio and is aspecting *Lagan* as well as *Karaka* Sun. Saturn is Lord of 6th house of accidents as well as *markesh* as 7th Lord.

Jupiter in transit is placed in Aquarius and is aspecting *Lagan* as well as *Karaka* Sun. Jupiter is Lord of 8th house of sudden accidents and death. The double transit has activated 6th, 7th and 8th houses as well as *Lagan*.

MARRIAGE IN OCTOBER 1987 :—

DASHA of *RAHU*/MARS/SATURN.

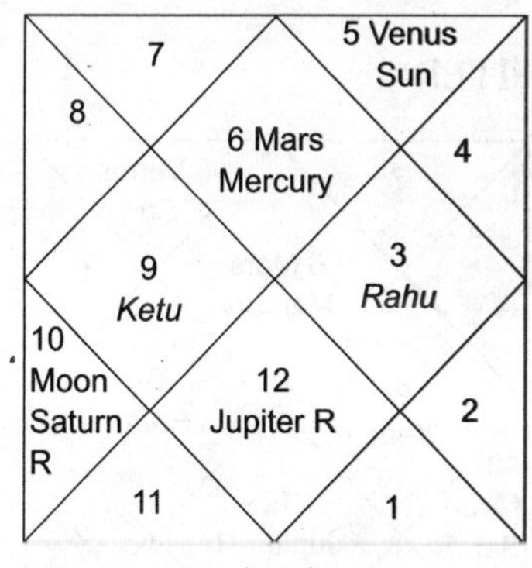

Birth Chart

11
9
Ketu
12
Jup.R
10 Moon
Sat.R
8
1
7
2
4
6
Mer.
Mars
3 Rahu
5 Ven
Sun

Moon Chart

Rahu is natural *Karaka* of marriage.

Rahu is aspecting 2nd house (family). *Rahu* is aspecting 12th (private life) house from Moon.

Rahu is aspecting 5th (romance and love) and 7th (life partner) houses from marriage *Karaka* Venus.

Mars is aspecting 7th house and seventh Lord Jupiter. It is posited in *Lagan* with *Lagan* Lord Mercury.

Saturn is posited in 5th house of romance and aspecting 7th house of marriage.

Saturn is posited in 5th house of romance and aspecting 7th Lord Jupiter.

Saturn is posited in 5th house of romance and aspecting Jupiter, *Karaka* of marriage.

Saturn is posited in 5th house of romance and conjunct with Moon, Lord of gains.

Saturn is posited in 5th house of romance and love and aspects 2nd house of family.

Saturn is aspecting 7th house of marriage in Moon horoscope.

Saturn is conjunct with 7th Lord Moon in Moon horoscope.

Saturn being retrograde, activates 2nd house and 12th house from Moon *Lagan*.

TRANSIT OF SATURN AND JUPITER

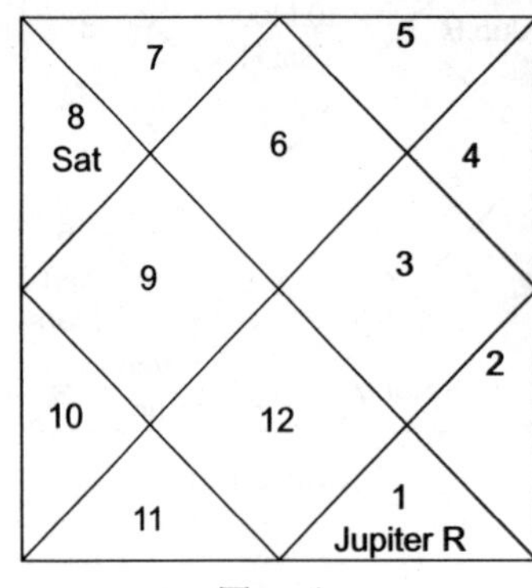

Transit

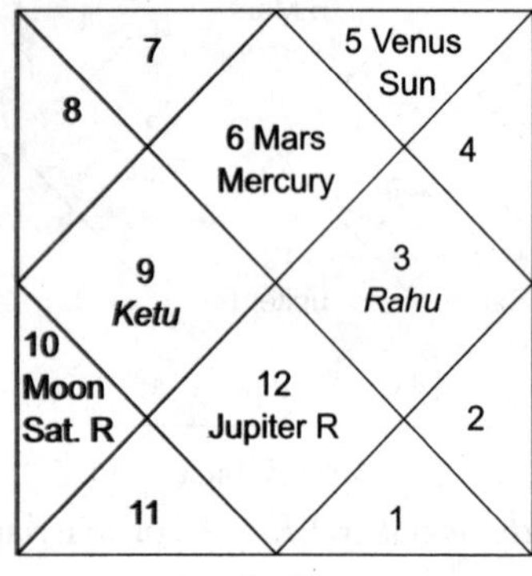

Birth Chart

Transit Over Birth Chart :—

Saturn in transit is placed in Scorpio the 3rd house and aspects 5th house as well as 5th Lord Saturn (house of love and romance) in birth chart.

Saturn aspects 5th house of love affair and 11th Lord Moon (Lord of gains) by 3rd aspect from 3rd house.

Saturn by retrogradation aspects 11th house of gains.

Saturn by retrogradation activates 2nd house and 2nd Lord Venus (house and Lord of family.)

Jupiter in transit is placed in Aries in retrogradation in 8th house and aspects Venus (Lord of 2nd house of family and 9th Lord of fortune.)

Jupiter in transit is placed in Aries in retrogradation in 8th house of family of partner and aspects 12th house of secret life/private life.

Jupiter in transit is placed in Aries in retrogradation in 8th house of family of partner and aspects Venus, *Karaka* of wife and glamour placed in 12th house of secret life/private life.

Jupiter in transit is placed in Aries in retrogradation in 8th house of family of partner and activates 7th house of partner and 7th Lord Jupiter.

Jupiter in transit is placed in Aries in retrogradation in 8th house of family of partner and activates 1st house and 1st Lord Mercury.

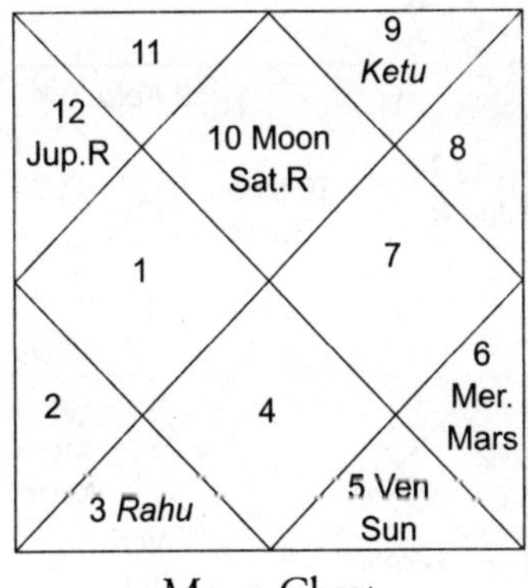

Moon Chart

11
9
12
10 Moon
8 Sat
1 Jup R
7
2
4
6
3
5

Transit

Transit Over Moon Chart :—

Saturn in transit is placed in Scorpio in the 11th house of gains and aspects *Lagan* as well as *Lagan* Lord Saturn in Moon *kundli.*

Saturn in transit is placed in Scorpio in the 11th house of gains and aspects 7th Lord Moon (Lord of house of life partner.)

Saturn aspects 5th house of romance and love by 7th aspect from 11th house of gains.

Saturn in transit is placed in Scorpio the 11th house of gains and aspects Venus (*Karaka* of wife).

Jupiter in transit is placed in Aries in retrogradation in 4th house and aspects 7th house of partner.

Jupiter aspects Venus (*karaka* of wife) by 5th aspect.

Jupiter in transit is placed in Aries in retrogradation in 4th house and is activating 12th Lord Jupiter of private life.

BOUGHT CAR IN MAY 1988 :—

For buying a vehicle, activation of 4th house/4th Lord/*karaka* for vehicles Venus should get activated by *dasha* and transit.

For buying a vehicle, activation of 4th house/4th Lord from Moon horoscope/*karaka* for vehicles Venus should get activated by *dasha* and transit.

DASHA of JUPITER/JUPITER/JUPITER

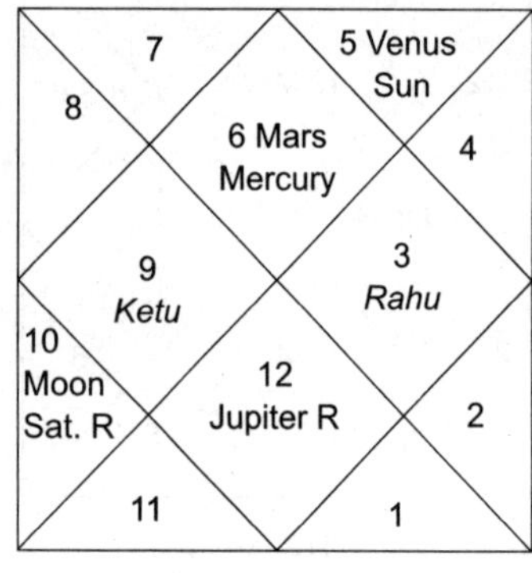

Birth Chart

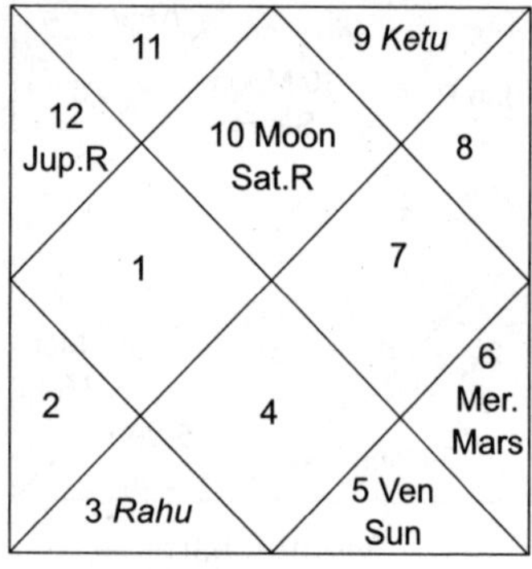

Moon Chart

Jupiter is Lord of 4th house of vehicles. 4th house is aspected by 8th Lord Mars.

4th house is aspected by retrograde aspect of Saturn.

Saturn is also aspecting 4th Lord Jupiter.

Jupiter is aspecting 4th Lord Mars in Moon horoscope.

Jupiter by retrogradation is aspecting Venus, *karaka* for vehicles.

TRANSIT OF SATURN AND JUPITER

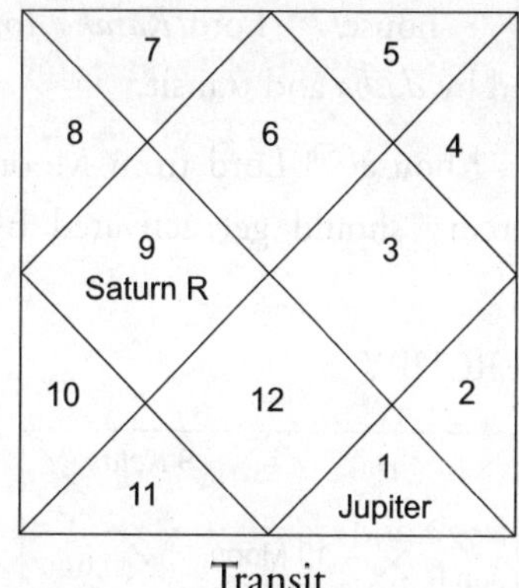

Transit

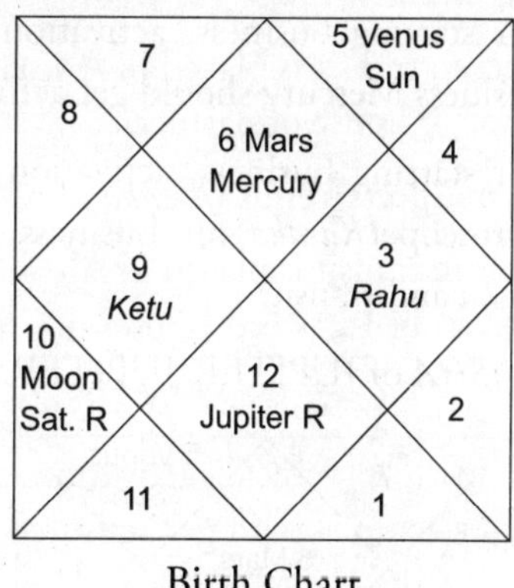

Birth Chart

Transit Over Birth Chart :—

Saturn in transit is placed in Sagittarius (4th house of vehicles).

Jupiter in transit is placed in Aries and aspects 4th house of vehicles.

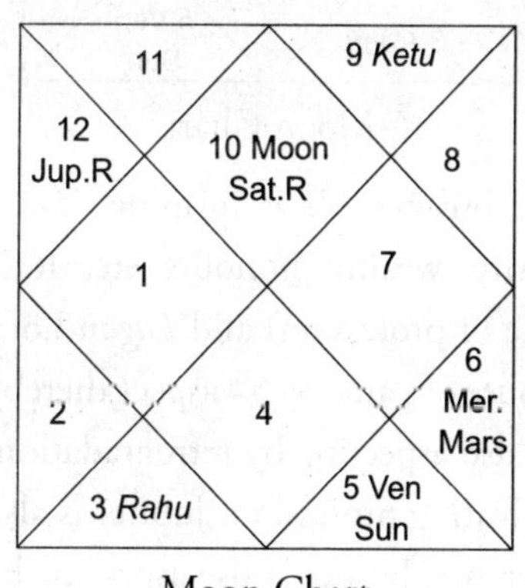

Moon Chart

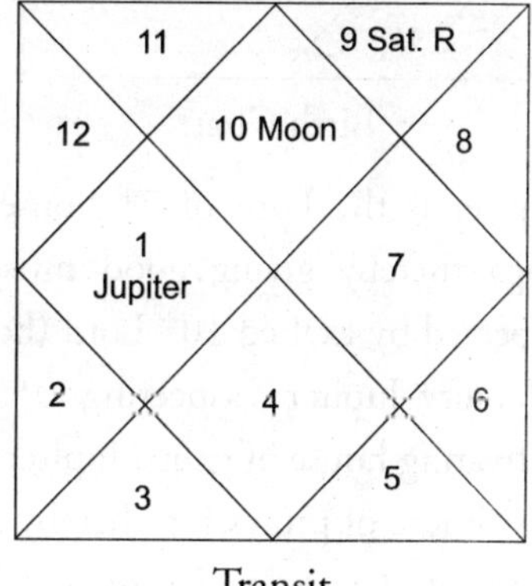

Transit

Transit Over Moon Chart :—

Saturn in transit is placed in Sagittarius and is aspecting 4th Lord Mars by 10th aspect.

Jupiter in transit is placed in Aries and is placed in 4th house of vehicles.

STARTS OWN BUSINESS IN FEBRUARY 89 :—

For starting business, activation of 7th house/7th Lord/*Karaka* for business Mercury should get activated by *dasha* and transit.

For starting business, activation of 7th house/7th Lord from Moon horoscope/*Karaka* for business Mercury should get activated by *dasha* and transit.

DASHA of JUPITER/JUPITER/MERCURY

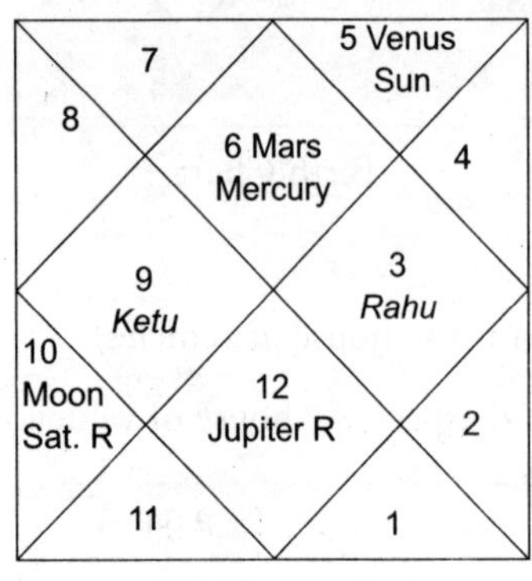

Birth Chart | Moon Chart

Jupiter is the Lord of 7th house of business. It is forming *Hansa* yoga thereby giving good prosperity, wealth, honours etc. It is aspected by exalted 10th Lord (house of profession) and *Lagan* Lord Mercury. Jupiter is aspecting 11th house of gains by 5th aspect thereby activating house of gains. Jupiter is also aspecting by retrogradation, 10th house of profession thereby activating profession. Jupiter is also aspecting *Lagan* and *Lagan* Lord Mercury. Jupiter is also aspecting by retrogradation second house of money as well as second house Lord of money, Venus. Mercury is also very strong forming *Bhadra* yoga.

Mercury is 10th Lord (house of profession) placed in *Lagan* in exalted state. It is aspecting 7th house (house of business) and seventh Lord Jupiter.

Simultaneous activation of *Lagan*, *Lagan* Lord, second house, second Lord, tenth house, tenth Lord, eleventh house, seventh house and seventh Lord gave him money, wealth, professional success during *dasha* of Jupiter.

TRANSIT OF SATURN AND JUPITER

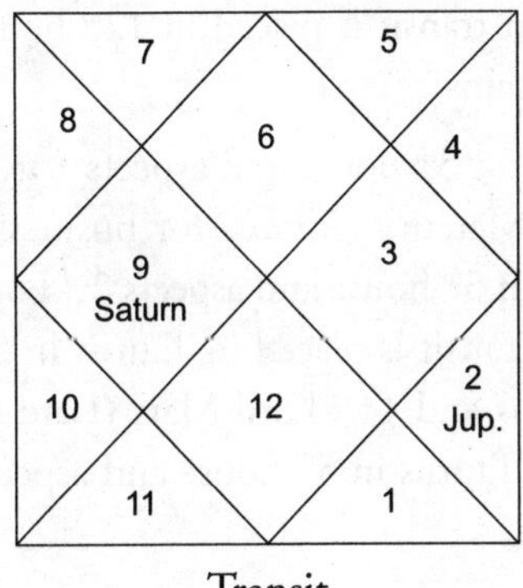

Transit

7
5 Venus Sun
8
6 Mars Mercury
4
9 *Ketu*
3 *Rahu*
10 Moon Sat. R
12 Jupiter R
2
11
1

Birth Chart

Transit Over Birth Chart :—

Saturn in transit is placed in Sagittarius and aspects 10th house and 10th Lord Mercury thereby activating profession. Saturn in transit is placed in Sagittarius and aspects 10th house and 10th Lord Mercury thereby activating business as Mercury is *Karaka* of business also.

Jupiter in transit is placed in Taurus in the house of fortune and aspects *Lagan* Lord and 10th Lord mercury. It aspects Mercury (*Karaka* for business).

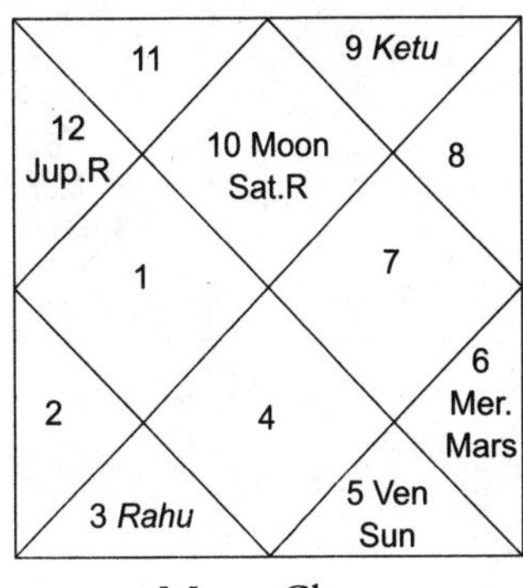

Moon Chart

11
9 Sat
12
10 Moon
8
1
7
6
2 Jupiter
4
3
5

Transit

Transit Over Moon chart :—

Saturn in transit is placed in 12th house and aspects 2nd house of money.

Saturn in transit is placed in 12th house and aspects 10th Lord . Saturn in transit is placed in 12th house and aspects 9th house and 9th Lord Mercury (Lord of fortune). Saturn in transit is placed in 12th house and aspects 11th Lord Mars (Lord of gains).

Jupiter in transit is placed in Taurus in 5th house and aspects *Lagan* and *Lagan* Lord Saturn. It aspects Mercury (*Karaka* for business). Jupiter in transit is placed in Taurus in 5th house and aspects 2nd Lord Saturn (Lord of money). Jupiter in transit is placed in Taurus in 5th house and aspects 11th house of gains and 11th Lord Mars (Lord of gains). Jupiter in transit is placed in Taurus in 5th house and aspects 7th Lord Moon (Lord of partnership).

So the houses of money (2nd, 5th, 9th), houses of profession and gains (10th, 11th) are getting activated along with 7th Lord of partnership thereby giving business partnership.

BIRTH OF DAUGHTER IN JULY, 1989 :—

DASHA OF JUPITER/JUPITER/VENUS

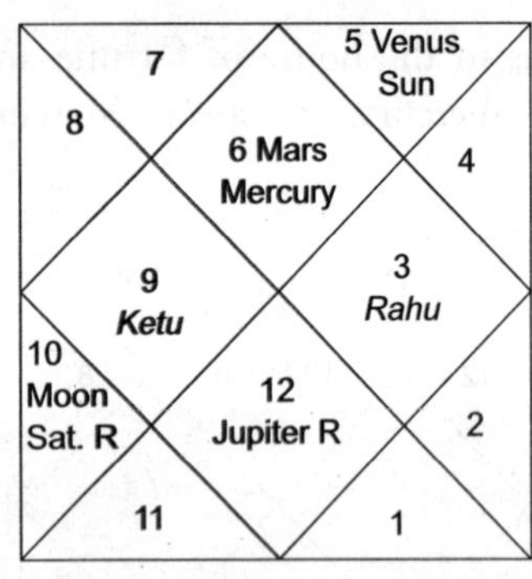

Birth Chart

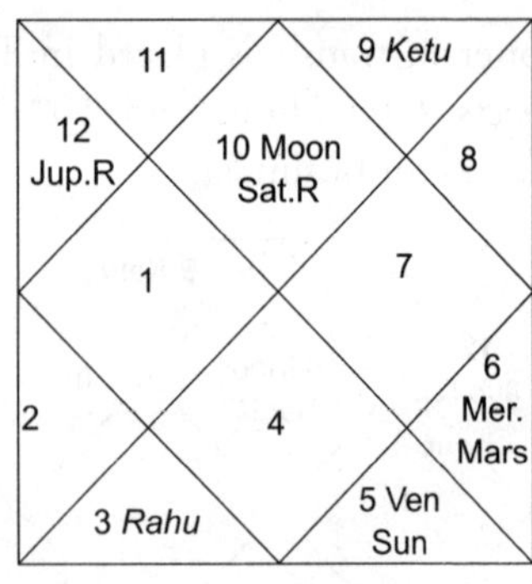

Moon Chart

Birth of a child takes place during the

— *dasha* of 5th Lord

— *dasha* of planets posited in 5th house

— *dasha* of planets aspecting 5th house

— *dasha* of planets aspecting 5th Lord

— *dasha* of planets having P.A.C. with *Karaka* Jupiter

— *dasha* of following planets from Moon

— *dasha* of 5th Lord from Moon

— *dasha* of planets posited in 5th house from Moon

— *dasha* of planets aspecting 5th house from Moon

— *dasha* of planets aspecting 5th Lord from Moon

— *dasha* of *putra karaka* Jupiter

Maha dasha of Jupiter can promise a child because it is natural *putra karaka* (child giver). It is aspected by 5th Lord Saturn from 5th house of progeny. It is conjunct with 11th Lord Moon (5th Lord from 7th house of partner). As per opinion of many astrologers, in case of males 9th house is taken for 1st child, 7th house for second child and 5th house for third child and so on. In this case of male horoscope, Jupiter is aspecting 9th Lord Venus by retrograde aspect.

Venus is 5th Lord from Moon and 9th Lord from *Lagan.*

Jupiter is aspecting Venus (5th Lord from Moon) by retrograde aspect.

Venus is 5th Lord from Moon *Lagan.* It is being aspected by *putra karaka* Jupiter.

So full activation of fifth and ninth (fifth from fifth) is there.

TRANSIT OF SATURN AND JUPITER

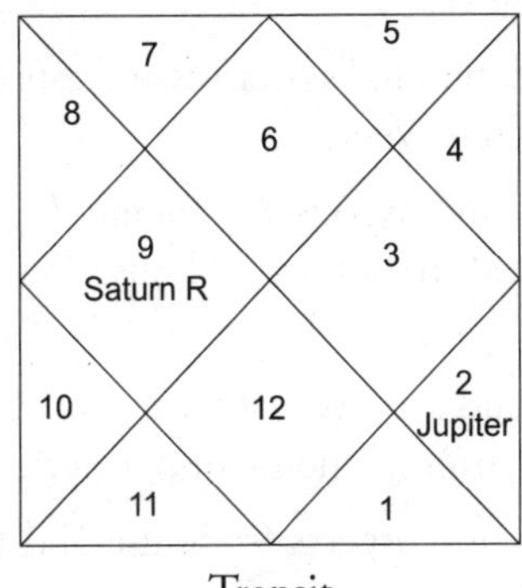

Transit

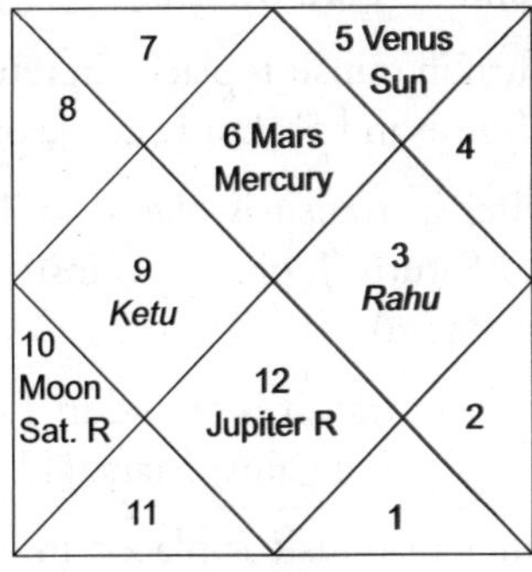

Birth Chart

Transit Over Birth Chart :—

Saturn in transit is placed in retrogradation in Sagittarius and aspects *Lagan* and *Lagan* Lord Mercury. Saturn in transit is placed in retrogradation in Sagittarius and aspects 5th house and 5th Lord (Lord of children)

Jupiter in transit was placed in Taurus during pregnancy and aspected *Lagan* and *Lagan* Lord Mercury. Jupiter in transit was placed in Taurus and aspected 5th house and 5th Lord (house of children) Saturn.

Jupiter in transit was placed in Taurus and aspected 11th Lord (Lord of gains) Moon. (11th is 5th from 7th house of partner).

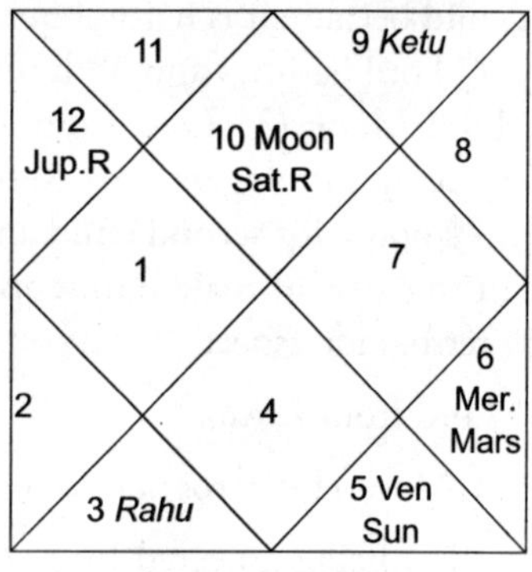

Moon Chart

11
9 Sat
12
10 Moon
8
1
7
2
Jup. R
4
6
3
5

Transit

Transit Over Moon chart :—

Saturn in transit is placed in retrogradation in Sagittarius and aspects 9th and 9th Lord Mercury.

Saturn in transit is placed in retrogradation in Sagittarius and aspects 5th house and 5th Lord (house of children) Venus.

Jupiter in transit is placed in Taurus and aspects *Lagan* and *Lagan* Lord Saturn. Jupiter in transit is placed in Taurus, 5th house (house of children).

Jupiter in transit is placed in Taurus and aspects 11th house and 11th Lord (Lord of gains) Mars. (11th is 5th from 7th house of partner).

Jupiter in transit is placed in Taurus and aspects 9th house and 9th Lord) Mercury (5th from 5th).

BIRTH OF SON IN1994 :—

DASHA OF JUPITER/MERCURY/SATURN

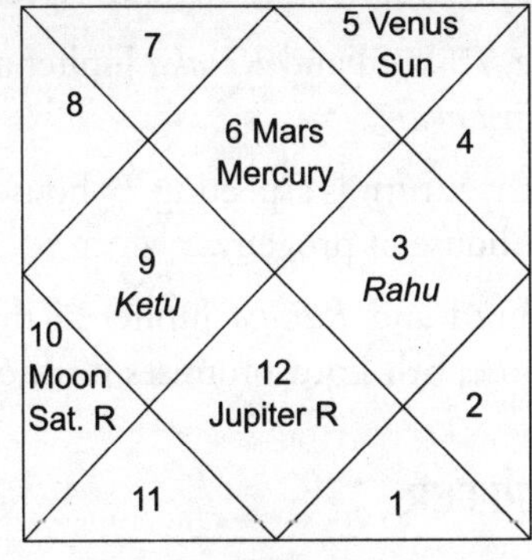

Birth Chart

Moon Chart

Birth of a child takes place during the

— *dasha* of 5th Lord

— *dasha* of planets posited in 5th house

— *dasha* of planets aspecting 5th house

— *dasha* of planets aspecting 5th Lord

— *dasha* of planets having P.A.C. with Jupiter

— *dasha* of following planets from Moon

— *dasha* of 5th Lord from Moon

— *dasha* of planets posited in 5th house from Moon

— *dasha* of planets aspecting 5th house from Moon

— *dasha* of planets aspecting 5th Lord from Moon

— *dasha* of *putra Karaka* Jupiter

Maha dasha of Jupiter can promise a child because it is natural *putra Karaka* (child giver). It is aspected by 5th Lord Saturn from 5th house of progeny. It is conjunct with 11th Lord Moon (5th Lord from 7th house of partner). As per opinion of many astrologers, in case of males 9th house is taken for 1st child, 7th house for second child and 5th house for third child and so on. In this case of male horoscope, Jupiter is placed in 7th house in own sign Pisces forming *Hansa* yoga.

Being second child activation of 7th house, 7th Lord and *Karaka* Jupiter are all getting activated at the same time in *dasha* of Jupiter.

Jupiter is aspecting Venus (5th Lord from Moon) by retrograde aspect.

Mercury is again activating 7th house, 7th Lord and *Karaka* Jupiter at the same time by seventh aspect from *Lagan*.

Saturn is Lord of 5th house of children. Saturn is aspecting 7th house, 7th Lord and *Karaka* Jupiter from 5th house of progeny.

So the activation of 7th house, 7th Lord and *Karaka* Jupiter at the same time with activation of 5th house, 5th Lord promises birth of second child.

TRANSIT OF SATURN AND JUPITER

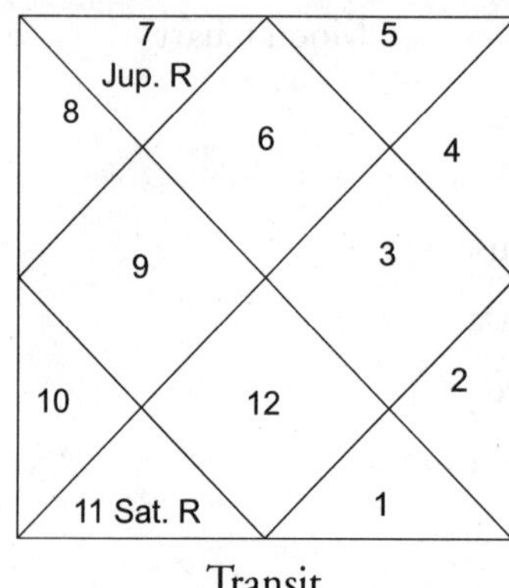

Transit

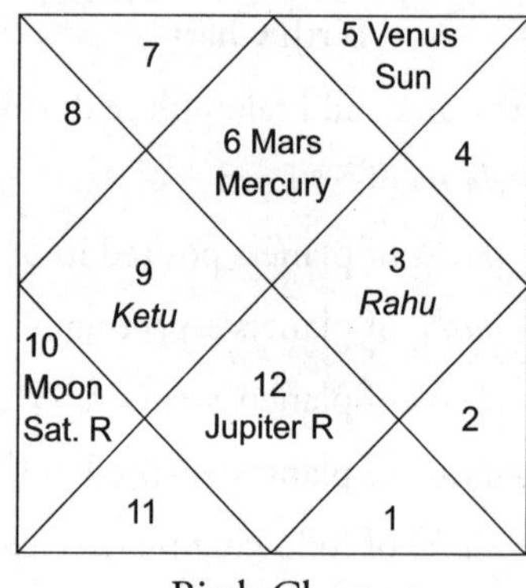

Birth Chart

Transit Over Birth Chart :—

Saturn in transit is placed in retrogradation in Aquarius and aspects 7th house and 7th Lord Jupiter (house and Lord of second child). Saturn in transit is placed in retrogradation in Aquarius and aspects Jupiter (*Karaka* of children).

Saturn in transit is placed in retrogradation in Aquarius and aspects 11th house of gains (11th house is 5th from 7th house of partner) and 11th Lord Moon by retrogradation.

Jupiter in transit was placed in retrogradation in Libra and aspected 7th house and 7th Lord Jupiter (house and Lord of second child).

Jupiter in transit was placed in retrogradation in Libra and aspects Jupiter (*Karaka* of children). Jupiter in transit was placed in retrogradation in Libra and aspects Moon,11th Lord of gains (11th house is 5th from 7th house of partner).Jupiter in transit was placed in retrogradation in Libra and aspected 5th house and 5th Lord Saturn (permanent house and Lord of children) in this horoscope.

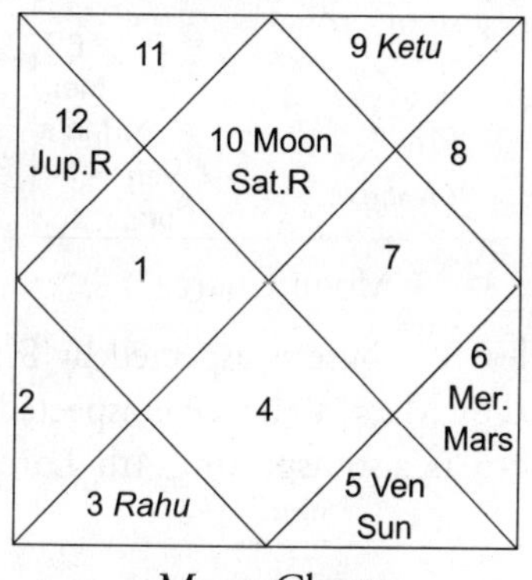

Moon Chart

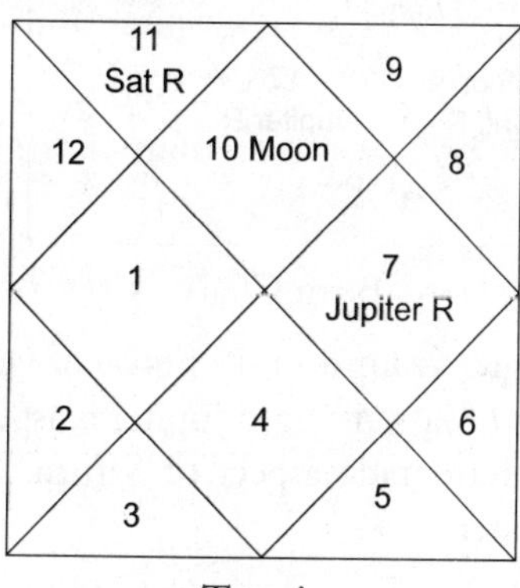

Transit

Transit Over Moon chart : —

Saturn in transit is placed in retrogradation in Aquarius and aspects 7th house and 7th Lord Moon (house and Lord of second child). Saturn in transit is placed in retrogradation in Aquarius and aspects Jupiter (*kara ka* of children).

Saturn in transit is placed in retrogradation in Aquarius and aspects 11th house of gains (11th house is 5th from 7th house of partner).

Jupiter in transit was placed in retrogradation in Libra and aspected 7th house and 7th Lord Moon (house and Lord of second child). Jupiter in transit was placed in retrogradation in Libra and aspected Jupiter (*karaka* of children). Jupiter in transit was placed in retrogradation in Libra and aspected 11th Lord of gains (11th house is 5th from 7th house of partner) Mars. Jupiter in transit was placed in retrogradation in Libra and aspected 5th house (permanent house of children).

BUYS A NEW CAR IN MARCH 1995 : —

DASHA OF JUPITER/MERCURY/SATURN

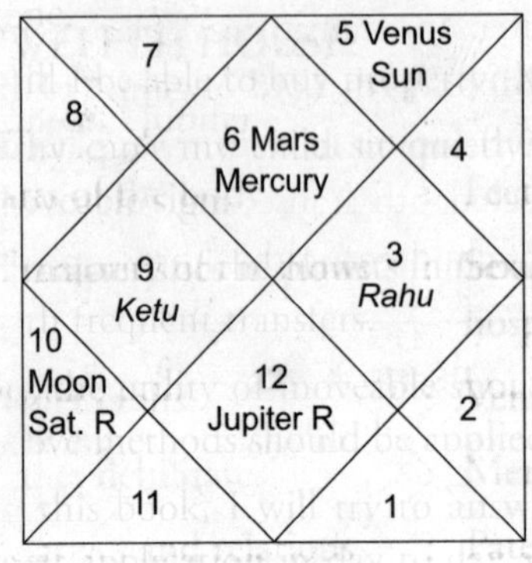

11
9 *Ketu*
12
Jup.R
10 Moon
Sat.R
8
1
7
6
Mer.
Mars
2
4
3 *Rahu*
5 Ven
Sun

Birth Chart Moon Chart

Jupiter is Lord of 4th house of vehicles. 4th house is aspected by 8th Lord Mars. 4th Lord Jupiter is aspected by Mars. 4th house is aspected by retrograde aspect of Saturn. Saturn is also aspecting 4th Lord Jupiter.

Mercury is aspecting 4th Lord Jupiter.

Saturn is aspecting 4th house and 4th Lord Jupiter.

All the three planets of above *dasha* are forming *panch mahapurush* yoga providing general prosperity with availability of all the facilities.

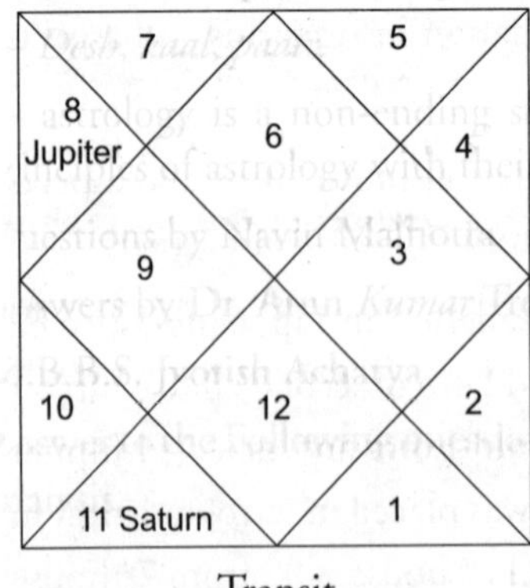

Transit

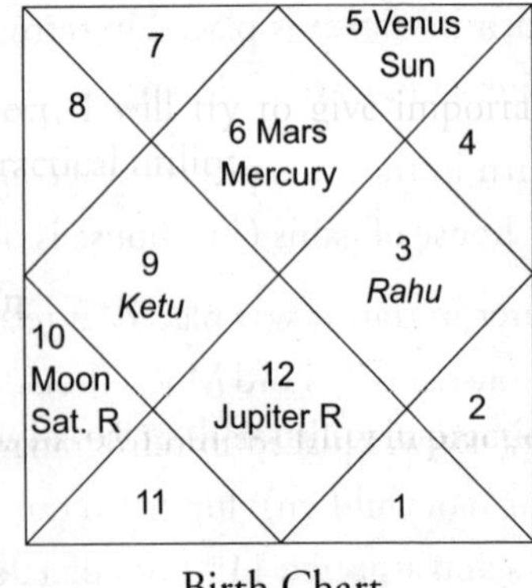

Birth Chart

Transit over Birth Chart :—

Transit of Saturn: Saturn aspects Venus (*Karaka* for vehicles) by 7th aspect.

Jupiter aspects 4th Lord Jupiter (Lord of house for vehicles) by 5th aspect.

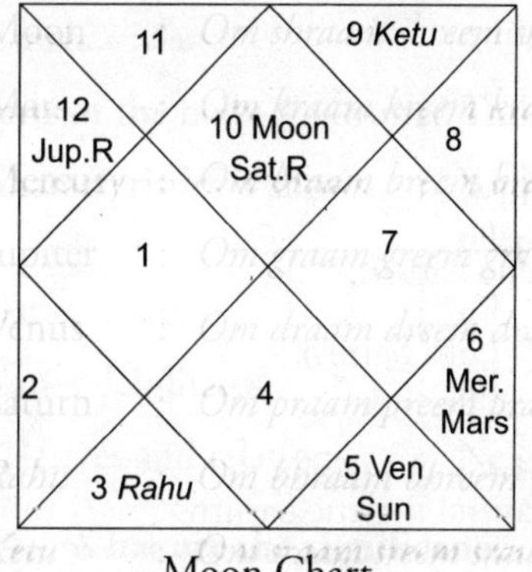

Moon Chart

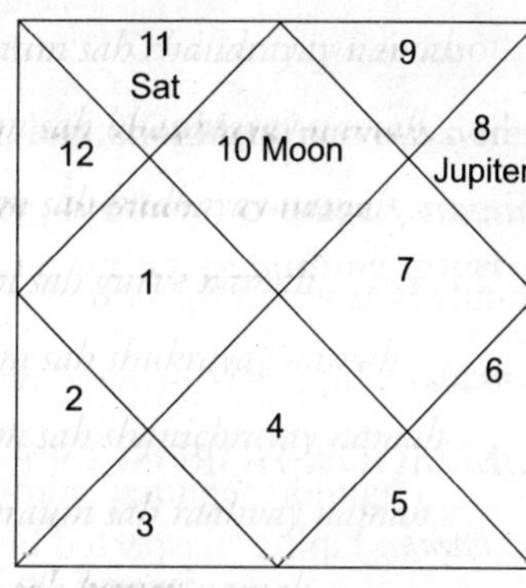

Transit

Transit Over Moon Chart :—

Transit of Saturn: Saturn aspects 4th house of vehicles.

Jupiter was in Libra earlier and aspected 4th house of vehicles by 7th aspect.

ROBBERY IN FEB., 1999

Dasha of Jupiter/Sun/Jupiter

For theft or robbery 2nd house of money and 11th house of gains should have P.A.C. with 6th Lord or there should be P.A.C. of malefics Saturn and or Mars.

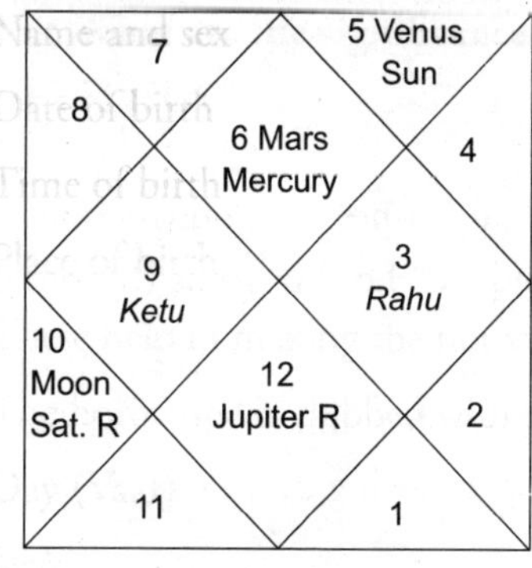

Birth Chart

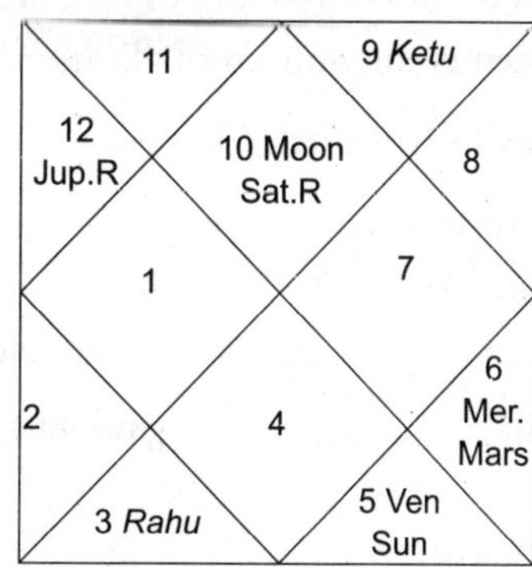

Moon Chart

11th Lord Moon is conjunct with 6th Lord Saturn.

11th Lord is conjunct with natural malefic Saturn.

11th house is aspected by 6th Lord Saturn.

11th house is aspected by natural malefic Saturn.

2nd house is aspected by 6th Lord Saturn.

2nd house is aspected by natural malefic Saturn.

Dhankaraka Jupiter is aspected by 6th Lord Saturn.

FROM MOON HOROSCOPE :—

Dhankaraka Jupiter is aspected by natural malefic Saturn.

11th Lord Mars is conjunct with 6th Lord Mercury.

11th Lord Mars is aspected by natural malefic retrograde Saturn.

2nd house is aspected by retrograde Saturn.

Dhankaraka Jupiter is aspected by natural malefic Saturn.

Dhankaraka Jupiter is aspected by natural malefic Mars.

Dhankaraka Jupiter is aspected by 6th Lord Mercury.

Dasha of Jupiter/Sun/Jupiter

Affliction of Jupiter has been explained above. Role of Sun as 12th Lord of birth chart and as 8th Lord of Moon horoscope explains the sudden event with hospitalization.

Transit Over Birth Chart :—

Saturn was transiting in 8th house of sudden-ness and obstructions. Saturn aspects 2nd house of money, and 11th Lord of gains (Moon). Saturn also aspects 6th Lord Saturn.

Jupiter was retrograde in Pisces in November and it activated 6th house, 11th house and 2nd house. It was transiting over *dhan karaka* Jupiter in 7th house.

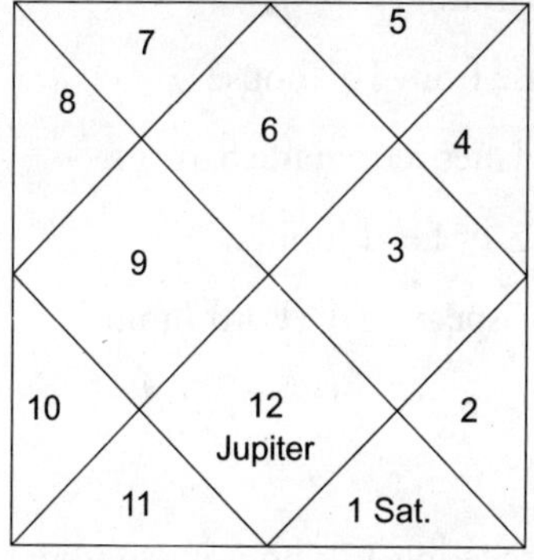

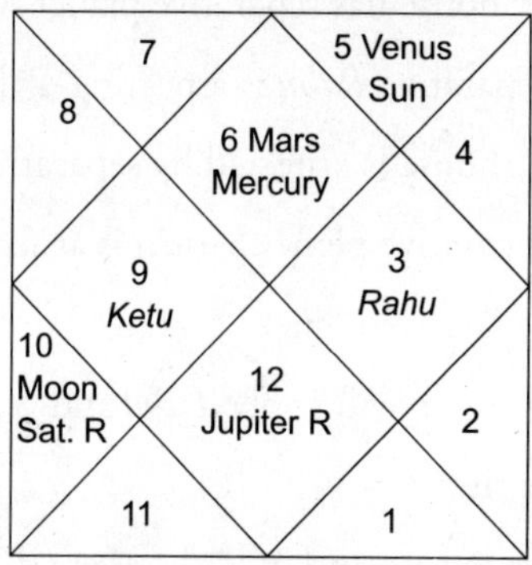

Transit Over Birth Chart :—

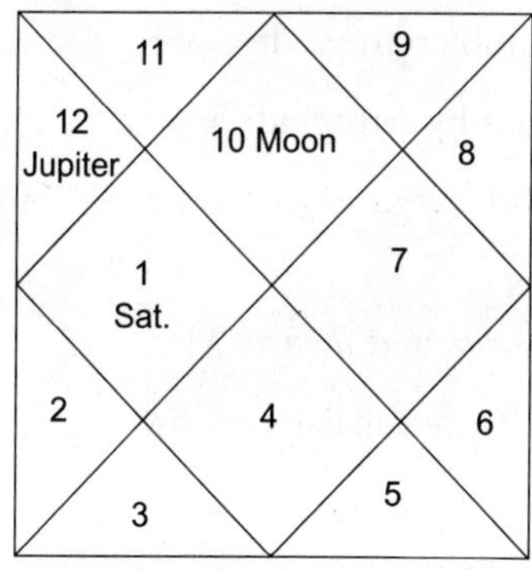

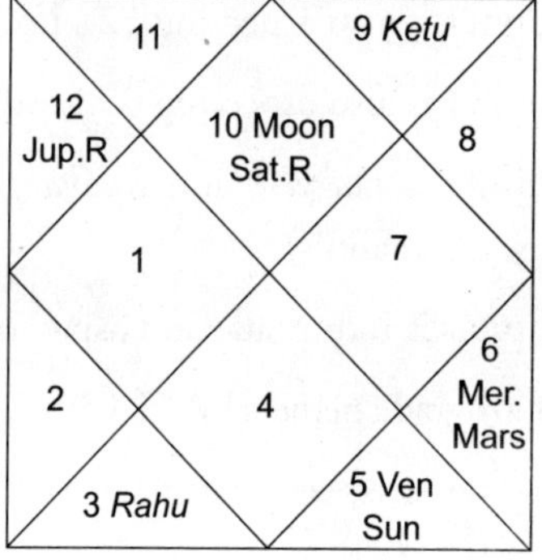

Transit Over Moon Chart :—

Saturn activated 6th house.

Jupiter was transiting in Pisces and was retrograde in November. It activated 2nd house, 6th house, 7th house and 11th house. It was transiting over *dhan karaka* Jupiter.

WENT ABROAD FOR SURGERY IN JUNE, 2001 :—

DASHA JUPITER/MARS /MERCURY

For going to foreign country, one must have afflicted fourth house of residence.

This should be followed by the activation of 7th house/9th house/12th house of foreign travelling by the *dasha* Lords.

Dasha of separative planets should be there.

4th house has separative planet *Ketu* in it.

Separative *Rahu* is aspecting 4th house from 10th house.

4th house is aspected by separative planet retrograde Saturn.

Separative planet Saturn is aspecting 4th Lord Jupiter.

Separative planet Mars (8th Lord) is aspecting 4th Lord Jupiter.

Now we will apply *dasha* and *gochar*.

Jupiter :—

Jupiter is Lord of 7th house and is aspecting 12th house by retrograde aspect.

Jupiter is also aspecting 12th Lord Sun by retrograde aspect.

Jupiter is also aspecting 9th Lord Venus by retrograde aspect.

Jupiter is *markesh* and *Badhakpati* for Virgo *Lagan* (for health and disease analysis).

Jupiter is retrograde and aspecting *Lagan* and *lagnesh* Mercury.

Retrograde planets P.A.C. with *Lagan/ lagnesh* makes one disease prone.

Jupiter is aspecting 8th Lord Mars (representing hips).

Jupiter by retrogradation is aspecting 12th house (house of hospitalization, abroad and expenses) and 12th Lord Sun (*karaka* of bones).

Mars is functional malefic for Virgo *Lagan* and is conjunct with *Lagan* Lord Mercury in *Lagan*, thereby fully capable of giving health problem with surgery.

Mars is *Karaka* for surgery.

Mercury although exalted is conjunct with 8th Lord (house of sudden and chronic diseases) makes it disease prone and accident prone.

Jupiter by retrogradation further makes *Lagan* and *lagnesh* mercury disease prone by its aspect from *Marak* and *Badhak* house (7th being *markesh* and *Badhakpati* both for dual *Lagan*).

TRANSIT OF SATURN AND JUPITER

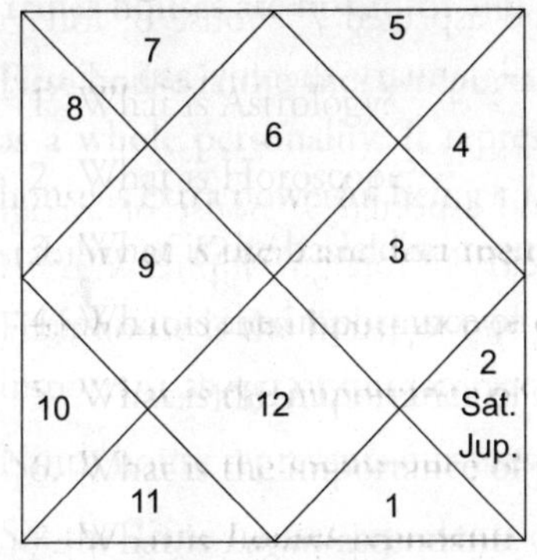

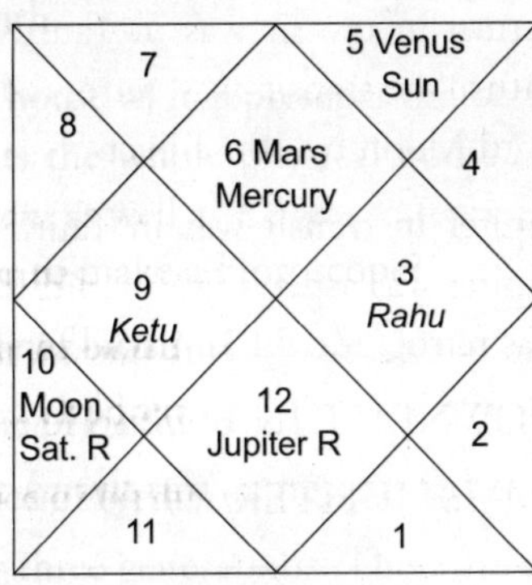

Transit Over Birth Chart :—

Saturn in transit was in Taurus in June and activated 9th house of foreign, 11th house (bad for health as it is 6th to 6th), 6th house (house of diseases).

Saturn in transit was retrograde till January thereby activating 9th house of foreign, 8th house, 11th house, 11th Lord Moon, 5th house and 5th Lord Saturn, and 6th house, 6th Lord Saturn

Jupiter in transit was in Taurus was transiting in 9th house of foreign and aspecting *Lagan*, *Lagan* Lord Mercury, 8th Lord Mars.

Jupiter in transit was retrograde till January thereby activating 9th house of foreign, 9th Lord Venus, 8th house, 11th Lord Moon, 5th house and 5th Lord Saturn, and 6th Lord Saturn, 12th house and 12th Lord Sun.

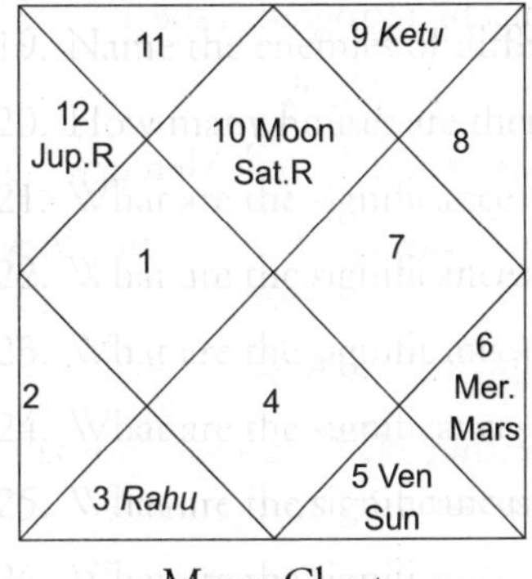

Moon Chart

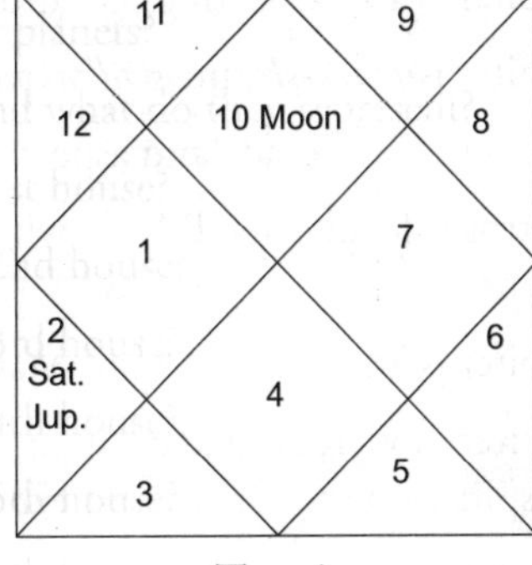

Transit

Transit Over Moon Chart :—

Saturn in transit was in Taurus and aspected 7th house of foreign. Saturn in transit was retrograde till January thereby aspecting 7th Lord Moon by 10th aspect.

Jupiter in transit was in Taurus and aspected 9th house of foreign. Jupiter was aspecting 9th Lord Mercury of foreign. Jupiter in transit was retrograde till January thereby aspecting 12th house of foreign.

DOWNFALL IN BUSSINESS IN 2002 ONWARDS :—

DASHA JUPITER/*RAHU*

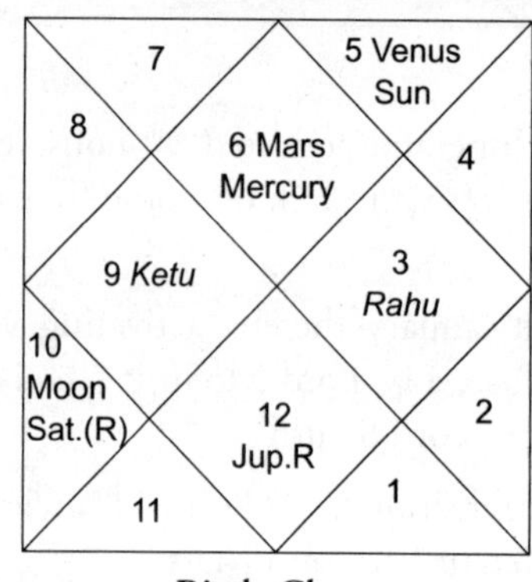

Birth Chart

11
9 Ketu
12 Jup.R
10 Moon Sat.R
8
1
7
2
4
6 Mer. Mars
3 Rahu
5 Ven Sun

Moon Chart

Jupiter is Lord of 7th house and is aspecting 12th house by retrograde aspect.

Jupiter is also aspecting 12th Lord Sun by retrograde aspect.

Jupiter is also aspecting 9th Lord Venus by retrograde aspect.

Jupiter is *markesh* and *Badhakpati* for Virgo *Lagan*.

Jupiter is retrograde and aspecting *Lagan* and *lagnesh* Mercury.

Retrograde planets P.A.C. with *Lagan/lagnesh* makes one disease prone.

Jupiter is aspecting 8th Lord Mars (representing hips).

Jupiter by retrogradation is aspecting 12th house (house of hospitalization, abroad and expenses) and 12th Lord Sun (*karaka* of bones).

Rahu is placed in 10th house of profession. Its dispositer is Mercury who is conjunct with functional malefic Mars Lord of 3rd and 8th house. *Rahu* is aspected by retrograde 6th Lord Saturn. *Rahu* is aspected by Jupiter by retrogradation. *Rahu* is posited in 6th house from Moon *Lagan* and aspects 10th house of profession and 12th house of losses and expenses. *Rahu* is also aspecting 2nd house of money from house of debts and loans.

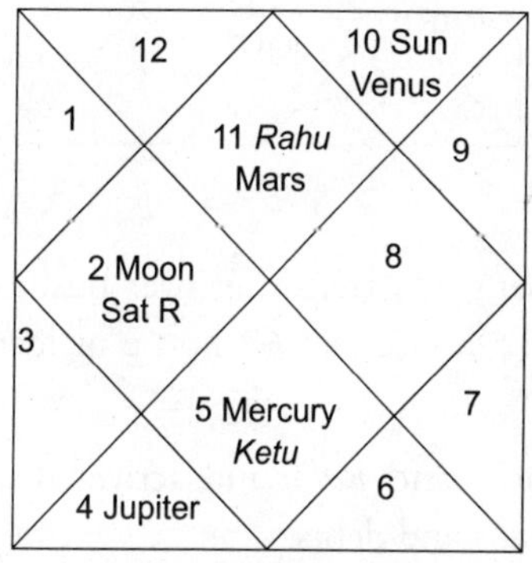

DASHAMSHA D10

4
2
5 Sun
Venus
3 *Rahu*
1
6 Mars
Mercury
12 Jup.(R)
7
9 *Ketu*
11
8
10 Moon
Sat.R

10TH HOUSE AS *LAGNA*

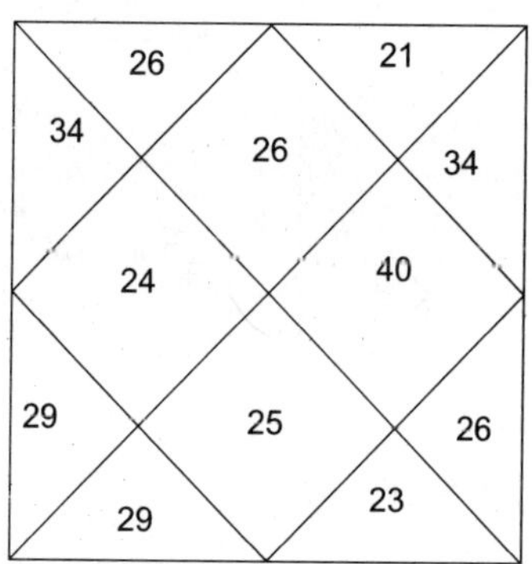

SARVASHTAKVARGA CHART

As per *Sarvashtakvarga*, Jupiter signs Sagittarius and Pisces signs have 24 and 25 *sarvashtak bindus*. Jupiter has 25 *sarvashtak bindus* in Pisces, where it is placed. Jupiter is very weak as it has less than 25 points (24+25+25 divided by three is less than 25 points).

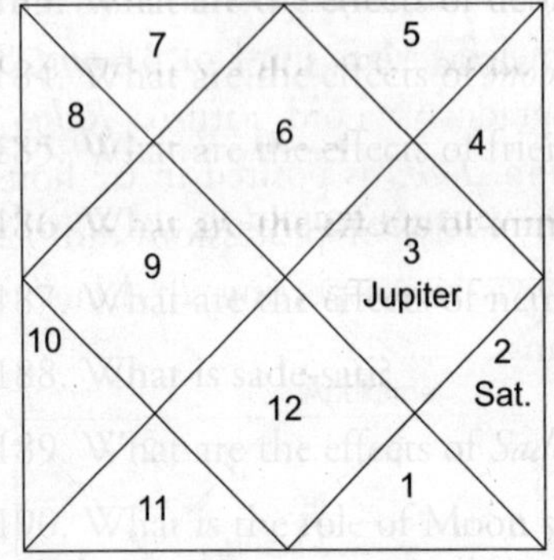

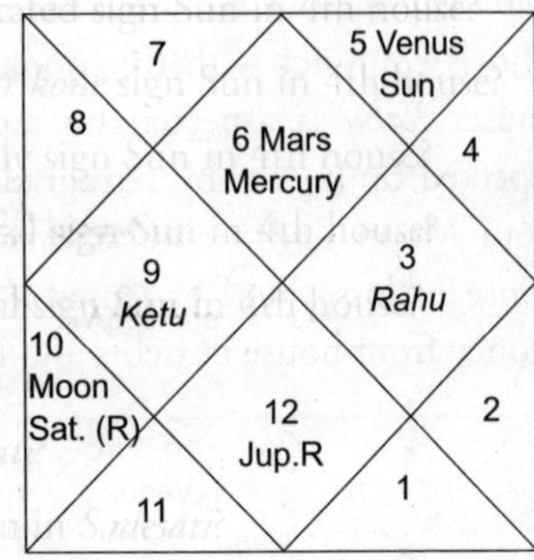

Transit Over Birth Chart :—

Saturn as 6th Lord of debts and loans was transiting over business *karaka* Mercury and it aspected 11th house and 6th house of loans and debts.

Jupiter was transiting over 10th house and *Rahu* and activated 2nd house of money and 6th house of loans and debts.

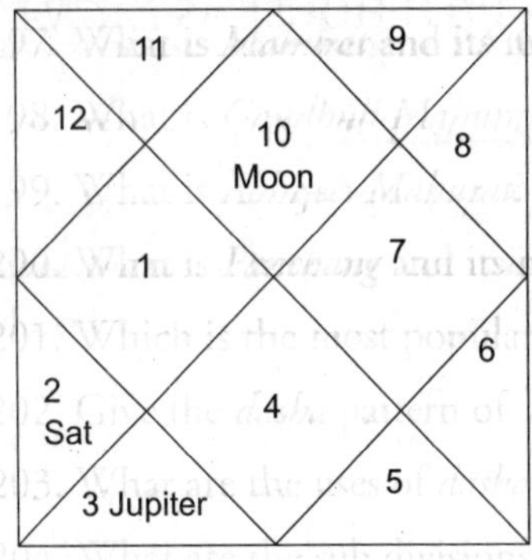

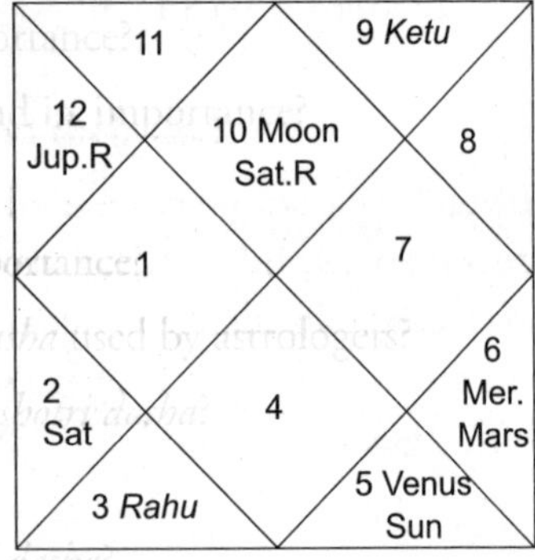

Transit Over Moon Chart :—

Saturn was transiting in 5th house and activated 7th house, 11th house and 2nd house.

Jupiter was transiting in 6th house of loans and debts and activated 10th house of profession with 12th house of losses and 2nd house of money.

CHARTS IN THE BOOK

BIBLIOGRAPHY

Set of Books by Indian Council of Astrological Sciences

Astrology, Destiny and Wheel of Time by K. N. Rao

Planets and Children by K. N. Rao

Elements of Vedic Astrology by Dr. K. S. Charak

Phaldeepika by Gopesh Kumar Ojha

How to Judge Horoscope by B. V. Raman

Prashna Shashtra by Deepak Kapoor

Dasha Nirnay by Z. Ansari

J. N. Bhasin